THE SEPTEMBER POPE

THE SEPTEMBER POPE

THE FINAL DAYS OF JOHN PAUL I

STEFANIA FALASCA

Foreword by Cardinal Pietro Parolin

Our Sunday Visitor
Huntington, Indiana

1st Edition © Piemme 2017
New edition © Copyright 2020 — Libreria Editrice Vaticana
00120 Vatican City
www.vatican.va; www.libreriaeditricevaticana.va

26 25 24 23 22 21   1 2 3 4 5 6 7 8 9

Published in English by Our Sunday Visitor Publishing Division, Our Sunday Visitor, Inc., 200 Noll Plaza, Huntington, IN 46750; 1-800-348-2440; www.osv.com.

ISBN: 978-1-68192-937-8 (Inventory No. T2676)
1. Biography & Autobiography—Religious.
2. Religion—Christianity—Saints & Sainthood.
3. Religion—Christianity—Catholic.

eISBN: 978-1-68192-938-5
LCCN: 2021945571

Cover and interior design: Lindsey Riesen
Cover art: Bridgeman Images
Interior portrait: Caroline Mazure

PRINTED IN THE UNITED STATES OF AMERICA

CONTENTS

FOREWORD

I gladly accepted the invitation to write the foreword to this book. I have a particular devotion to John Paul I, and I admire his everyday holiness. Being from Venice, Italy, myself, I am filled with emotion when I remember how, on August 26, 1978, Cardinal Albino Luciani, Patriarch of Venice, became John Paul I. The cardinals certainly did not make their decision based upon a political strategy; rather, they simply followed an ecclesial definition of what a bishop should be: He should be a pastor.

His sudden and unexpected death, after a pontificate of little more than a month, has given rise — over the decades since September 1978 — to a myriad of theories, suspicions, and assumptions. He died too soon and too suddenly, especially after we had experienced his humble spirit of genuine evangelical newness. Albino Luciani — priest, bishop, patriarch, and later pope — was and remains an instrumental benchmark in the history of the Italian and the universal Church. His is the story of a bishop who had experienced the Second Vatican Council and put it into practice. He was a man of sharp and open intellect. He was a pastor who was close to the holy and faithful people of God, who was centered on the essentials of faith and had an extraordinary cultural and social sensitivity. He was a mild man of the Church and at the same time firm in governing. He was wise and capable of expressing himself in a way that was simple and accessible to everyone. He was a brilliant writer and a journalist, as demonstrated by his book *Illustrissimi*, which he wanted to correct and reprint during his pontificate.

His closeness to others, his humility, his simplicity, and his emphasis on God's mercy and tenderness — all were salient features of a Petrine Magisterium that attracted people forty years ago as it does today, for it is more relevant than ever.

Yet his message has often been obscured by theories and suspicions surrounding his death, a death that took place in the papal apartments on the evening of September 28, 1978. After so many inferences, after so many reconstructions based on unconfirmed rumors, we can now know what happened in the last hours of the life of this pope, whose importance — as suggested by his successor, John Paul II — is inversely proportional to the duration of his very short pontificate: *Magis ostentus quam datus,* "more shown than given." Finally, we have a reconstruction carried out with a rigorous methodology of historical research, based on exceptional, previously unpublished documentation, which is presented here by Dr. Stefania Falasca, the deputy postulator of the Postulation of the Cause of Beatification and Canonization of Albino Luciani. Moreover, I would like to underline the importance of doing the essential work of research, of acquiring sources and completing drafts, and the importance of all of this from a historical and historiographic point of view, given the scarcity of scientific works about the life and the work of Luciani. This was a work that had not yet been undertaken; an effort that, since the beginning of the Roman phase of the cause of canonization, has subsequently been carried out with tenacious zeal and conscientiousness, especially by Doctor Falasca. It is a needed reconsideration of the memory of John Paul I, so that his historical value can be fully restored with the propriety and seriousness that is his due, allowing us to investigate new fields of study within his work. It is a laudable effort, therefore, one carried out in a relatively short time period, especially when compared to the causes of other popes of the twentieth century, obviously with the exception of the cause of Pope Saint John Paul II.

The research now found in this book is intended to retrace the last hours of the life of the pontiff from Venice. It uses the documentation and oral sources available. It was conducted according to historical-critical criteria, thorough documentary verification, and the dry and precise comparison of the testimonial evidence. Thus, it sheds light on the epilogue to Pope Luciani's life, finally clarifying the points that were left in limbo, amplified, and misrepresented in mystery-writer reconstructions. It also outlines the points made by those who deny conspiracy hypotheses.

Finally, we must not forget the value of the introductory pages of this book, which, before getting into the heart of the discussion on the last hours of Albino Luciani's life, give a concise and effective overview of the man. They are a useful vade mecum for those who are interested in the unpublished details about the death of Pope Luciani, but know little about his life and magisterium.

His short pontificate was not a shooting star, which flares out after a brief journey. His death did not close this moment in the history of the Church, thus serving worldly interests. He did not close a chapter or start a new one. Even if John Paul I was not able to add important gestures to the governance of the Church, he nevertheless contributed *explevit tempora multa* to strengthen the design of a conciliar Church which is to be close to the suffering of the people and to their thirst for charity. This is not insignificant, since this is a story of grace entering the world — namely, a story destined to go down in history.

Cardinal Pietro Parolin
Secretary of State of His Holiness

ACKNOWLEDGMENTS

T he final days of the life of John Paul I that is described here was written following the practice of critically examining the documentary and testimonial sources. It is the fruit of research work initiated by the cause of canonization. I would first like to thank all those who, with care and dedication, have supported the cause over the years, as well as the systematic work of finding and acquiring sources, something that had never been done before for John Paul I. In particular, I am grateful to Archbishop Marcello Bartolucci, secretary emeritus of the Congregation for the Causes of Saints and to Undersecretary Fr. Bogusław Turek. I am grateful to Fr. Vincenzo Criscuolo, the general relator for the congregation, for his exemplary dedication, and I am grateful to the postulator of the cause, Cardinal Beniamino Stella, for his paternal care. I warmly thank the scholars who shared my work of reviewing Luciani's documents: the historian Mauro Velati and Fr. Davide Fiocco who collaborated in drafting of *Positio super virtutibus*. With grateful affection, I thank the nieces of John Paul I, Pia Luciani and Lina Petri, to whom I am indebted for their painstaking attention in revising the text during its draft phase. I would also like to thank Dr. Antonella Litta and Roi Bernard, whose generosity made it possible to give this book a new editorial format. I would also like to thank Maria Stella Adario and the *Press Up* printing company. Finally, thanks to Paolo Ruffini, Andrea Tornielli, and Friar Giulio Cesareo for their farsightedness in making this the first book of a series dedicated to the writings of Albino Luciani and the study of his work. The series is being published by Libreria Editrice Vaticana, in collaboration with the new John Paul I Vatican Foundation.

INCIPIT

The English say a fact is like the Mayor of London, that is, only he has true, undisputed dignity. Therefore, when deliberating, take account only of facts that have been checked. I say *facts*, not opinions or rumors. I say checked and not only certain, because it is not enough that proofs are valid for me, they must be valid for everyone and stand up to examination.

Albino Luciani, *Illustrissimi*, 1976

L ate Thursday evening, on September 28, 1978, Albino Luciani, Pope John Paul I, suddenly died in a room of the papal palace in the Vatican after only thirty-four days of Petrine ministry.

News of his sudden death, broadcast in the early hours of the next day, provoked surprise and disbelief. From his first appearance immediately after his election on August 26, he spoke in an offhand manner in first person, and thus Pope Luciani had suddenly opened up a new era of relationship with the contemporary world.

Subsequent meetings increased empathy for him. He was a very original personality who taught using language that was persuasive and universally comprehensible, which brought him closer to believers and nonbelievers alike.

The conclave that elected him had unanimously chosen him to be a shepherd close to the people, a man capable of carrying the Church forward along the lines of the Second Vatican Council.

However, an unexpected turn of events upset that choice: his death. His sudden death rapidly became a work of theater, a poetic myth that ended up engulfing everything about John Paul I and his magisterial consistency. His death gave rise to a genre of best-selling thrillers, such as *In God's Name* by David Yallop, followed over the years by a trail of tabloid trash. However, the story also attracted surprising interest from characters of a very different caliber. This is the case with the theologian Hans Urs von Balthasar. As editor of the writings of the German nun Erika Holzach, he reported, if not endorsed, her "vision" of two assassins who killed the pope in his bed, making the *année charnière* ("pivotal year") 1978 — the year of the three popes — also the setting for a conspiracy theory that, given the viral nature of the internet, has been endlessly reproduced. One need only type in "John Paul I + killed" to see more than 83 million results on Google.

Historical research may record this as a phenomenon, but it definitively points in other directions. This research aims at understanding this man and restoring the depth and scope of who he was in his historic times. The cause of canonization has made this possible, giving me access to documentary sources. Thus I worked on this and was involved in archival research for a decade. These are the only sources that allow one to delve into analytical investigation and talk of Luciani in scientific terms.

It is on this documentary and procedural bases that we now want to retrace the sudden ending of his life, but not, however, before briefly reviewing his short pontificate.

Being very respectful of the sources, I chose to do this using a chronological format. This lets one fast-forward the story and start telling it from the end, from the final scenes of his life which occurred on the evening of September 28, scenes which show the

263rd successor of Peter retiring to his room, alone. They show him pause for a brief moment outside the door of his private study with the four nuns who were on duty at the papal apartments. This is the critical hour that we need to understand. We need to hear again the voice of John Paul I having a brief conversation with the young nun who would be among the first to find him dead the next day. Moreover, we need to hear again the final words he said, as he stood outside his door, to those nuns who were the last to see him alive.

This is not a novel. Pirandello's play *Right You Are — If You Think You Are* is now dated. This was how it went, like it or not, according to the facts.

Finally, we hear: "Goodnight, see you tomorrow, God willing."

ABBREVIATIONS

AAS   Vatican City, *Acta Apostolicae Sedis.*

ArBL   Belluno, Episcopal Archive.

ArCV   Vatican City, Archive of the Congregation for Bishops.

AcDVV   Diocesan Archive of Vittorio Veneto.

ArILS   Rome, Luigi Sturzo Institute Archive.

ArPAL   Vatican City, Private Archive of Albino Luciani (already at the Historical Archives of Venice).

ArPost   Rome-Belluno, Postulation Archive.

DVAM   *Albino Luciani dal Veneto al mondo. Atti del convegno di studi nel XXX della morte di Giovanni Paolo I* (Canale d'Agordo, Vicenza, Venezia, 24-26 settembre 2008), edited by G. Vian, Viella, 2010.

OpOm   Albino Luciani — John Paul I, Opera omnia, vols. I-IX, Messaggero, 1988-1989.

Positio I   Information to the Congregation for the Causes of Saints, from the Diocese of Belluno-Feltre on the beatification and canonization of Servant of God John Paul I (Albino Luciani) (1912-1978). Position on the life, virtues, and reputation of sanctity, Vol.

	1, Belluno 2016.
Positio II	Summary of witnesses in the Congregation for the Causes of Saints, from the Diocese of Belluno-Feltre on the beatification and canonization of Servant of God John Paul I (Albino Luciani) (1912-1978). Position on the life, virtues, and reputation of sanctity, Vol. 2, Belluno 2016.
Positio III	Summary documents to the Congregation for the Causes of Saints, from the Diocese of Belluno-Feltre on the beatification and canonization of Servant of God John Paul I (Albino Luciani) (1912-1978). Position on the life, virtues, and reputation of sanctity, Vol. 3, Belluno 2016.
Positio IV	Biography documents from the Congregation for the Causes of Saints, from the Diocese of Belluno-Feltre on the beatification and canonization of Servant of God John Paul I (Albino Luciani) (1912-1978). Position on the life, virtues, and reputation of sanctity, Vol. 4, Belluno 2016.
Positio V	Diocesan supplementary investigation to the Congregation for the Causes of Saints, from the Diocese of Belluno-Feltre on the beatification and canonization of Servant of God John Paul I (Albino Luciani) (1912-1978). Position on the life, virtues, and reputation of sanctity, Vol. 5, Belluno 2016.

PART ONE

THE BREVITY
OF THE
PONTIFICATE

A confidential dispatch from the U.S. State Department quickly pointed out the distinguishing feature of the papal election: speed. Moreover, the clerk of the U.S. Embassy in Rome understood the reason for that speed as "the convergent will of the College of Cardinals to demonstrate unity," a unity that was "reaffirmed also by the newly elected himself" in his unprecedented choice of joining the names of his two predecessors: John and Paul.[1] This combination was certainly intended to generate, in the desire for momentum, a leap forward for their common legacy — the Second Vatican Council.

After an "almost plebiscitary" consensus "that had the flavor of acclamation" ("a royal three-thirds," according to the expression attributed to Cardinal Léon-Joseph Suenens of Belgium), and after a very brief conclave lasting only twenty-six hours, Albino Luciani ascended to the throne of St. Peter on August 26, 1978.[2] Or rather, he descended there, as a *Servus servorum Dei*. He lowered himself to the height of authority in service to the will of Christ, given that he wrote at the bottom of his personal agenda of the pontificate that ministers of the Church were "servants, not masters of the truth."[3]

Cardinal Eduardo Francisco Pironio of Argentina, in an unpublished homily, remembered the exact moment when the Bishop of Rome was elected: "I was right in front of him, and I was looking at him. And all of us cardinals were waiting for his 'yes.' His 'yes' to Christ: a 'yes' to the Church as a servant and a 'yes' to humanity as a good shepherd. I saw in him a deep serenity, which came from an interiority that cannot be improvised."[4]

In a flash, his words became biographical. At the same time, the speed of that conclave, which upset the predictions made by the press in the previous days, took many by surprise and left them amazed.

Who is Albino Luciani? Simply put, this was the question the public posed in August 1978. However, it is also a question that needs historical research — because, during that sweltering August conclave, the cardinals answered that question by electing John Paul I.

Albino Luciani grew up in northeastern Italy, a region marked by endemic emigration. It was an area scarred by two world wars which caused particular hardship and social division. Luciani grew up in a peripheral, but not marginal, border area. However, its open borders also made it a place of human and cultural enrichment. It was an environment where religion had never been the overriding structure but an underlying, connective, and integrating foundation. Luciani had lived out his childhood, acquired an education, and served as a priest and as the vicar general for the Diocese of Belluno, Italy, until he was forty-six years of age. Moreover, not even his subsequent appointments as the bishop of Vittorio Veneto and as Patriarch of Venice ever caused him to move from his native territory around Venice — until his election. To the cardinals of the first conclave of 1978, these confines did not seem to be a limitation, but an important opportunity.

It had been an important opportunity for Luciani himself, given that his love for study, research, and his wide exposure to universal literature gave him a human and cultural background that went far beyond the ecclesiastical preparation in his Tridentine seminary, a seminary where he worked as vice-rector and professor of dogmatics and other disciplines, starting when he was only twenty-five. He served there for more than twenty years,[5] combining pastoral ministry with administrative duty.

The result of this care was an ever-stronger attention to the dimensions of the human being, to serving people. Moreover, Luciano did not see people — as they were, with the concrete events of their lives — as merely recipients of his magisterium; he saw them as brothers and sisters in a common vocation; he saw everyone united in the common need for mercy. As a bishop, he chose *"Humilitas"* for his motto and then maintained it as Bishop of Rome, because it represented for him the essence of Christianity, the virtue Christ brought into the world, and the only one that leads to him. Moreover, humility would be the theme of the first of the four audiences of his pontificate, the key to opening his subsequent audiences on faith, hope, and charity — part of a magisterium that, rooted in time, anticipated the times.

The conclave that gathered to elect the successor of Paul VI was the first conclave held after the conclusion of Vatican II. It was the first conclave to exclude cardinals over eighty years old.[6] It was the first conclave in which the new legislation promulgated by Paul VI in 1975 was applied, which, with the *sede vacante*, rescinded the curial government, leaving the successor full freedom in his choice of collaborators.[7] It was the first conclave to take place in which the conclave members received heightened media exposure.[8]

Moreover, while the media did not skimp in publishing profiles of candidates,[9] for the first time the heads of delegations of the accredited diplomatic corps and a representative of the journalists were allowed to visit the enclosure of the conclave.[10] For the first time the Italian military secret services collaborated in the electromagnetic isolation of the conclave areas.[11]

In the early morning of August 10, after spending a few days at the Stella Maris Heliotherapeutic Institute at the Lido, Patriarch Albino Luciani departed Venice.[12] A photographer, in collaboration with the director of the patriarchal archive, surprised him by taking his picture as he was getting aboard a motorboat.[13] He reached Rome by car with his secretary and stayed at the Augustinian College, a few steps away from St. Peter's Basilica. He immediately paid homage to the body of Paul VI and, as was customary in those days, refrained from any informal meetings with the cardinals.[14] He preferred to spend his time[15] drafting letters and going over the latest findings[16] of his pastoral visit, as the minutes of his 1978 personal agenda attest.[17] Moreover, he had already noted — quoting Cardinal Franz König — that "at the next conclave, someone will have to use a stick to get one of the cardinals to agree to lead the Church."[18] In fact, writing confidentially from Rome, he considered himself "out of danger."[19]

In the press review of the candidates for the pontificate, his name remained in the shadows. In the newspapers, "Luciani's name received very marginal mention here and there."[20] His name did not even appear in the listings of the London bookmakers.[21] In an interview released in August 1978, Cardinal Aloísio Lorscheider of Brazil, president of the Latin American Bishops' Conference, had, however, painted a portrait of the most likely candidate, which closely resembled the profile of the Patriarch of Venice:

> The new pope should be first of all a good father, a good shepherd as Jesus was, someone who carries out his ministry with patience and willingness to dialogue ... he should be sensitive to social problems ... he should respect and encourage the collegiality of bishops ... he should not try to impose Christian solutions on non-Christians.

Those characteristics — he later stated — expressed the orientation of that college of cardinals searching for "a pope who would be first and foremost a good shepherd."[22] Moreover, "they still believed it right to choose an Italian."[23] In the informal meetings of the cardinals, especially among those from outside of Europe, a consensus was gradually created around the Patriarch of Venice,[24] as suggested by Cardinal Hyacinthe Thiandoum, archbishop of Dakar, Senegal, who was a friend and admirer of Luciani. He affirmed, "For my part I had no doubts that Cardinal Luciani would soon occupy the throne of St. Peter … in Rome, before the opening of the conclave, I invariably replied: 'Cardinal Luciani.'"[25]

Choosing Luciani was not, as Gabriele de Rosa observed:

> a sudden choice, a choice that arose during the few hours of the conclave or during the course of quickly made agreements and brief meetings in Rome: It came as the result of more distant and careful reflection, perhaps even before of the death of Paul VI; meaning, in that regard, the news channels and other information sources were already off the mark.[26]

It was therefore significant that there was a massive and spontaneous convergence of the 111 electors, the majority of whom were attending their first conclave and seemed disinterested in just a "changing of the guard." Suffice it to say that their choice was an expression of a "common ecclesial mentality."[27] Moreover, it was precisely in this unanimity that we see he was not a pope chosen for a specific political project. Since the conclave that elected Paul VI's successor was the first since the conclusion of Vatican II, that election indicated a willingness to make progress in implementing its guidelines. The cardinals had therefore decisively aimed at the virtue of pastoralism. Luciani was not chosen to be a pastor; he was chosen because he already was one. They chose a pastor.

His name did not require particular evaluation or compromise.[28] Luciani's long-recognized value was his characteristic focus on what was essential. He was a shepherd nourished by serene and human wisdom along with strong evangelical virtues; one who led the flock by example, living among them, drawing no distinction between his personal and pastoral life, between his spiritual life and his exercise of government, harmoniously combining what he taught with what he lived.

He was an expert in humanity and the wounds of the world, the needs of the immense multitude of the destitute who lived outside of affluence. He was a priest with vast and profound wisdom who knew how to combine the new and the old into a happy and ingenious synthesis. Moreover, since the Second Vatican Council was intended to be "a sign of the Lord's mercy upon his Church," as envisaged in the Johannine *Gaudet Mater Ecclesia* (and it was actually there that the Church chose to apply the term "medicine of mercy"), he was elected as an apostle of the council, someone who had made the Council his episcopal novitiate, whose teachings he correctly explained with crystalline lucidity.

Moreover, he showed persevering courage in putting its directives into practice. Indeed, he embodied the directives: *naturaliter et simpliciter.* Of primary importance was poverty — which for Luciani constituted the very fiber of his priesthood and his being *propter homines* ("for humans"), and doing the everyday work of the Gospel.

With his unprecedented choice of the double name "John Paul," he erected an arch that connected those who had been the pillars of this work; pillars that some had judged were detached. Luciani was aware of this spreading dissension within the Church and considered it offensive to the truth and an enemy to unity and peace. His choice to combine the names was therefore one of the expressions of his brilliant intuition, intuition by which the pope from Belluno was able to readily grasp the issues, to see to the bottom of them with certainty, and thus untie the knots caused by difficult situations and problems in the Church.[29]

In the days that followed, even the cardinal electors — "always subject to the rigorous discipline of secrecy" — emphasized the convergence that had been achieved and the "eminently ecclesial and nonpolitical point of view which motivated their actions to the point of bringing them to a rapid consensus and, as some said, almost a moral plebiscite."[30]

Congratulatory messages from civil authorities reached the Vatican immediately. One of them was from the American president, Jimmy Carter.[31] Later, various Italian politicians expressed their support for the election.[32] The Soviet press, on the other hand, waited until September 1 before issuing a public response from the Soviet president, Leonid Brezhnev. He wished the new pope success in his efforts to "consolidate peace and international détente and to strengthen friendship and cooperation among peoples."[33] The presidents of the nations adhering to the Warsaw Pact followed suit. A highly confidential dispatch from Italian diplomatic channels also noted the reaction of the Central Committee of the Communist Party of the Soviet Union (CPSU):

> As proof of Soviet interest in maintaining normal relations with the Holy See, it was noted that, after sending a telegram of condolences, Moscow would send a telegram of congratulations, which, when received by the Holy See, would have made clear to the USSR ambassador in Rome that the Committee would like him to represent them at the solemn ceremony in St. Peter's. The Ambassador requested, and obtained, authorization from the Central Committee.[34]

Amid the almost unanimous satisfaction, some discordant voices were heard from Venice, from the small circle of priests and lay people who had already opposed Luciani during his years of ministry around the Lagoon. In the ideological context of the time, they did not consider him "up to the task entrusted to him as head of the Church." They believed "that his cultural experience was too far removed from the demands of modern culture and that he was too attached to a certain way of understanding ecclesial obedience."[35] This image of his ineptitude and unsuitability for the task could plausibly be traced back to some magazines that were circulating at the time[36] in which this image was crystallized into a cliché by the followers of the "progressive" or "conservative" labels. These were labels that Luciani escaped because of his characteristic focus on what was essential, a focus that later, in the arena of public opinion, was used by outsiders to fuel their narrative against the Curia.[37]

It is significant that the first decision made as soon as Luciani was elected was to refrain from opening the conclave immediately in order to invite the elderly cardinals who had been left outside to listen to the first message with the rest of the college. The course of his pontificate was clearly outlined in the six "we wish" points that he made in his *Urbi et orbi* speech and in his early speeches, in which, on several occasions, he declared in every way possible that he would continue to implement the Second Vatican Council, preserving its legacy and preventing any interpretative drift.[38]

Thus, having been given the "unique and singular title of this Roman See 'which presides over the whole society of love,'" his pontificate began with the utmost simplicity. There would be no coronation or use of the royal "we" and these gestures testified to a decisive desire to rediscover the basic pastoral dimension of the papal office.

During his brief pontificate, as the pontiff advanced the Church along the main avenues indicated by the Council, he made clear his priorities:[39] a return to the sources of the Gospel, a renewed missionary spirit, episcopal collegiality, service in ecclesial poverty, dialogue with the contemporary world, a search for unity with the Christian Churches, interreligious dialogue, and the search for peace.

On September 20, during his General Audience on hope, John Paul I said:

> Let me explain. At the council, I, too, in 1962, endorsed the "Message to the World" of the council fathers ... I endorsed *Gaudium et Spes*. I was moved and enthusiastic when *Populorum Progressio* [Paul VI] came out; I spoke about it, I wrote about it. Even today, I am not really persuaded that the Magisterium of the Church will ever sufficiently insist in presenting and recommending the solution of the great problems of freedom, justice, peace, development; nor will the laity ever fight sufficiently to solve these problems.[40]

This next affirmation, which was omitted in the official editions, although immediately rebutted by the chancelleries, still leads us straight to his list of commitments which were interwoven and embedded in his short pontificate, particularly, his search for peace: "At this time an example comes to us from Camp David. The day before yesterday, the American Congress broke out in a round of applause, that we too heard, when Carter quoted Jesus' words: "Blessed are the peacemakers." I truly hope that that applause and those words will enter the hearts of all Christians, especially us Catholics and will truly make us agents and makers of peace."[41] This was precisely why he wanted to foster reconciliation and brotherhood among peoples, to invite collaboration so as to "safeguard and increase peace in our troubled world"; to stem nationalism and curtail within nations that "violence which can only destroy and sow seeds of ruin and sorrow."[42] This was what John Paul I prioritized in his programmatic speech, along with his ecumenical and interreligious commitment, documented by his full agenda of audiences with the representatives of non-Catholic churches.[43]

These same perspectives were clearly seen in his address to the Diplomatic Corps held on August 31, in which Luiciani, freeing himself from the presumptions of geopolitical attention seeking, defined the nature and particularity of the Holy See's diplomatic work, both of which arise from the point of view of faith. Therefore, in the wake of the conciliar constitution *Gaudium et Spes*, as in many of the messages of Pope Saint Paul VI, he moved in the wake of great diplomacy, bearing much fruit to the Church, nourishing her with charity.[44] Then on September 4, having received more than one hundred representatives of international missions, he reemphasized the same reasoning and emphasized that "our heart is open to all peoples, all cultures and all races." He then affirmed:

> Of course, we do not have miraculous solutions for the great world problems, however we can offer something very precious: a spirit that helps to dissolve these problems and view them from an essential prospect, that of openness to the values of universal charity … so that the Church, humble messenger of the Gospel to all peoples of the earth, might contribute to create a climate of justice, brotherhood, solidarity, and hope, without which the world cannot live.[45]

Each of these priorities thus punctuated the words and gestures of the thirty-four days of his pontificate, as the fruit of his long-standing labor and through his unprecedentedly persuasive and attractive magisterium, rooted in the radical theological choice of simple, conversational, and accessible language, of that *sermo humilis* approved by Saint Augustine, which is clear to the world and people, and engages them using understandable dialogue so that the message of salvation might reach everyone.[46]

Moreover, it is through a direct connection with these priorities that the most brilliant pope of the twentieth century is reunited with the present, rolling back the stone of his tomb.

PART TWO

ON THE THIRD FLOOR OF THE APOSTOLIC PALACE

So I went up with him to the private apartment which was then unsealed in the presence of Monsignor Martin and Cardinal Villot. The pope and I found ourselves alone in the empty apartment.[47]

It was the afternoon of August 27 and the newly elected John Paul I made his first visit to the private apartments of the pontiffs on the third floor of the Apostolic Palace. As required by law, the apartments had been sealed after the death of Paul VI. The secretary, Fr. Diego Lorenzi, recounted this moment during his tribunal deposition. He was the last of the secretaries that Luciani had hired to work for him in Venice and whom he took with him to Rome for the conclave.[48] The previous evening, Father Lorenzi had witnessed the election from St. Peter's Square, together with the crowd. As soon as Luciani's name had been proclaimed, he rushed up to the Apostolic Palace. However, the pope sent word that he should return the following day. Thus the cloister of the conclave, which had lasted until that morning, came to an end. Lorenzi stated that after Luciani recited his first Angelus, he stopped for lunch at the apartment of the Vatican Secretary of State, Cardinal Jean Villot,[49] and did not take possession of his private apartment until after 3:00 p.m. that afternoon: "He then ate a meal in Cardinal Villot's apartment, where I met him around 3:00 p.m."[50]

By that time, however, the secretary and the pope were not alone in the rooms previously occupied by Paul VI. Also present were the brothers from Venice, Guido and Giampaolo Gusso, who had been papal butlers for John XXIII and Paul VI. Lorenzi recalls that "at that moment a phone call came from Bishop Maffeo Ducoli, the bishop of Belluno-Feltre, who was about to go to the town of Canale d'Agordo and wanted to bring the pope's blessing to the people."[51] Before departing for Canale d'Agordo, the bishop had in fact tried to contact the pope, who was in the chapel at the time. When the pope was informed of the phone call, he called the bishop personally and gave him a greeting for his family and for his home parish.[52] The pope then had his personal belongings brought over from the nearby Augustinian college where he had been staying during the pre-conclave period. He also sent two messages of gratitude to the prior, Fr. Prosper Grech, and to the vicar general of the Augustinian order, Fr. Gioele Schiavella, to whom he again expressed his surprise at having been called to the papal throne:

> On Saint Augustine's day, one must really thank the Augustinian fathers for the courteous and religious hospitality they offered to someone who — without knowing it or even

suspecting it — was on his way to a position of fearsome responsibility.[53]

That afternoon, the Sisters of the Holy Child Mary arrived to organize the rooms of the papal apartments. John Paul I had contacted the religious community by telephone, expressing his desire that the sisters of this congregation — who had already provided assistance in Vittorio Veneto and Venice — also continue in the Vatican. The superior general, Angelamaria Campanile, immediately accepted the request.[54] Moreover, by the afternoon of August 27, some sisters from the nearby general house of the Institute came to the apartments to organize them and to prepare a frugal dinner. Srs. Gabriella Cacciamalli and Assunta Crespani arrived first. They had already served under Paul VI.[55] Next came Srs. Vincenza Paradiso and Clorinda Moschetti who remained provisionally for the first week of the pontificate. On August 29, they were joined by the elderly Sr. Vincenza Taffarel, who had been with Luciani since the time of his episcopate of Vittorio Veneto. However, the superior general soon selected the definitive team for the new community. The final team members were Srs. Elena Maggi, Vincenza Taffarel, Cecilia Tomaselli, and Margherita Marin.[56]

These nuns were from Venice and remained with John Paul I until his death. Their significant presence remained in the shadows until it was reconstructed during the recent investigations initiated by the canonical process of canonization.

The specific tasks of each were described as follows by Sr. Margherita Marin, the youngest of the group:

> I oversaw the wardrobe and the sacristy, but I also carried out other services when needed. Sister Cecilia was the cook, Sister Vincenza was a nurse, while Sister Elena coordinated our work; she was the group leader. Sister Vincenza was the oldest; she had known the Holy Father for many years. She met him in Belluno at a time when, as a young priest, he had some health problems and she assisted him as a nurse. Later, when he became a bishop, he requested a small com-

munity of the Sisters of the Holy Child Mary for the episcopal apartments, and he wanted her to assist him. Sister
Vincenza also followed him to Venice and was the only one
of the nuns who was with him in Venice to come to the
Vatican. … He greeted us with simplicity, without making
us feel uneasy. He told us to pray, that the Lord had given
him a great burden, but that, with his help and everyone's
prayers, he would carry it through. The day he saw us all together for the first time, he was almost apologetic; he knew
that I was the youngest, and he said, "I'm sorry for taking
some young nuns away." He showed a lot of regard for us
sisters. He immediately treated us with familiarity.[57]

The superior of the Institute in Rome, Sr. Giulia Scardanzan,
in her extra-tribunal testimony, also described the respect and cordial benevolence John Paul I had for them and how he immediately
made them fully-fledged family members in the apartments:

I got a phone call from His Holiness's secretary. My Provincial, Sr. Vincenza Calabrese and I were expected the following day in the Holy Father's private chapel for Mass. But
the biggest surprise was after Mass, when the sisters told
us: "The Holy Father wants you to stop by for breakfast" …
we took a seat at a table in a small room and he came and
sat down with us, with great simplicity, and again, he took
an interest in our community and our religious province.[58]

The nun was from Luciani's home region and had been an acquain-
tance of his for many years. She, too, mentioned the special regard
Luciani always had for the sisters, which was decidedly different
from the detachment shown by his predecessor Paul VI and his secretary, Msgr. Pasquale Macchi, toward the sisters in the apartment.
John Paul I closed the private chapel where Paul VI used to celebrate
Mass with his secretaries, and he dispensed other Vatican personnel
from having to attend.[59] He wanted to celebrate daily Mass in the
small private chapel of the papal apartments, attended by the secre-

taries and the sisters.

As Sr. Margherita Marin attested:

> I remember the day after our arrival, I was sent, together
> with the secretary, to collect the vestments and to close the
> pope's private chapel, the one where Paul VI used to cele-
> brate morning Mass with his secretaries, because John Paul
> I wanted the morning Mass to be celebrated in the private
> chapel inside the apartments with the sisters present to-
> gether with his secretaries: "We are a family and we cele-
> brate together," he said.[60]

Even this gesture, not observed by the outside world, appeared
symptomatic of that conciliar orientation which was synonymous
with the ministerial style that Albino Luciani intended to continue.
Moreover, during his pontificate, he reconfirmed the respectful familiarity he had always shown the sisters, even while he was bishop
and patriarch. There was none of the haughtiness, which too often
reduces nuns to mere attendants: "He went to the sisters in the evening after dinner to say goodnight, keeping himself updated about
their health and about their work commitments for the following
day, as he had always done."[61]

Furthermore, a witness from his time in the city of Vittorio
Veneto recalled: "In Vittorio Veneto, one of the sisters in his service
worked late to finish some housework and was found dead on the
floor the next morning. The bishop stayed up all night to pray beside
her body."[62]

Therefore, it is not surprising that on September 3, the solemn
day of the beginning of his pontificate, he also invited the nuns who
had assisted him in the Patriarchate of Venice to lunch, accompanied by their provincial uperior, Maria Teresa Zambon.[63]

Sr. Margherita Marin once more gives us an impression of the
convivial atmosphere he created while he was the pontiff:

> Sister Vincenza told us that she had not so willingly agreed
> to come, because she felt she was getting too elderly, but lat-

er she was fine. She had been experiencing health problems and I remember the Holy Father said to us, "You know, Sister Vincenza is suffering from a heart condition and I told her not to walk too much and also to take the personal elevator if she needs it."[64]

Finally, Pia Luciani, the niece of John Paul I, left us this portrait of him:

> Sister Vincenza assisted my Uncle Albino with dedication and he let himself be helped. She was a very good nun and quite capable of organizing the work at the bishop's residence where she was assisted by one or two of the Sisters of the Holy Child Mary. My uncle got to know the Sisters of the Holy Child Mary because they served at the Sperti Orphanage in Belluno where he had been the chaplain. When he was made bishop of Vittorio Veneto, he asked their superior to send Sister Margherita, one of the Sperti nuns, to help him at the bishop's residence. Sister Margherita was elderly by then, and when she died at the bishop's residence, two more sisters followed. After them came Sister Vincenza, who eventually followed my uncle to Venice and the Vatican. She was very devoted to her bishop, but she still knew how to make him respect her when she asked him to follow certain instructions regarding health and food. I remember that when she saw that my uncle was eating too little, she would leave the kitchen, enter the dining room, and reprimand him with a certain energy … my uncle was attentive to the sisters' dignity and their needs … he often read his homilies to them to get their opinion before he delivered them. … He very much valued their participation as auditors at the Second Vatican Council.[65]

Inside the papal apartments, the nuns had their own rooms.[66] The secretaries occupied private rooms on the floor above, which were accessed via an internal staircase. The apartments — as the witness Sr. Margherita Marin reports — were not large and allowed us to see each other "all the time, even if we were doing different things."[67] In the short time they were there, the nuns kept busy with their duties. They were, however, unable to finish installing John Paul I's private library, which had come from Venice:

> Each of us, as I said, had her own duties to perform, so the day was full. There was also a lot to do in order to set up and arrange the apartment left by Paul VI and we didn't have enough time to complete everything in one month. I remember a few days before the end of that month we had just begun to unpack the crates of books from Venice and place the volumes in the library. There was no time to organize all those books from Venice and arrange them in the library of his private study. The only volumes we managed to organize were the *opera omnia* of St. Francis de Sales. There was no time.[68]

Luciani had asked Fr. Mario Senigaglia, his secretary in Venice before Father Lorenzi, to send him his notebooks.[69] He felt he urgently needed his papers and his library. This included all the material of his personal archives, which had built up over the years, along with his well-stocked library, which could be defined as his "workshop," a sort of a work in progress that he could draw upon or add to and from which he was never separated. He had arranged to have these personal effects brought to the Vatican the day after his ascension to the Throne of Peter.[70] The date that the possessions were transferred from the Patriarchate of Venice to the papal apartments is documented as September 13. On that occasion, there was also a brief meeting with the Jesuit Roberto Busa, Luciani's former seminary classmate, who had organized the shipment and who introduced him to the managers and workers of the Borghi Trasporti Company. Under the supervision of Fr. Carlo Bolzan from Vittorio Veneto, the workers transferred about fifty crates from Venice to Rome. The crates contained books from the library and the papers from the archives,[71] along with the pope's personal effects. The pope wanted to meet the workers and greet them personally in order to thank them for their service.[72]

Now we come to the other members of the papal apartments family.

As his leading secretary, Luciani confirmed Fr. John Joseph Magee, an Irish priest who was a member of the Missionary Society of St. Patrick. He had been Paul VI's secretary since March 7, 1975, and was now collaborating with Pasquale Macchi to clear the office of the deceased pontiff. According to his testimony, on the morning of August 30, the newly elected pope met with Magee in the papal apartments and the next day proposed that he be his secretary. When Magee consented, the pope immediately directed him to the Secretariat of State to formalize the appointment.[73] Given his previous experience, Magee was mainly to work on the correspondence coming from the Secretariat of State.[74]

John Paul I retained Fr. Diego Lorenzi, a member of the Don Orione Fathers, in the post of personal secretary. Lorenzi had followed him from Venice to the Vatican. However, there was a good deal of reservation regarding his suitability for the office, which John Paul I himself confided to Msgr. Pasquale Macchi, Paul VI's secretary and the executor of his will.[75] This also emerged in a report by Sr. Margherita Marin:

> We communicated more frequently with Father Magee. He was close to the Holy Father and gave us instructions. With Father Diego, it was less often. I heard from Sister Vincenza that he was not suitable for that office. A week before the pope died, Sister Vincenza told us that the Holy Father would soon be changing him. He was going to be replaced by a certain Father Mario, the secretary he had previously in Venice.[76]

The same household members, due to the knowledge they had from the Venice period, recognized that "this priest probably had some character problems."[77] In the first days of his pontificate, Monsignor Macchi and Mario Cardinal Casariego actually suggested that the pope should bring in Fr. Mario Senigaglia.

The cardinal went about facilitating Father Senigaglia's release from his employment in Venice so that he could go immediately to the Vatican, as Loris Capovilla reported:

> In the days following Pope Luciani's election, Mario Cardinal Casariego confided to me that to get the papal household off to a good start he had suggested that the pope bring in Monsignor Mario Senigaglia, who had been his secretary until October of 1976, and was the Pastor of Santo Stefano in Venice for two years. The cardinal spoke with the father general of the Somascan Fathers, suggesting that the order take charge of the parish of Santo Stefano or, in any case, facilitate Senigaglia's departure from Venice so that he could immediately go to the Vatican. Even the Most Reverend Giuseppe Carraro, bishop of Verona, passing through Loreto right after meeting the new pope in the Vatican, told me that the young member of the Don Orione Fathers [Fr. Diego Lorenzi] was not in the right place.[78]

During a conversation a year earlier, in Venice, the then Bishop Capovilla reported his own impression from a personal interview with Fr. Diego Lorenzi:

> He told me: "I confine myself to typing. He does not confide in me. He talks more with the nuns in the kitchen than with me!" I understood that something was wrong. I said to him, "It is already a great honor to be close to such a holy man, to a venerable father of the Church. If he is not very outgoing, it is due to his being from the mountains and his long service as a teacher and curial officer. Help him."[79]

A comparison of the depositions also reveals that during the course of the short pontificate, there was a certain disharmony between the secretaries John Magee and Diego Lorenzi.[80] As reported by the Augustinian Fr. Prosper Grech, Magee was asked to assist the pope during the time that the secretary, Lorenzi, went to Venice to collect the pope's personal effects.[81]

Monsignor Macchi, during his stay in Rome, also offered to help set up the papal apartments and the private secretariat. On September 10, about to depart Rome, he wrote, "Being among the people in St. Peter's Square on these Sundays for the Angelus, I was able to see the affection that the faithful have for your Holiness." Moreover, he assured the pope of his availability for "any humble service that may be required of me."[82]

From Sr. Margherita Marin we learn that it was the pontiff himself who agreed to Father Lorenzi's absence: "He had already gone out at other times in the evening. I know that the Holy Father had once told the secretaries that they could go out if they wanted to and Father Diego had gone out several times."[83]

While Luciani was a bishop in Vittorio Veneto, he never allowed his secretaries to serve as a filter. Luciani himself would often answer the phone himself, go to open the door, and personally look after his appointments and his mail.[84] Even as pope, at least on one occasion for which there is evidence, he answered the phone himself.[85]

The duties he required of all his secretaries over time were the same duties he required of Father Diego:

> In being my secretary, he shall have an unvaried life. He shall be my master of ceremonies at liturgical functions. He shall drive my car when I travel. He shall take interest in the poor who come asking for help, and he shall join me for meals.[86]

With the exception of Senigaglia, who remained secretary for six years, all of the other secretaries never exceeded three years of service. From the testamentary documentation and correspondence, reasons emerge supporting his preference for not keeping young priests with him for a long time and thereby depriving them of the opportunities of their apostolate. Luciani was worried that their physiognomy or pastoral personality would be lessened by occupying themselves "almost exclusively in bureaucratic matters," that their physiognomy would be deformed by the aspirations for a *carrieretta* ("little career"). This was shown in one of the letters he wrote to his fifth secretary in Vittorio Veneto:

> The problem of your physiognomy … by prolonging itself in these things, at your age, you run the risk of it becoming deformed — to the detriment of your apostolate … and I would not like it said how your bishop, who often regrets that young priests, even after the Second Vatican Council, are still being employed in little careers as kindergarten teachers, could himself employ a priest with fine gifts for a long time doing little more than driving his car.[87]

Also as regards Father Lorenzi, in the diocesan bulletin of Venice issued in October 1976, the then patriarch made Lorenzi's appointment official in these terms:

> The patriarch has asked the Reverend Fr. Diego Lorenzi to lend himself for a while in service as a private secretary. Father Lorenzi is currently the assistant pastor at San Pio X Church in Marghera and recently graduated from Padua.[88]

The decision to release Father Diego in order to assign him to other positions therefore seemed to have been supported by his brother Edoardo, when he stopped at the Vatican on September 20, according to a statement by his niece Lina Petri:

> We all sensed that he [Father Lorenzi] was unsuitable for his post as the pope's private secretary, the post he held at the time of the election. Years later, my uncle Berto told me that when he was passing through the Vatican on his way to Australia, Uncle Albino told him that within a week or so Father Diego would have to leave office and that he had already spoken to him about it.[89]

In fact, the priest held the post until September 28.

However, there was another member of the papal-apartments family besides the nuns and the secretaries: the papal butler.

During the first week, the Gusso brothers had initially performed this service. Then, Luciani asked Msgr. Giuseppe Caprio, the Vatican Vice-Secretary of State, to talk to Camillo Cibin — a native of Vittorio Veneto and a commander of the gendarmerie — and ask him to indicate a trustworthy person who could carry out the task with discretion. Angelo Gugel had been employed in the Legal Office of the Governorate; the pope had known him from the time of the Second Vatican Council. Gugel was soon summoned and began service on September 6.[90]

Gugel resided with his family, however, not in the Vatican. The witness himself described his duties:

> I arrived before 8:00 a.m. and made myself available to the pope. I accompanied him to audiences and served him during lunch. I took a break in the afternoon, then resumed work around 5:00 p.m. for the "table" meetings and for dinner. I finished serving by 8:00 p.m. … I took directions from time to time from Monsignor Magee.[91]

In his deposition, the papal butler pointed out the "very natural" way the pope related to people.[92]

Finally, also among the pope's household members there was his confessor. At the end of the pope's audience with journalists on September 1, his secretary, Father Lorenzi, approached the Jesuit Fr. Bartolomeo Sorge, Director of *La Civiltà Cattolica*, and instructed him on behalf of the pope and in a confidential way to tell the Jesuit Fr. Paolo Dezza that John Paul I wanted him as his personal confessor. This was not the first time that Luciani chose a priest of the Society of Jesus as his personal confessor; he had done so previously as the Patriarch of Venice.[93] The Jesuit reported that "when he called back (as agreed upon) that same day at 12:30 p.m., the pope answered the phone himself and not his secretary."[94]

Seen from up close, the days of John Paul I over that short period of time showed his desire to maintain a rhythm and a style that he had already acquired some time ago. In the Vatican, in fact, Luciani continued the habits he had developed as a bishop and a patriarch. He woke up early, around 4:30 a.m.[95] After a sip of a coffee in the sacristy, he would go into the chapel around 5:20 a.m. and pray alone for more than an hour and a half.[96] Mass was at 7:00 a.m. with the secretaries and the sisters. Occasionally guests attended the celebration. When other celebrations were scheduled for the day, the Mass was presided over by Father Magee, while John Paul I attended "like a simple altar boy."[97] The secretary reported that there were three occasions when the pope asked him to celebrate the Mass in English, allowing him "to be an altar boy." The last time was on September 26.[98]

After the morning Mass, he had breakfast and carefully read the newspapers. Around 9:00 a.m., there were the planned audiences, scheduled by the prefecture of the papal household,[99] which lasted until lunchtime.[100] A short rest followed and work resumed in the early afternoon, his speeches were prepared and documents were studied in view of the meeting with the Cardinal Secretary of State.[101] He often spent time reading and walking in the roof garden.[102] In the late afternoon, his work audiences with collaborators from the Curia were conducted in his private study.[103]

Between 7:30 and 8:00 p.m., he had dinner with the secretaries and sometimes with some guests.[104] After dinner, he would go into the sitting room to thank the sisters for their work and retire to his room to read before going to sleep.[105]

This was the profile of the living quarters on the third floor of the Apostolic Palace and the daily schedule that John Paul I wanted.

Only once, during the thirty-four days of his pontificate, did Luciani ever go down from the apartment to take a walk in the Vatican Gardens. Cardinal Villot accompanied him that afternoon on Sunday, September 17.

However, the cardinal pointed out to him that whenever he went down to the Vatican Gardens, the staff would have to close all public access. Thus, for the time being, Luciani preferred to forego the walks.[106] However, this was not the only time he chose restraint.

He made a similar choice when Msgr. Dino Monduzzi, prefect of the papal household, prescribed "that whenever the pope was inside the apostolic palace there should be an escort of four Swiss Guards with the retinue of prelates. The second time this happened, [John Paul I] decided to eliminate the escort and the retinue."[107]

Meanwhile, even in the apartments, there were those who came and went, and guests were registered as well.

THE
UNDISCLOSED
APPOINTMENT

On September 20, the pope was contacted by his brother Edoardo who wanted to meet with him before leaving for an institutional mission in Australia. This was in connection with Eduardo's role as president of the Belluno Chamber of Commerce.[108] Edoardo arrived at the apartment and spent the night as a guest: "We dined together and continued talking while walking in the roof garden until midnight." The pope spoke to him about African Cardinal Bernandin Gantin, in particular about an original homily he had given, and about the Vatican Secretary of State Villot, whose resignation he had refused, insisting that he remain:[109] Cardinal Villot intended to respect the freedom of the newly elected pope and hoped to be able to pass his last years in a French monastery.[110]

"Albino was very peaceful. He wasn't even tired," Edoardo reported about their meeting. "I remember that he said to me: 'If I had been told to be a road worker, I would have done it with the same tranquility.' Moreover, he added, 'I have never looked for any position, except the one you know about,'" referring to the only personal project for which he had expressed a desire, in 1947 — to be the custodian of a church in Falcade, Italy. Edoardo attended the morning Mass in the chapel of the apartment and they then had breakfast together.[111]

This was not the only meeting he had with his brother at the papal apartments. On Saturday, September 2, they met and had a conversation lasting about two hours.[112] The meeting was then extended to his other family members who had arrived at the Vatican for the beginning of the pontificate.[113] Antonia, the pope's sister, reported what he said to her: "Be at peace as I am at peace, because I haven't done anything to get here."[114]

On Thursday, September 14, he received other relatives who arrived from Marysville, Michigan, in the United States, where they had emigrated.[115] His niece, Pia Luciani, was also a guest for lunch in the apartment. In her report of the event, she emphasized her uncle's usual calm resolve.[116] For the occasion, the pope gave them a medal with the image of Our Lady of Guadalupe for their daughter, Morena.[117] The handwritten notes in his personal appointment book used during his pontificate suggested that he was thinking of the piscatorial ring with the image of Our Lady venerated at the Mexican shrine. In fact, at the bottom of his appointment book he wrote: "Ring with Our Lady of Guadalupe?"[118]

These were not the only private meetings that the pope granted. Besides the aforementioned Fr. Carlo Bolzan, who had been asked to organize the contents of the crates from Venice, another frequent visitor to the papal apartments was Dr. Antonio Da Ros. He had served as Luciani's personal physician ever since his ministry in Vittorio Veneto. On September 3, after the meeting with the group from Vittorio Veneto, the doctor and his wife were invited to visit at 3:30 p.m.[119] They visited again on September 13 and 23.[120] On September 8, Cardinal Antonio Poma, president of the Italian Episcopal Conference, was a guest for dinner along with the pope's private secretary.

During their conversation, John Paul I encouraged the archbishop of Bologna to continue as President of the Conference. The pope talked about Metropolitan Nikodim of the Russian Orthodox Church of Leningrad who died in his arms during the audience in the apostolic palace on September 5. He also spoke about the quest for Christian unity.[121] Later, he spoke of his ministry in Venice, the relevance of the Cini Foundation, and the Piperno family from Bologna who were his benefactors during his formative years in Belluno.[122]

On September 13, the pope's lunch guest was Msgr. Fortunato Marchi, the treasurer of the Patriarchate of Venice. The day before, Marchi had contacted the secretary, Lorenzi, about the pope's pension plan, as required by Italian law, since the pope had reached age sixty-five. Their conversation covered various topics: from the exposition of the Shroud of Turin to the possibility of a trip to Puebla, Mexico, for the next General Conference of the Latin American Episcopate,[123] which seemed unapproved by the pope because the Latin American state had no diplomatic relations with the Holy See. During lunch, John Paul I also began to correct the drafts of his speeches in *L'Osservatore Romano*.[124] In the pontiff's hand-written papers, there is also a confirmation of the private audience with Valerio Volpini, the director of the Vatican's newspaper.[125] The pope wrote a note about this audience: "Volpini = not binding - 20 thousand copies OR - Center for the production of video cassettes; the TV for transmitting them."[126]

The bishop of Belluno-Feltre, Maffeo Ducoli was present for dinner on Friday, September 22. On that occasion, the pope told him that to restore the parish church in Agordo he had offered the copyrights he received from the publisher of *Illustrissimi* for the collection of imaginary letters, which Luciani had published in 1976. The prelate recalled that after saying farewell, the pope invited him to go back and thank the sisters who had prepared dinner.[127]

Among the private audiences in the Apostolic Palace, Luciani records one on September 7 with Vittore Branca and his wife. Branca was a philologist, a professor in Padua, and a member of the Cini Foundation in Venice. He had enjoyed a cordial friendship with Pope Paul VI, and maintained the same friendship with Luciani.

The pope welcomed the couple into his study "that clear, early September morning, after we had passed through still-deserted loggias and the Vatican rooms." Luciani was worried that he would not be able to offer them even a cup of coffee.[128] Luciani signed a message for the Cini Foundation, informing the president that he had asked Capovilla to substitute for him at the commemoration of the first anniversary of Count Cini's death. The pope had even expressed his concern to the prefect of the Congregation for Bishops, Sebastiano Cardinal Baggio, that during his patriarchate in Venice he had been unable to follow the institution fully. However, he considered the institution "important for its influence, not only on the city and region, but throughout the country."[129]

There is no actual documentary evidence of other strictly private audiences during the course of his pontificate.[130] Nor do we know — considering what Luciani had to face a few years earlier regarding the Catholic Bank of Veneto — whether, or how, he might have been interested in the contingent financial problem, which — one should stress — manifested itself during the time of the previous pontiff and continued with his successor. Regarding the possible choices John Paul I had in mind, in his notes dating back to the pontificate we find only one note on the *Lex Ecclesiae Fundamentalis*, a topic on which debate had begun during the pontificate of Paul VI.[131]

As can be seen from the numerous texts and plentiful tribunal documentation, there is instead ample evidence of the balance and serene mastery that Luciani demonstrated from the beginning as he dealt with the tasks and issues that were placed in front of him. "He immediately showed that he was up to the task of being the successor of Peter and faced all the problems at that time with wisdom and without hesitation," said Giovanni Cardinal Battista Re, then an official of the Secretariat of State.[132] John Paul I did not appear distressed or crushed by the weight of his new responsibility; he had been prepared by his twenty years of episcopate during a difficult era. Indeed, he seemed to exhibit great serenity in governance.[133] Observing John Paul I closely on a daily basis, the papal butler, Angelo Gugel, stated that:

In his day-to-day work of audiences and meetings, he never complained about being tired or fatigued. He was resistant to fatigue, always serene and was not worried about the various problems he would eventually have to face. A cardinal coming out of an audience with the pope told me one day how very happy he was because after months of looking for a solution to a problem, the pope had given him a clear and definitive answer. The pope was confident and determined in his decisions.[134]

Even the commander of the Vatican Gendarmerie at the time, Camillo Cibin, noted that he was "very attentive to people and their problems,"[135] and was facing "his new tasks with serenity,"[136] and confirmed, while in his new office, his extraordinary memory, which he used to recall facts, problems, and people down to the smallest detail.[137] Observing him from within the papal apartments, Sr. Margherita Marin herself confirmed that she never found him "anxious or worried ... not even a headache," and recalled having seen him "always calm, serene. He knew how to work with his collaborators ... I never saw him show signs of impatience with anyone."[138]

Cardinal Caprio, then the Substitute for General Affairs to the Secretary of State, stated in his testimonial report that those days "were full of commitments, many of which were quite burdensome, but the pope accepted them and carried them all out calmly, masterfully, and so naturally one would think he had been prepared for them for a long time."[139] Cardinal Giovanni Coppa, then a councilor in the Secretariat of State, highlighted the pope's "freedom from bureaucratic schemes" and stated that he was "serene, open, even joking; he stayed high above the fray."[140]

The observations by the deputy of the Secretariat of State, among others, help lessen some of the lingering clichés, that painted Pope Luciani as "bewildered," "isolated," "naive" and "crushed by the enormous stress that followed his election":[141]

The pope did not hide the gravity of the task that the Lord had entrusted to him, nor the importance of the problems that were submitted to him for judgment. He studied everything calmly and his decisions were clear, firm and precise. I confess that at first his spontaneity disconcerted me: but, as the days passed, I noticed that his knowledge of people and his preparation ahead of confronting a situation were far superior to what his humility made it seem; the faith and trust he placed in divine assistance knew no bounds. He never smiled to be misleading. He listened, he inquired, and he studied. However, once he made a decision, he did not backtrack, unless new facts were introduced.[142]

Finally, Cardinal Baggio, who in his role as prefect of the Congregation for Bishops, met the pope at least twice during his pontificate, acknowledged that "he treated problems with great clarity and practicality ... the qualities of governance that I admired most in him were his wisdom and calmness."[143]

These were the qualities of governance that John Paul I exhibited during the last week of his pontificate. He moved resolutely ahead with ecumenical meetings, promoting dialogue and peace, and emphasized the call to poverty and the responsibilities of the universal Church, as evidenced by his actions and ordinary magisterium.

The final week opened with the pope's efforts to promote peace. Those efforts were made concrete in two particular situations. The first was his letter dated September 20, addressed to the bishops of the episcopal conferences of Argentina and Chile. Because of this mediation by the Holy See, the two countries avoided an impending clash caused by a border dispute over the sovereignty of the islands in the Beagle Channel.[144] The second was his letter dated September 21, which he personally sent to the president of the United States, Jimmy Carter. It concerned an international issue that was a recurrent theme throughout the entire pontificate: support for peace talks that took place in Camp David on September 17, between the American president, the Egyptian President Anwar Sadat and the Israeli Prime Minister Menachem Begin. During the pope's first General Audience held September 6, on the theme of humility, he asked those present to pray:

> For an intention that I have much at heart ... that these
> talks may pave the way towards a full and just peace. Just:
> that is, to the satisfaction of all the parties in the conflict.
> Full: without leaving any problem unresolved; the problem
> of the people of Palestine, the security of Israel, the Holy
> City of Jerusalem.[145]

The pope's support for the summit was immediately taken up by
the American diplomatic community and interpreted in the light of
the pope's previous meeting with U.S. Vice President Mondale, as
evidenced by the confidential notes of the U.S. State Department.[146]

On September 10, Luciani spoke extensively about the summit.
He dedicated the Sunday Angelus to its success and emphasized
how the three leaders — Carter, Sadat, and Begin — had prayed for
the success of the talks.[147] The three had expressly asked the people to pray with them "so that peace and justice might emerge from
these deliberations."[148] Diplomatic channels again echoed the pope's
endorsement. A few days later, after thirteen days of intense and at
times dramatic negotiations, which had repeatedly given the impression of not being resolved positively, the summit concluded with
the signing in Washington of the Framework for Peace in the Middle East and the Framework for the Conclusion of a Peace Treaty
between Egypt and Israel. On September 17, President Carter wrote
to the pope to inform him of the results that had been achieved, declaring that he had received "great inspiration from your prayers for
the Camp David summit and for peace in the Middle East," as documented by a secret note of the U.S. State Department.[149] On September 21, Pope Luciani, in turn, wrote directly to President Carter.

The letter, which was signed at the bottom and reported in the
confidential note of the American Embassy in Rome to the U.S. Secretary of State, reads as follows:

> We are profoundly grateful for your courteous message of
> September 17, in which you kindly and promptly informed
> us of the results obtained at the Camp David summit. We
> have taken careful note of the points of convergence reached

in the talks, as you have indicated to us in detail, which concern both the overall peace plan for the Middle East and the future peace treaty between Egypt and Israel. Noting with pleasure the intensive and effective work that you brought to fruition in the difficult search for an agreement at Camp David, we wish to express our ardent desire that the result obtained may actually constitute an important step on the way to a definitive solution to the problem of the Middle East, and the full reconciliation of the peoples who have suffered so much from the sad and prolonged conflict.

John Paul I concluded:

> Rest assured that the Holy See will continue, as in the past, to follow with deep interest the efforts to achieve this goal. It is ready to collaborate by every possible means compatible with its activity. Likewise, we will continue to lift up our prayers for that path which is so necessary for the Middle Eastern states and the whole world and we pray for the progress of the American people and their leaders.[150]

Even in his final week, the programmatic commitment to the search for peace extended into the busy schedule of audiences and ecumenical meetings which wove throughout his pontificate.[151] Maronite Patriarch Antoine Khoraiche of Antioch revealed, in a statement released to Vatican Radio on September 30, that John Paul I

> was thinking of making a special visit to Lebanon to personally work towards restoring peace among the children of that nation. He had also graciously promised to receive us a second time in a private audience before we returned to Lebanon, at which time we would have a discussion with His Holiness on the subject of such a visit.[152]

Moreover, these priorities were taken up and continued through his final days, without lessening his responsibilities regarding the universal Church. Again, on September 21, the day of his letter to Carter, he received the bishops of the 12th pastoral region of the United States of America for an *ad limina* visit. During this audience, for the first time after an official speech, the pope invited the prelates to ask him questions. After a moment of amazement at this unprecedented request, they asked the pope to talk about his pastoral experience in Vittorio Veneto and Venice. Leaning on the auxiliary bishop of New York, Anthony Francis Mestice to be his interpreter, Luciani responded. He concluded, saying, "For us bishops, the personal encounter with the people is more valuable than our great speeches."[153]

Among the last acts of John Paul I was the appointment of his successor in Venice. It was an appointment that led directly to the last of his thirty-four days in the Chair of St. Peter.

Not many residential bishops were received in audience during his brief pontificate.[154] On the first page of the personal appointment book he used during his month at the Vatican, noted under "visiting senior cardinals" were the names of Alfredo Ottaviani, former prefect of the Holy Office, and Cardinal Alberto di Jorio, former pro-president of the Pontifical Commission for Vatican City.[155] Subsequent pages show the names of Pericle Felici, prefect of the Apostolic Signatura, and Stefan Wyszyński, archbishop of Warsaw and Primate of Poland.[156]

The appointments of eleven bishops were published, nine of whom were residential, while the other two were diplomats.[157] However, it was primarily the vacancy of the See of Venice, led by Luciani from 1970 until his election to the Chair of Peter, which affected the whole course of the month of his pontificate: "Venice" recurs twice in his personal appointment book.[158]

Initially, it was proposed the pope should keep the title of the Patriarchal See at the Cathedral of San Marco, as Patriarchs Sarto and Roncalli had already done, by appointing one of his vicars at the Lagoon.[159] However, on August 29, while waiting to identify a successor for the Chair of St. Mark, Luciani preferred instead to appoint an apostolic administrator for the patriarchate and conferred upon him the powers of a diocesan ordinary with the onus of reporting directly to the pope. He also confirmed the pastoral and presbyteral councils.[160] The administrator, Giuseppe Bosa, who was given permission to suspend the implementation of a reform of the Curia, which had been announced with the appointment of three episcopal vicars,[161] was entrusted with a message to deliver to the faithful of Venice[162] while the pope wrote a letter directly to the seminarians of Venice.[163]

The names of several potential candidates for the Venice office immediately began to circulate. Among them was Pasquale Macchi, the former secretary of Paul VI and his executor.[164] However, the documentary sources acquired by the Congregation for Bishops for the records of the cause have made it possible to eliminate all hypotheses and inferences.[165]

As far as it appears, the first candidate for the Chair of St. Mark was the Jesuit Fr. Bartolomeo Sorge, director of *La Civiltà Cattolica*. At the time, he had only heard about it from "well-informed" people; but it was in fact confirmed for him a few months later by John Paul II and, later, from the Jesuit Fr. Paolo Dezza, whom Luciani had chosen to be his confessor.

According to Sorge, he had become associated with the "progressive" label, something about which Cardinal Giovanni Colombo of Milan would have expressed uncertainty.[166] What is certain is that on August 30, Cardinal Sebastiano Baggio, prefect of the Congregation of Bishops, in a confidential note *ex audientia Summi Pontificis*, wrote:

> The Holy Father spoke to me, *motu proprio*, about appointing the new Patriarch of Venice: it was not very urgent, because he had appointed the Vicar General Monsignor G. Bosa as Apostolic Administrator *"sede vacante cum onere referendi ad ipsum Summum Pontificem."* His preferred candidate would be Fr. Bartolomeo Sorge, SJ, Sardinian by origin, but born in the Veneto region, where he has family. See if there are precedents and start a very discreet investigation.[167]

The "very discreet investigation" began immediately. On August 31,

Baggio already received information from Fr. Pedro Arrupe, the superior general of the Society of Jesus, who, after a detailed report, wrote in conclusion that "Father Sorge could respond well to the concrete responsibility of an episcopal ministry if, all things considered, the Holy See believed it necessary to entrust it to him."[168] On the same day, the prefect of the Congregation of Bishops, in a confidential note, wrote that he had questioned the Cardinal Vicar of Rome Ugo Poletti about the Jesuit's candidacy. Poletti said he was "completely favorable" and considered Father Sorge "worthy and capable," noting:

> He will be a great contribution to the Italian Episcopal Conference which from an intellectual point of view is quite weak, even in the permanent council. Above all, he will be a comfort to many lay people who are very faithful, and much attached to the Church, but who feel that the Church hierarchy does not fully grasp the many urgent issues of the contemporary world.

Alongside this consideration, Baggio noted, "He certainly does not talk about those who have already made a different political and cultural choice." Thus he concluded that his possible appointment, according to the Vicar of Rome, would "certainly be criticized in certain sectors, but would do honor to the pope by creating much sympathy for him."[169]

The Jesuit Dezza was also solicited for his opinion, and on September 2 he responded to the ad hoc questionnaire by attaching a final consideration of this tenor:

> Your Eminence rightly observed that the episcopate today is more than a position of honor, it is a service that involves commitment and suffering. However, it seems to me that in countries, such as Italy, which have a good diocesan clergy, it is preferable that this pastoral office be entrusted to diocesan priests rather than to religious, and especially to Jesuits. … In any case, regardless of this consideration, and looking

at the person of Father Sorge, I feel I must give a positive response to the questions contained in the attached questionnaire. The only difficulty comes from some of his attitudes and statements regarding certain religious-social-political problems, which are hotly debated today, and which seem to be too extreme for some and have created opposition against him in certain ecclesiastical and lay circles. It seems to me that these are debatable opinions, which may be contradicted by others, but which do not contain doctrinal errors; on the contrary, one must acknowledge his sincere and ready disposition to comply with any directives of the Holy See. Therefore, I believe that these attitudes of his do not constitute a difficulty in themselves unless the opposition, which I mentioned above, in ecclesiastical and lay circles, is such as to discourage his appointment for reasons of prudence.[170]

On September 4, another positive opinion came from the Benedictine Paul Augustin Mayer, then secretary of the Congregation for Religious.[171] On the same day, Cardinal Antonio Poma, archbishop of Bologna and president of the Italian bishops' conference, expressed a different opinion, pointing out, among other things, that:

> The aforementioned priest, after Berlinguer's letter to Monsignor Bettazzi, publicly called for cultural dialogue with Italian Communism. Such a position is not conducive to the unity of the Italian episcopate. He is pursuing, with a concrete plan, a precise intention to consolidate some Catholic groups or forces, different from others, in view of any possible national convention. [An attempt, though not fully successful, had already been made].[172]

The cardinal of Bologna therefore maintained that this did not coincide "with the national program of the Italian bishops' conference," and therefore concluded, "All things considered — despite the recognition of the great gifts of the aforementioned priest — the vote for the proposed See, undoubtedly important and significant for all of Italy, is, it seems, negative."[173]

Having received this information, Pope Luciani took pen and paper and on September 10 wrote in his own hand to Archbishop Giovanni Colombo of Milan:

> Your Eminence, among the candidates for the Patriarchate of Venice is Father B. Sorge. My informants agree in recognizing his personal piety, his fidelity to the Holy See, and his cultural preparation. Some point to him enthusiastically. A few others have reservations because of his seemingly apparent ties to somewhat suspicious Catholic currents, due to some expressions he may have let slip in the past. On the positive side, it would be difficult to find a successor in Triveneto and Sorge is partly from Veneto (his mother and brothers live there and Monsignor Carraro was his spiritual advisor in the past), the bishops of Triveneto greatly appreciated the Spiritual Retreat Courses he preached. The clergy and the laity in Venice like him.
>
> Can you give me some advice? *Sub secreto sia m.* Blessings, with all my heart,
>
> I. Paulus PP. I.[174]

Evidently, the council would have had a different opinion if the pope were to turn to another candidate. The next candidate was the Salesian, Fr. Angelo Viganò, then active in the Ambrosian diocese and already well known by Luciani for his collaboration in the renewal of catechesis in Italy.[175] However, the priest may not have wanted to read what Cardinal Baggio wrote in his register on September 27:

> After a long, frank, and cordial conversation this evening, Fr. Angelo Viganò asked me if he could consult the former rector major of the Salesians, Father Ricceri (the current rector major, his brother Egidio, is away in South America). He will send me his written answer by tomorrow night. His uncertainly comes from not recognizing himself as having

a theological culture adequate to the needs of pastoral ministry today; from not knowing any foreign language other than a little French (but then he admitted that he can read a little English, too); from not having had any other experience except those related to the fields of organization, formation, and religious life; from the consciousness of having been overestimated both in Turin and Milan, so much so that he thinks that someone may have confused him with his brother Father Egidio, who has a personality far superior to his own.[176]

The records reflect, therefore, that the recalcitrant Father Viganò had actually been appointed to the Chair of St. Mark, as shown in the note for the audience with John Paul II, regarding what was provided for Venice. Baggio summarized what had been done:

The individual responses were submitted for the pope's consideration who, after reading them, focused his attention on Fr. Angelo Viganò, a Salesian, already approved for the episcopate, and designated him as his successor in Venice. However, Father Viganò, with whom I had a long and cordial conversation on September 27, sent me a letter the next day in which he begged the Holy Father to excuse him from accepting the appointment to the Patriarchate of Venice, indeed, not to consider him for any other diocese in the future, as he believed that he possessed neither adequate theological culture nor the proper pastoral experience and that he had been overestimated in both Turin and Milan. Father Viganò's letter, in its original text, was quickly sent to the Cardinal Secretary of State who immediately brought it to the attention of the Holy Father.[177]

Thus we come to September 28, the last day of the life of John Paul I, a day in which the pope expected to meet with the Secretary of State Jean Villot in order to examine the letter from Father Viganò of Milan, in which he had clearly and decisively expressed his reservations about being appointed the Patriarch of Venice. Not giving up, Luciani was counting on the support of Cardinal Colombo in an attempt to convince the Salesian to accept.[178] Moreover, this was precisely the subject of the pope's final phone call with the Archbishop of Milan on the evening of September 28.

It would be his last call before closing the book of his earthly existence.

SEPTEMBER 28: THE LAST DAY

"In the morning, he went into the chapel to pray at the usual time, and he celebrated Mass with us at seven. He normally had breakfast, and then stopped for a while to read the newspapers. Then, around nine o'clock, he went downstairs for his morning audiences."[179]

The chronicle of the last day of John Paul I, Thursday, September 28, 1978, began by mirroring, without significant variations, those of previous days. Moreover, the day is reported in great detail by the eyewitness Sr. Margherita Marin, the only one still alive of the four nuns from the Sisters of the Holy Child Mary who were called to assist him in the pontifical apartments. They served from August 30 to September 29, 1978. She was thirty-seven at the time, making her the youngest of the group.[180] The sequence of events that day, recounted by the nun who has since maintained complete confidentiality, remains an essential point of reference, given the credibility of the witness, even though her testimony has only recently been entered into the records.[181]

As scheduled, during his morning audiences that day Pope Luciani received Cardinal Julio Rosales and the bishops of the Philippines for an *ad limina* visit. He gave them a speech in English about the spread of the Gospel in the Far East.[182] Then he received two apostolic nuncios, the one to Brazil, the other to Holland, as well as the editor of the newspaper *Il Gazzettino,* who had published his articles in the past, for Luciani was well-known as a brilliant writer among the Italian episcopate. This was followed by a meeting with Cardinal Gantin of Africa,[183] in the cardinal's dual capacity as president of the Pontifical Commission *Iustitia et Pax* and president of the Pontifical Council *Cor Unum.* He was accompanied by the secretaries of the two dicasteries: the Jesuit Roger Heckel and the Dominican Henri de Riedmatten.[184] They met to coordinate the Church's activities in the field of human promotion, justice, and peace from the perspective of the directives issued by the Second Vatican Council. "He welcomed us with great kindness," Gantin recalls. "He arranged the chairs himself so that we could be at his side ... No one could imagine that a few hours later he would pass into eternity."[185]

Margherita Marin stated that around noon the pope returned to the apartments asking the nuns in the kitchen for a coffee, and then immediately went to his private study.

"Around noon he came back upstairs to the apartments," the sister said, "but I remember that he came into the kitchen, as he often did, asking us for a coffee: 'Sisters, do you have any coffee? Could you make me a coffee?' He sat down to wait, took the coffee, and went to his study." He then had lunch with his secretaries. Later, he retired for his usual short afternoon rest. That afternoon, he stayed in the apartments[186]: "I don't remember exactly when he went back to his rooms," the nun asserted, "but he stayed home that whole afternoon. He never left the apartments, and he received no one because he told us he was drafting a document for the bishops. However, I do not know to which bishops he was referring."[187] The witness assures us:

> I remember it well because that afternoon I was ironing in
> the wardrobe room with the door open, and I could see him

going back and forth. He was walking around the apartment with papers in his hand that he was reading. Every now and then he would stop to make a few notes, and then he would start walking again while reading. As he was walking, he would pass by where I was standing. I remember that, seeing me ironing, he also said to me: "Sister, I make you work so hard … but you don't need to iron that shirt so well because it's hot. … Just iron the collar and the cuffs — you can't see the rest, you know." He told me this in his Venetian dialect, which he often used with us. That's how he spent the whole afternoon.[188]

In the apartment that afternoon, according to Sister Margherita's observations, were both secretaries, Frs. John Magee and Diego Lorenzi.[189] The pope kept his appointment scheduled for 6:00 p.m. with the Secretary of State, Cardinal Villot. Then, he recited Evening Prayer in English with the secretaries and had dinner around 8:00 p.m. With him at table were his secretaries and the papal butler, Angelo Gugel, serving as usual, while the nuns were in the small room reserved for them.[190] After dinner, around 9:00 p.m., he had a phone call with Cardinal Giovanni Colombo, archbishop of Milan: "I had already heard the Holy Father talking that morning to Father Magee about this phone call," confirmed the nun. She added: "I don't remember exactly how long their conversation lasted, maybe half an hour. Afterwards he came to us, as he always did, to say goodnight before he retired."[191] The nun also spoke about her last image of Pope Luciani. She remembered him in front of his private study, next to the bedroom, when, after having already said goodnight to the sisters, he turned around once more and waved goodnight to them before closing the door.[192]

Therefore, the last people to see him enter his room were the nuns, not the secretaries. In addition to the tranquility the nuns observed in him as he retired, the witness also stated that, as usual, the pope's secretaries did not accompany him to his room. Thus, that last evening, "he went alone to his room, as usual, and did not need to be accompanied."[193]

That summarizes the last day of the life of John Paul I, reconstructed from all the documentary and testimonial sources entered into the records during the proceedings of the investigation. In order to establish what really happened and the exact order of events during those last hours of the life of John Paul I, a comparison of the eyewitness testimony can only be the beginning. As far as that afternoon and evening are concerned, the depositions of the secretaries Fr. Diego Lorenzi[194] and Fr. John Magee[195] show glaring divergences. The first of these, in the reports provided by the two secretaries, concerns an alleged illness from which the pope supposedly suffered in the afternoon. According to Father Magee's account, the pontiff had experienced this ailment in the early afternoon:

> I was in the private secretariat, a few steps away from the hall. At a certain point, I heard the voice of the Holy Father calling me. I went immediately and found the Holy Father standing by the table with his hand on his chest. He explained to me that he had a pain in his chest and asked me to call Sister Vincenza, the nurse, because according to him she had some fabulous medicine. Sister Vincenza came with the medicine and a glass of water. The pope took the medicine, and I was going to accompany him to his bedroom to get some rest. Then I spoke with Fr. Diego Lorenzi, who was then returning from outside. I told him that I intended to call the doctor, but he told me that the Holy Father would not want that. A short time later, the Holy Father called me to tell me that the pain had passed and that he was ready to receive Cardinal Villot.[196]

These details were then reiterated by Magee on several occasions until the conference held in Canale d'Agordo on September 27, 2008, when they were further amplified as an addition to his testimony:

> On the afternoon of September 28, the pope did not go to the roof garden because the air was quite chilly and he wanted to walk around the great hall. ... I remember that

afternoon when I was in the secretariat, Father Diego was out, and I was alone in the secretariat. At a certain point, I heard the pope calling me. I went to him and saw him standing next to the table and he said to me: "Can you call Sister Vincenza for me?" and I said: "Yes, Your Holiness right away … are you not feeling well?" "Uh, I have a pain here," he said, putting his hand to his chest.[197]

The Irish secretary again emphasizes Sister Vincenza's involvement in a passage that almost has the flavor of *excusatio non-petita* in the way he colors the alleged intervention while distancing himself from responsibility.

So I went to get the nun and she immediately came with some medicine, the kind you put under your tongue. After Sister Vincenza gave him the medicine, I helped the Holy Father to his bedroom to rest. … Then, when I returned after the meeting with Cardinal Villot, I asked him: "Your Holiness, how do you feel?" And he struck his chest three times with a clenched fist saying: "I feel really good. Sister Vincenza's medicine works miracles, Sister Vincenza always comes through."[198]

Later, Magee again took care to ask the pope for reassurances about his health, even after the meeting with Cardinal Villot, with whom Luciani stayed until about 6:30 p.m. "I asked the Holy Father how he was, and he replied, 'Very well! That medicine of Sister Vincenza's is really good.'"[199]

Fr. Diego Lorenzi mentions the same episode in his deposition, but — after asserting, unlike Magee, that the pope that afternoon had gone up for "a short walk in the roof garden of the palace"[200] — he indicated the incident took place at dinner and stated:

At about 8:00 p.m. the pope, Monsignor Magee and I had dinner. Rather suddenly, the pope put his hands to his chest saying, "I am having some pains, but they are passing." Our immediate reaction was to say, "There is a doctor within easy reach, let's call him." He replied, "It is passing, there is no need."[201]

It should be noted that Father Lorenzi revealed these details for the first time on October 2, 1987, nine years after the death of Pope Luciani, during a live television broadcast;[202] and that Magee revealed his the following year, in 1988, during an interview he granted the international monthly *30giorni*.[203] The episode of the illness and, even more notably, the involvement of Sr. Vincenza Taffarel and the medicine she administered that afternoon, finds no confirmation in the account by Sister Margherita, who declared with certainty that John Paul I did not feel any pain and affirmed that she did not see "any particular activity either by Sister Vincenza, or by the secretaries that would make me suspect otherwise."[204]

Dr. Antonio Da Ros, Luciani's personal physician since his episcopate in Vittorio Veneto,[205] declared during the tribunal hearing that on the evening of September 28 he had communicated by phone with Sister Vincenza: "Let me point out that I made a telephone call to Sister Vincenza around 7:30 in the evening of September 28. She assured me that the pope, despite having had an intense day, was fine and there was nothing new to report."[206] Also in his diary notes, written at the time of the events and deposited in the tribunal records, the doctor recorded, "At 7:30 p.m., I telephoned the Vatican and, as usual, the pope was fine."[207] Moreover, this data was confirmed in the statements given by the pontiff's close relatives following the meeting they had with Sister Vincenza herself, a few days after the pope's death.[208]

Regarding the statements of the two secretaries, the pope's niece, Lina Petri, expressed some reservations. She recalled how, the next morning, after discovering the pope's death, Sister Vincenza did not mention any episode of illness whatsoever. In fact, she pointed out "that Lina's uncle was in better health in Rome than he had been in Venice."[209] Even the eldest daughter of his brother Edoardo, Pia Luciani, referred to the conversation she and her family had with Sister Vincenza, a nun who had assisted the pope since his episcopate years in Vittorio Veneto:

> Immediately afterwards, we spoke with Sister Vincenza, who had always been attentive and close by. ... She also told us that there had been no problems, neither the previous day nor before. Sister Vincenza had such knowledge and respect for our uncle, and we trusted her so much that we had no reason to doubt her.[210]

Dr. Renato Buzzonetti,[211] who was then officially the Coadjutor to the Director of the Vatican Health Service and who confirmed the death of the pontiff, also certified in his statement that at his explicit request "the Vatican Pharmacy denied having received any request for drugs from the pope's private apartments in the evening hours of September 28."[212]

However, although the details were decidedly creative and there were differences in the reported time of certain events, and despite having been kept quiet for a decade by both secretaries, the episode of a possible illness occurring around 7:30-8:00 p.m. was reported the next day, in the findings of the confirmation of death. The report was made by the secretary, Magee, to Doctor Buzzonetti, who notes in a confidential document, bound by professional secrecy, dated October 9, 1978, and addressed to the then substitute of the Secretariat of State Msgr. Giuseppe Caprio:

> The episode of pain, localized in the upper third of the sternal region, which the Holy Father suffered around 7:30 p.m. on the day of his death, lasted for over five minutes and occurred while the pope was seated and intent on the recitation of Compline[213] with Father Magee. It regressed without any therapy. In this regard, the (nonliteral) testimony of Father Magee was as follows: "The pope repeatedly brought his hand to his chest, the pain was quite strong; it was a disorder that the Holy Father had already experienced on previous occasions and that he interpreted as being 'rheumatic' in nature. His Holiness decisively refused the intervention

of a doctor." The pope's secretary gave his own version of the Holy Father's interpretation of this morbid event.[214]

This was confidential documentation in the keeping of the doctor, strictly contemporary with the events and acquired only recently after its release was authorized for the tribunal process. Its importance can be seen from the declaration signed by Doctor Buzzonetti, in which he stated that in the days following the death of the pontiff, he wrote "some confidential reports bound by professional secrecy, signed only by me or jointly with Professor Mario Fontana, director of the Vatican Health Service, destined for the Secretariat of State and the College of Cardinals gathered in the Congregation."[215] Therefore, referring to the episode described in the report of February 28, 2013, which was included in the records, Buzzonetti himself further specified:

> Father Magee, next to the bed of the deceased, reported to me that around 7:30 p.m. the Holy Father: 1. repeatedly brought his hand to his chest; 2. complained of a rather strong retro-sternal pain; 3. [the pain] was not accompanied by breathlessness; 4. It lasted for over five minutes; 5. It regressed without treatment; 6. It occurred while he was seated, intent on the recitation of compline together with the secretary Magee; 7. The pope refused to involve the doctor of the Vatican Medical Guard, asserting that these painful episodes were not infrequent for him and were to be classified as "rheumatic in nature."[216]

Therefore, one should note that if this symptom, underestimated at the time, was experienced by the pope in the evening hours, it was such that it was noticed only by the secretaries and not by the sisters, who in fact made no mention of it, either in the above-mentioned phone call from Doctor Da Ros or in the subsequent meetings with the pope's closest relatives. In any case, if the indisposition manifested itself, Luciani spent both the afternoon and the evening completely calm, as noted in the testimony of the witness Sr. Margherita Marin.

The *de visu* witness accounts agree that the pope's audience with Cardinal Villot took place around 6:00 p.m. The cardinal gave the pope the letter he received from the Prefect of the Congregation of Bishops concerning a priest from Lombardy, Fr. Angelo Viganò, who had refused the appointment as Patriarch of Venice.[217] The witnesses further agree that once the cardinal had departed, the pope celebrated Evening Prayer in English with the secretaries. Dinner followed around 8:00 p.m., with the papal butler serving.[218]

However, there are still inconsistencies in the secretaries' accounts of what took place during and after dinner. Using an imitative style, Magee narrated the conversation that took place at dinner: He asked the pope if he had chosen someone to preach the spiritual retreat for the Roman Curia during the first week of Lent. The pope said he had, adding, "But the retreat I would like to have now would be for a good death." Moreover, while the other secretary tried to change the subject, the pope recalled together with Father Diego a prayer for a good death that he had learned from his mother: "God, give me the grace to accept the death with which you will strike me."[219]

Magee does not report the episode of the illness during the dinner, which was otherwise reported with some emphasis by Fr. Diego Lorenzi in his deposition, and so in his last published report:

> After that day's audiences — the last of which was with Cardinal Secretary of State Villot — we were at table for dinner, [the pope] was already seated, and he began telling the two secretaries: "Strange … I'm feeling some chest pains … but I notice they are getting less intense." My surprise was shared by Monsignor Magee, who took care to say: "There is always a doctor on call; it doesn't cost anything to have him come over." He dissuaded us from doing so and — I must add, almost as an apology — that in the past, I had never allowed myself to contradict him. My inexperience, then, regarding the premonitory symptoms of heart problems linked to those pains, played a notable part in our continuing with dinner.[220]

The eyewitnesses all agreed about there being a telephone conversation with the archbishop of Milan, Giovanni Colombo, around 9:00 p.m. After the audience with Cardinal Villot, Luciani asked Father Lorenzi to contact the cardinal, but "he was away, so I decided I would contact him later."[221] Magee affirmed that they were still at the table:

> The pope turned to Father Diego and said to him: "I would like to call Cardinal Colombo on the telephone, you go and get him and I will come right away." … Father Diego left the room; then, standing at the end of the corridor, he said to the pope: "Your Holiness, Cardinal Colombo is on the telephone."[222]

Therefore, the pope and the cardinal were finally able to talk and their conversation lasted for about half an hour.[223]

As for the content of the phone call, the papers from the Congregation for Bishops dispel, as we have said, all the assumptions that were made over time.[224] The purpose and object of the conversation was to designate his successor in Venice, during which Luciani asked the Archbishop of Milan to speak with Fr. Angelo Viganò and insist that he accept the appointment as Patriarch of the Chair of St. Mark.[225] In fact, during the telephone conversation, they certainly "tackled the subject of the appointment to the Patriarchate of Venice" and the cardinal — back from a trip to Boston for the inauguration of a monument to Father Orione — would also have brought the pontiff "the enthusiastic devotion of the Americans towards him." Finally, Colombo also learned "that the pope had already retired from his work desk and was about to go to bed," as stated in the testimony of Msgr. Francantonio Bernasconi, the last secretary of the Archbishop of Milan, who at the request of the postulation provided the documentation in his possession.[226] The archbishop of Milan himself stated:

> He spoke to me personally and for a long time in a voice that was very normal; it conveyed no evident weariness nor

was it possible to infer any physical illness from it. In his final farewell, he invoked some prayer and was full of serenity and hope.[227]

Regarding the final moments of that day, Father Lorenzi stressed in several speeches (but did not reiterate during the tribunal hearing) that he had spent the evening in the papal apartments using "that moment of calm to prepare some notes for a homily."[228] However, one should note that immediately after passing the telephone call to the pope, Fr. Diego Lorenzi left the papal apartments, as he had done before on other occasions, and which was unanimously reported by the witnesses.[229] It was also reported by Sr. Margherita Marin[230] and was confirmed by the papal butler, Angelo Gugel, during his interview with the relator for the cause of John Paul I.[231] Gugel also mentioned in his deposition that he lingered in the papal apartments that evening to prepare "a package with a pectoral cross that the pope wanted delivered to the bishop of Belluno-Feltre, Gioacchino Muccin. Father Lorenzi was supposed to take the package with him when he went by car to Venice the following day."[232] The next day, in fact, the priest would have had to travel back to the Veneto region where he was to celebrate a wedding. After dinner, around 9:00 p.m., the pope also personally said goodnight to the butler.[233]

The secretary Magee, on the other hand, stopped to talk to the nuns. He was leafing through the Pontifical Yearbook directory and commenting on it. Sr. Margherita Marin stated in her report:

> When dinner was over, after Father Diego handed over the phone call from Cardinal Colombo, he left the papal apartments. He had gone out in the evening other times. I know that the Holy Father had once told the secretaries that, if they wanted to, they could go out. And Father Diego had gone out several times. However, I don't know where he went. Father Magee, on the other hand, stayed there with us. He stopped by with us nuns to talk a little bit, to keep us company. I remember that he had the volume of the papal

yearbook with him. Perhaps he had to check something. He was leafing through it and began to read the list of popes: who they were, how long they had lived, etc. ... I remember that detail. He stayed with us for maybe half an hour. Then he too retired.[234]

The sisters retired last, around 10:30 p.m. or a little later.

With regard to the final courtesies paid to the pontiff, right up to the threshold of his bedroom, the versions offered by the secretaries once again diverge and therefore do not appear to be fully credible.

Magee, after the phone call with Cardinal Colombo, claims to have accompanied the pope alone to his room, "noting that he took a sheet with his homily"[235]— that is, he selected one from a collection of typed homilies,[236] and in the conference Magee gave during his testimony, he offered additional details, such as the following:

> After saying goodnight to the pope that evening, I went to the kitchen to say good night to the nuns, and I asked Sister Vincenza again how the Holy Father was, and she told me there had been other times when he was sick but, with these medicines, he was fine. I said: "But if he feels sick at night, we have this system now; you just press a button," and I had explained it to the pope and showed him where he should call me, and I went up to my room, sure that if he needed me I was ready to go immediately.[237]

The Irish secretary concluded: "His last words to me were, 'Thank you. Good night! See you tomorrow, God willing!' It was 9:30 p.m."[238] According to his version, Magee went to the kitchen to say goodnight to the nuns and to check again with Sister Vincenza on the normality of the afternoon episode of the illness.[239]

Lorenzi's reconstruction, formulated during the tribunal hearing, also seems to be pervaded by apologetic concerns.[240] He assures us that he and his colleague accompanied the pontiff to the threshold of his bedroom:

At the end of the conversation [with Cardinal Colombo], Father Magee and I accompanied the pope to his bedroom, and Father Magee thoughtfully pointed out to the pope the button on the headboard of his bed so that he could call us in case of need. The pope acknowledged the thoughtful suggestion, and we wished each other good night.[241]

The description is also inconsistent with what he himself said in the article he penned that appeared in *Il Gazzettino* in September 1979. In it, he stated that, immediately after the end of the telephone conversation with Cardinal Colombo, "the pope appeared at the door of our study wishing us a 'good night,' as he did every evening."[242]

These examples add to a multitude of contradictory and flowery details — overlapping over the years, up to the aforementioned statements by Lorenzi in the magazine *Messaggi di Don Orione* and by Magee at the aforementioned conference held in Canale d'Agordo. They highlight the unreliability of both secretaries in objectively reporting the sequence of events just before the pope's death.

Sr. Margherita Marin — as noted — denies their versions, stating that the pope went to sleep as usual and that as usual he "did not need to be accompanied."[243]

Thus concludes the last day of Pope Luciani's life:

After [Cardinal Colombo's phone call] he came to us, as he always did, to say goodnight to us before retiring to his study. I remember that he asked me which Mass I had prepared for him for the following day, and I answered him, "The Mass of the Angels." He wished us a good night saying what he used to say to us every evening: "Until tomorrow, sisters; if the Lord wishes, we'll all celebrate Mass together." There is a detail from that moment that remains imprinted in my memory: We were all together in the small living room with the door open, the door faced the door of his private study [adjacent to his bedroom], and after he said goodnight to us, the Holy Father stood at the door of his study, turned around again and waved goodnight to us, smiling. ... I feel like I can still see him there at the door. It is the last image I have of him.[244]

SEPTEMBER 29:
THE DISCOVERY

On the morning of Friday, September 29, the lifeless body of John Paul I was not found by his secretary, John Magee, as was later officially announced by the Vatican Press Office. The discovery of the death is attributed to Sr. Vincenza Taffarel, who was not alone at that juncture: Sr. Margherita Marin accompanied her. Sister Margherita's testimony, never before revealed and released only during the tribunal process, reported the moment of the discovery. She added: "How all those rumors came out, I really don't know. We were there. I can tell you, and I have told you, everything I know and have seen."[245] These are her words:

> I got up as usual around 5:00 a.m., because at 5:30 the groceries we ordered arrived and the flowers were deposited just outside the elevator. That morning, I went to collect everything, and after I put it all away, I returned to pray with the other sisters. The papal apartments were so small that we could always see each other, even when we were doing

different things. We were praying in the little room near the kitchen, all four of us together.

Around 5:10 that morning, like every morning, Sister Vincenza had left a cup of coffee for the Holy Father in the sacristy, in front of the chapel, just outside the pope's apartment. When the Holy Father came out of his room, he would have some coffee in the sacristy before he entered the chapel to pray. That morning, however, the coffee remained there. About ten minutes later, Sister Vincenza said: "He hasn't come out yet? Why not?" I was there in the corridor. So I saw that she knocked once, then she knocked again, but he did not answer ... there was still silence. Then, she opened the door and walked in. I was there as she entered, but I stayed outside. I heard her say, "Your Holiness, you shouldn't pull these jokes on me."

Then she called me as she came out, shocked, so I immediately went in with her and saw him. The Holy Father was in his bed, the reading light over the headboard was on. He had two pillows under his back that propped him up a bit, his legs were outstretched, his arms were on top of the bedsheets, he was wearing pajamas, and in his hands, resting on his chest, he was clutching some typewritten pages. His head was turned a little bit to the right with a slight smile, his glasses rested on his nose, and his eyes were half-closed ... he really seemed to be sleeping. I touched his hands; they were cold, I noticed and was struck by his fingernails, which were a little dark.[246]

The nun confidently reported that her attitude was calm and composed and that nothing in the room was out of place:

No. Nothing. Nothing. Not even a crease. Nothing fell to the floor, nothing was disheveled that could suggest there had been any noticeable illness. He looked just like someone who had fallen asleep reading. Who fell asleep and stayed that way.[247]

A few months later, the then Bishop of Belluno-Feltre, Maffeo Ducoli, asked her to tell him how the pope had really been found. The nun repeated that he had been found reposing in his bed and that "it hadn't even been creased."[248] The witness' statement fully agrees with what Doctor Buzzonetti confidentially certified regarding his objective examination of the body and the specific circumstances of his death,[249] definitely dispelling any conjecture or rumors that had subsequently been spread by the press.[250]

Immediately after the discovery, Sister Vincenza went to the upper floor of the apartments to call Magee,[251] while Sister Margherita ran to awaken Father Diego who "woke up with a start."[252] The first secretary to go down turned out to have been Magee, at 5:25 a.m., according to his story:

> I immediately went down with the nuns to see if it was true. I asked the nuns to stay outside and went into the bedroom alone. I found the Holy Father in bed, almost seated, with his glasses on and with the page of the homily in his hands, as if he were reading at that moment. I touched his hands and they were cold. I knelt beside the bed. I prayed. I cried.[253]

Soon after, Magee telephoned the Vatican doctor and the Camerlengo, Cardinal Jean Villot. In his testimony, the Irish cleric painted these moments with pathos, feeling at the time that he had been invested with the "great responsibility … to reveal to the whole world that the pope was dead." Moreover, he worried about having to communicate it immediately to Secretary of State Villot, considering the cardinal's precarious health, given that he had already suffered two heart attacks.[254]

According to his account, he telephoned Dr. Renato Buzzonetti at 5:42 a.m. from his private secretary's office. This is confirmed in the doctor's testimonial report:

> At dawn on September 29, 1978, at 5:42 a.m., (the time on my watch), I was awakened by a telephone call from Father

Magee: "The pope is dead." He urged me to hurry to the Vatican. At around 6:00 a.m., I entered the pontiff's bedroom, an environment I knew from the many professional meetings I had with Paul VI.[255]

Father Magee called Doctor Buzzonetti to attend to the emergency rather than Professor Mario Fontana, the then director of the Vatican Health Service and primary pontifical physician. It should be noted that the reason for this was not because the professor was ill and resided away from the Apostolic Palace. It was because — unbeknownst to the professor — Doctor Buzzonetti had already been designated by the pontiff as "the Roman coadjutor of Doctor Da Ros, who had retained his post as the pope's personal physician, despite residing in Vittorio Veneto."[256] Forty years later, the circumstances of Doctor Buzzonetti's appointment have now been clarified. In his report, Buzzonetti explained that on September 23, Magee had summoned him to a confidential meeting with Doctor Da Ros, who communicated "brief hints of the pontiff's medical history." On that occasion, it was proposed that Doctor Buzzonetti should be a second doctor for John Paul I.[257] At that juncture, Buzzonetti had reservations about his decision "because he considered the proposal risky and scarcely valid from an operational point of view." However, the following day he wrote to Magee and declared he was "willing to accept the assignment" that was "proposed to him on behalf of the Holy Father." On September 24, the Irish secretary responded to Doctor Buzzonetti in writing, noting his availability "but without mentioning his actual appointment to the new post."[258]

In a confidential letter sent to the deputy of the Vatican Secretariat of State, dated October 9, 1978, the doctor in fact wrote:

I also consider it my duty to send you a photocopy of the letters that were exchanged between myself and Father J. Magee after the proposal Doctor Da Ros and Father Magee made to me regarding the medical assistance for the Holy Father of venerable memory. It stipulated that — alongside Doctor Da Ros, who would take on the role of "personal physician to the pope" while maintaining his residence in Vittorio Veneto — I would be in charge of the assistance service during the Pontifical Ceremonies and Audiences as well as any emergency services. Due to rapidly unfolding events, the proposal was not followed up, and I never received an explicit mandate. Finally, let me take this opportunity to inform Your Most Reverend Excellency that on Friday, October 6 of this year, at 8:30 p.m., in fulfillment of the task I received from you, I telephoned Doctor Da Ros in Vittorio Veneto (area code 0438) and invited him, on your behalf, to transmit to the Secretariat of State any documentation in his possession regarding the state of health of Pope John Paul I during the thirty-three days of his pontificate and over the last few years. Doctor Da Ros replied that he would ask for an audience with you "at the earliest opportunity" and report back to me in person.[259]

It was not until about ten years later, on January 7, 1988, during a conversation with Magee — who had since become Bishop of Cloyne in Ireland — that the doctor learned that John Paul I had given his consent to the post between September 24–28. Doctor Buzzonetti affirmed:

 Let me emphasize that I did not know about this assent until the aforementioned meeting with Monsignor Magee. In fact, up until that late date, I wondered why they had called me. I had assumed that I had been called on that famous morning of September 29, 1978, only because I was the assistant of the Director of the Vatican Health Service. I lived near the Vatican, Father Magee knew me well and Professor Fontana, the Director of the Vatican City State Health Service, was seriously ill.[260]

At about 6:00 a.m., Cardinal Villot and Doctor Buzzonetti arrived almost simultaneously. The doctor immediately ascertained the death "due to the cessation of all cardiac, respiratory and nervous activity" and validated "the necropsy examination with the electro-cardio-thanatogram, which was conducted for more than twenty minutes."[261] In the confidential documentation on the certification of Luciani's death, addressed to the second in charge at the Vatican Secretariat of State, the doctor gave the following detailed report:

> Following the telephone call made by Fr. John Magee to my home at about 5:42 a.m. on September 29, I arrived at the bedroom of His Holiness about 6:00 a.m. I immediately ascertained the death of the Holy Father due to the cessation of all cardiac, respiratory, and nervous activity.
>
> His Holiness was lying in his bed; he was covered with blankets up to the height of the upper thorax; his head, the back of his neck and the upper part of his back were resting on two pillows. The covers, the bedclothes and the pillows were in order. The Holy Father had his head slightly tilted towards the right side, he wore glasses (which had not slipped from his nose). His upper limbs were upon the covers, his arms were abducted and internally rotated, and his forearms were flexed beyond 90°. He gripped some printed sheets with both hands, which he was holding in the correct position for reading. His eyelids and mouth were partly open. His attitude was composed and serene. The light from the lamp above the headboard was on. The bell hung a few centimeters above the Holy Father's head.
>
> On examination of the body, I found intense cadaveric rigidity in the jaw and in the upper and lower limbs. The stiffness affected the joints of the fingers and toes, so much so that it was necessary to exert a certain amount of tractive force to pull the sheets out from between the fingers of his hands.
>
> Hypostatic spots were present on the posterior regions of the neck, trunk, limbs, shoulders, and superior-anterior regions of the thorax in the form of a cape. On digital pressure, the hypostatic spots faded significantly. The nail beds were cyanotic. The face was not cyanotic.

The uncovered parts — face and hands — were distinctly cold to the touch. Also cold, but to a lesser extent, were the covered parts, especially the lower limbs. Only the dorsal and lumbar regions, resting directly on the bed surface, maintained a slight warmth.

The lower limbs had uniform edema at the feet and legs and the overlying epidermis was taut and shiny, with no obvious signs of inflammation. There had been no incontinence of urine or feces.

The main findings of thanatological objectivity in relation to the identification of the time of death are therefore the following:

    a. widespread and intense cadaveric rigidity;
    b. widespread but still migratable hypostatic spots;
    c. the skin temperature remarkably cold with slight warmth maintained only in the most covered and protected regions.

For these reasons it is correct to assume that the death of the Holy Father took place approximately at 11:00 p.m. on September 28, 1978.[262]

In the meantime, the nuns had vacated the room, as Sr. Margherita Marin recalled: "Father Magee came up to us afterwards and said: 'He didn't suffer, he didn't even notice it,' reporting what the doctor had told him, and he also said that his sudden death had occurred around eleven o'clock at night."[263] In the detailed report on the "thanatological exam," followed by the medical arguments that led to the clinical diagnosis of death, Doctor Buzzonetti further noted: "The attitude presented by the body indicated that in the passage from life to death, a symptomatology of alarm or malaise did not arise and there was no period of agony of any importance."[264] In his observations, he also noted that on the bedside table, he had not seen "the presence of a glass, which could contain drugs," after he first personally made sure that the Vatican Pharmacy did not receive re-

quests for drugs from the pope's private apartment, either that evening or in the previous days of his pontificate.[265] In the report, the
doctor also added that he had learned "that the first discovery of
the death had been made *by the nuns* of the private apartment" and
that upon his arrival at 6:00 a.m. "the other secretary, Father Lorenzi, was not present."[266] In fact, in the tribunal hearing, Father Diego
did not mention the discovery, confirming his delayed awakening,
already pointed out by Sr. Margherita Marin and Father Magee. In
a paper published in 2000, in the magazine of his religious congregation, Father Lorenzi again presented his personal version of the
facts:

> I was awakened by Sr. Vincenza Taffarel who had noticed
> that the pope had not picked up his tray with the coffee that
> had been left outside his room. She knocked and perhaps
> opened the door somewhat to discover that the pope was
> dead. I rushed to the pope's room. It was five minutes to
> six. The other secretary, Magee, was already there. After a
> moment of bewilderment, Cardinal Villot was immediately
> called first and then he took charge of the situation.[267]

After the death was confirmed, Father Diego was asked to inform
Doctor Da Ros in Vittorio Veneto. "I made an immediate phone call
to Doctor Da Ros and informed him of the death."[268] He then moved
on to call the pope's relatives, starting with the pope's niece, Pia Luciani, the eldest daughter of his brother Edoardo. At the tribunal
hearing, she recalled the phone call that morning and was critical of
the particular indelicacy of the communication:

> I was informed of his death by Father Diego. At about six in
> the morning, on September 29, he called me and said: "You
> must be brave. Your uncle is dead. The official version that
> the Curia wants to have announced on the radio is different
> from what I am telling you. We secretaries did not find him
> this morning. Sister Vincenza did. I am going to warn you
> right now that there is no money. You know very well that

he had been giving everything away.[269]

The witness added, "Even when we relatives arrived in Rome, [Father Diego] insisted that we should not expect anything." For their part, the relatives made no requests whatsoever, "especially at such an agitated time, when we had other thoughts on our minds."[270] With Doctor Buzzonetti present, the secretaries dressed the body in a white cassock from the room.[271] The pope had been found while he "gripped some printed sheets with both hands, which had been held in the correct position for reading" and "it was necessary to exert a certain amount of tractive force to pull the sheets out from between the fingers of his hands."[272] According to the description of the witness, Sr. Margherita Marin, "they were typewritten sheets, or rather two or three half sheets; I am sure they were not handwritten, but I cannot say what they contained because I did not read them at that moment. Someone out in the corridor told us that they were the papers for Wednesday's audience."[273] Her observation agrees with what was said by the secretaries as well as Doctor Buzzonetti, who wrote: "In his hands he held some printed sheets. I took these sheets from the hands of the deceased and, without reading them, placed them on the desk located near the bed. Later I learned that they were pages containing one of his homilies."[274]

It may very well be that the pope was re-reading one of his old essays in anticipation of the Angelus,[275] which was to have been held on Sunday, October 1, the liturgical memorial of St. Thérèse of Lisieux. However, it was more likely in anticipation of the General Audience for the following Wednesday, which would have focused on the cardinal virtue of prudence, as attested by the last autograph notes taken from the appointment book John Paul I used during his pontificate. In it, he wrote: "Seven lamps of sanctification. Make them shine. I do not know if the Holy Spirit will want to use me to make these seven shine a little."[276] His successor, John Paul II, knew that he planned to dedicate a General Audience to this virtue:

I have learned from the notes of the late pontiff that it was his intention to speak not only of the three theological virtues, faith, hope and charity, but also of the four so-called cardinal virtues. John Paul I wished to speak of the "seven lamps" of the Christian life, as Pope John XXIII called them. Well, today I wish to continue this plan, which the late pope had prepared, and to speak briefly of the virtue of prudence.[277]

Not only was it Luciani's established habit to read in bed, even when working on homilies or speeches, it was part of his style to reexamine and rework his writings, something also demonstrated by the meticulous work he did for the Angelus and the General Audiences of his pontificate.[278]

Regarding the fate of those sheets, the eyewitness, Sr. Margherita Marin, stated: "I cannot say who took care of them. Nor did I ask. We left him holding them; we didn't touch anything. … The study with his papers, and his room, were then sealed. They were reopened by his successor."[279] On several occasions, the Postulation questioned the secretaries about the fate of the papers that Pope Luciani was holding, but they were unable to give a thorough response. The papers could not be located in the Historical Archive of the Patriarchate of Venice — where the other papers taken from the pope's private apartment were kept[280] — nor in the Vatican Secret Archive, nor in the Archives of the Secretariat of State for which the Postulation requested and carried out ad hoc surveys.[281]

As for the destination of his other personal effects, Sr. Margherita Marin clarified: "I remember that Father Magee told us to take some of the Holy Father's personal effects. He gave Sister Vincenza his glasses, slippers, and other objects. I took his little radio, which I still keep as a relic."[282] Some of the objects — including the glasses that Luciani wore at the time of his death (and which were subjected to the fervent imagination of the press[283]) — were given by Sr. Vincenza Taffarel, as personal mementos of John Paul, to his last secretary in Vittorio Veneto, Fr. Francesco Taffarel. They were subsequently kept in the Archive of the Postulation and finally delivered, through the Vatican Secretary of State, Cardinal Pietro Parolin, to the museum of Canale d'Agordo on August 26, 2016.[284]

The Vicar of Rome, Ugo Poletti, came to the pope's room immediately after Cardinal Villot and Doctor Buzzonetti. Shortly afterward, he celebrated a Mass of suffrage together with the nuns.[285] The canonical act of the *Recognitio cadaveris* was drafted, marking the beginning of the *sede vacante*.[286] As the prelates came and went, the sisters could sense their discomfort at having to "give the world the news that the pope, who had won everyone over in such a short time, had died like that, and so, only two hours after we nuns had found him, they put out the official news."[287] According to Magee's reconstruction, Cardinal Villot insisted that the secretary be designated as the one who found the body. Magee objected, to which the cardinal replied: "We cannot say that a nun went into the pope's room in the morning. You officially found the pope dead, alone, didn't you?"[288] Thus the official communiqué of the Vatican Press Office falsely indicated who made the discovery:

> This morning, September 29, 1978, about five-thirty, the private secretary of the pope, Rev. Fr. John Magee, when contrary to custom, he had not found the Holy Father in the chapel of his private apartment, looked for him in his room and found him dead in bed with the light on, like one who was engaged in reading. The physician who hastened to the pope's room verified the death, which took place presumably toward eleven o'clock yesterday evening, as "sudden death that could be related to acute myocardial infarction." The venerated body will lie in state in the Clementine Hall of the Apostolic Palace.[289]

Magee asked the nuns to go along with the official version which reported that the secretary was the first to have found him.[290] Fr. Diego Lorenzi then reiterated this in a brusque manner to Sister Vincenza, ordering her, according to the pope's niece, Lina Petri, who was present at the time and therefore an eyewitness: "Sister, what happened here tonight must not leave here and you are forbidden to talk about it with anyone. Is that clear?"[291] The sisters complied, but when the pope's siblings, Edoardo and Antonia, visited Sister Vincenza on the evening of October 2, the nun confided to them that she had been the one who found their deceased brother. The siblings kept this confidence a secret, as the pope's niece, Lina Petri, attested:

> It was only sometime later that I learned from my mother that during the meeting Sister Vincenza wanted to uplift their broken hearts a little, so she encouraged them to be at peace and told them that she had been the one who found Father Albino dead. Clearly, her conscience informed her that the obligation to keep that secret was secondary to her duty to comfort the pope's brother and sister, by confiding to them my deceased uncle was found by someone who loved him very much and had been familiar to him for years.
>
> However, what Sister Vincenza had confided to my mother seemed to me, at least at the moment, to corroborate Father Diego's abrupt words that morning.[292]

The pope's other niece, Pia Luciani, reported the same thing: "We spoke with Sister Vincenza ... and she confirmed what Father Diego had already told me, that she had been the first to find him, and this reassured us."[293]

Within the walls of the Vatican, once word got out about the death of John Paul I, Commander of the Gendarmerie Camillo Cibin immediately proceeded "to block the access ways and provide the necessary services, following instructions from the Cardinal Secretary of State [Jean Villot]."[294] The director of Vatican Radio, Fr. Roberto Tucci, announced the death at 7:30 a.m. At 7:42 a.m., a reporter broadcasting the news on RAI Two radio was interrupted on-air by the Program Director, Paolo Orsini, who laconically announced: "The pope was found dead this morning." At 9:30 a.m., Italian television began a series of special programs.[295] Once the news started to spread, requests and allegations from journalists multiplied, to which someone responded by releasing a devout news item that stated the last thing the pope had read was the *Imitation of Christ*. The Jesuit Fr. Francesco Farusi, Vatican Radio News director, was the first to put out this item. Later, Father Farusi issued a correction:

> What I reported was, unfortunately, a big lie. But the information had been given to me that morning by Father Lorenzi, one of the pope's two secretaries. Then, I did some more checking and discovered that Luciani had not been reading the *Imitation of Christ* when he died. So, I felt it was my duty to make the correction.[296]

Pia Luciani rightly commented about this in her deposition: "I believe that the Roman Curia was not very prudent in giving inaccurate information about his discovery; it paved the way for allegations."[297]

Meanwhile, news reached the pope's sister, Antonia, in Levico She informed her daughter, Lina Petri, then a medical student in Rome, living at one of the dormitories of Catholic University, not far from the Vatican.[298] Lina Petri, the pope's young niece, was the only relative to view the pontiff's body in the private apartment. She reached the Vatican by bus, accompanied by Msgr. Giovanni Nervo, vice president of *Caritas*. She passed through the gate of Porta Sant'Anna at around 8:15 a.m. and with some difficulty was able to enter the papal apartments, and then the pope's room, after which, she stayed off to the side with Sister Vincenza.[299] This is her account:

> My uncle was lying on the bed, wearing his white papal cassock. I was feeling enormous grief, but I was immediately struck by my uncle's face, which was wrapped in a towel and turned a little to the right and towards the door I was entering. He seemed to be welcoming me with a slight smile. It seemed as though he were smiling at someone coming through the door and at that instant I instinctively thought: "The Lord came to take him and he smiled at him." They gave me a chair and left me there at the foot of the bed, alone. The door that led to his study was open (the one with the Angelus window), and I think there was more than one person in there because of the sounds I heard coming

from there. However, I soon became distracted with other thoughts and paid no attention to anyone. I spoke with him mentally and prayed. I don't know how long I was alone there, it seemed like a very long time to me, but in reality, I probably stayed about twenty minutes or so.

All I remember about the room is that from where I was sitting I could see his bed in front of me, on the left, and on the right, between the two corner windows of the room, was his desk. It was completely empty of papers and books. There was only a crucifix and a photograph of my maternal grandparents (the pope's parents) holding my cousin Pia, their first niece.

As I looked at my uncle in bed, I was quite struck by the sleeves of his cassock; they were all wrinkled from the elbow to the wrists. I kept thinking about that over the years. I always wondered if he was dressed when he died and if his sleeves were so wrinkled because he had been lying for a long time like that at his desk or in bed.[300]

Twenty years after the events, the detail about the wrinkled sleeves noted by the pope's niece, Lina Petri, was amplified and distorted in the reconstructions by the English journalist John Cornwell.[301] In reality, as noted above, the secretaries had dressed the pope shortly before, after he had been discovered. The doctor stood by as they dressed the pope in the white cassock he used to wear in private.[302] The news of the pope's sudden death spread quickly among all the cardinals, not just those in *Urbe degentes*. One of those surprised by the news was Cardinal Karol Wojtyła in Kraków, Poland. He had been intent on celebrating the twentieth anniversary Mass of his episcopal ordination and, before returning to Poland, had tried in vain to have an audience with John Paul I.[303] The news also reached Cardinal Joseph Ratzinger at the Marian Congress in Guayaquil, Ecuador, where he had been sent by the pope to serve as his papal legate.[304]

The exceptional testimony acquired from Pope Emeritus Benedict XVI, and entered in the records in June 2015, was nothing less than a historical novelty as far as canonization processes were concerned. It was, in fact, the first time that a pope had ever given *de visu* testimony about another pope. Pope Benedict recounted the details of the situation:

> On the day of the pope's death I was asleep in the bishop's residence in Quito[, Ecuador]. At one point, in the middle of the night, I woke up and heard the door open and someone enter. When I turned on the light, I saw a monk in a brown robe. He looked like a mysterious messenger from the beyond, so I doubted if I was really awake. He came in and told me that he had just received news that the pope had died. At first, I could not believe it, but then I did not doubt the veracity of the information. Curiously enough, I went right back to sleep, but then the following morning I definitely learned the unthinkable news. That monk was an auxiliary bishop of Quito. He had put on his religious habit in order to communicate the news that night. At Mass, during the Prayers of the Faithful, a concelebrant prayed for the late Pope John Paul I. My lay secretary, who was present there, winced, wondering how it was possible to get confused like that. We only referred that way to Paul VI. In the end, we were all truly shocked by that news. There was no longer any doubt that it was true.[305]

On September 29, between 8:00 a.m. and 9:00 a.m., the pope's body was dressed in papal vestments for lying in state in the Clementine Hall. According to the testimony of Doctor Buzzonetti, who was present, the nuns were asked to prepare the vestments for dressing the deceased.[306] The vestments were then provided to the secretaries: Msgr. Virgilio Noè, Master of Pontifical Ceremonies; Brother Augusto, one of the members of the Fatebenefratelli of the community of the Vatican Pharmacy;[307] and the Primary Pontifical Physician Mario Fontana.[308] The nuns then had to vacate the apartments, which according to practice had to be sealed by the staff of the Apostolic Chamber, under the orders of the camerlengo.[309] The pope's niece, Lina Petri recalled:

> After what seemed like a long time to me, around nine o'clock, I heard some commotion and murmuring in the other room. Someone whispered to me that it was time to go because the camerlengo had arrived and they needed to dress my uncle in his sacred vestments for exposition in the Clementine Hall, and, in fact, Cardinal Villot entered at that moment, dismayed and in tears. The nuns escorted me into the dining room. I cried —especially after Sister Vincenza told me that they had just recently been planning a small party for my uncle's birthday, which would have been October 17.[310]

Prelates, officials of the Curia, and civil authorities, began flowing into the Clementine Hall. The first to arrive was the president of the Italian Republic, Sandro Pertini, accompanied by Giuseppe Caprio, the then substitute of the Vatican Secretariat of State: "A few minutes after the lying in state of the pope's body began, I accompanied President Pertini to make the sad visit followed by the honorable Fanfani and Andreotti."[311]

In the meantime, Professor Fontana had summoned the staff in charge of the preservation treatment for the body to lie in state. This was a team of forensic doctors from the Institute of Forensic Medicine at the Sapienza University in Rome, directed by the head physician, Cesare Gerin,[312] and composed of Professors Fausto Meriggi, Franco Marracino, and Pietro Fucci, supported by technicians Ernesto and Arnaldo Signoracci, of whom only one actually collaborated in the treatment. These forensic doctors were the same who, a few weeks earlier, had treated the body of Paul VI. Cardinal Silvio Oddi spoke out on behalf of the Catholic University's request to fulfill the pitiful task, but Cardinal Villot confirmed the decision taken by Fontana.

The preservation treatment was conducted in the Foconi Room, adjacent to the Clementine Hall, in the second loggia of the Apostolic Palace, without removing entrails, organs, or blood. The opera-

tion took place in the late afternoon of September 29. It began shortly after 7:00 p.m. and was completed around 3:30 a.m. the following
morning,[313] to allow for the resumption of the endless procession
of the faithful, which continued until the evening of September 30.

THE MEDICAL
HISTORY OF
ALBINO LUCIANI

Returning to the morning that the deceased pope was discovered, the pope's niece, Lina Petri, recalled the meeting she had with Sr. Vincenza Taffarel in the papal apartments. The nun, who was also a nurse, kept repeating to her: "And to think that he was fine, his health was better here in Rome than in Venice, where the humidity did not help him. He would always say to me: 'Sister Vincenza, isn't it true we are better off here than in Venice?'"[314] His niece commented:

> During the private meeting on September 2, Uncle Albino had also told my mother that his health was better in Rome. At that time, Mom had no impression that he thought his end imminent, as she heard from other quarters. During a three-way conversation with her brother Berto, he assured her that nothing had changed in their relationship, and he

91

expressly gave her an appointment for Christmas, so that we could continue our habit of meeting together, as we did in Venice. We family members never had the impression that he had serious health problems. I remember that my mother would get very angry when anyone talked about the tuberculosis her brother was supposed to have suffered as a young man.[315]

Therefore, on the subject of her uncle's health, Lina Petri — who graduated with a medical degree — although she never practiced — made a detailed report on the health documents found in the hospitals where Luciani had been hospitalized over the years. Her report is filed in the records of the cause, together with the clinical documentation she found.[316] Regarding these health episodes, it suffices to mention the diagnoses and specify the conclusions.

Looking back at the patient's case history based on the medical records compiled when he last stayed at the Provincial General Hospital in Mestre, Italy (December 2–8, 1975), Albino Luciani underwent seven hospitalizations and four operations during his whole life.

The first operation was in Padua, at age eleven, for a tonsillectomy. The second was an adenoidectomy (first and second hospitalization). The patient's case history also contains a document written at the patient's bedside by Dr. Luciano Caprioglio during the patient's hospitalization in 1975, at the hospital in Mestre.[317] It shows deletions and corrections, because Luciani himself probably mixed up the order of his first two operations, a point of confusion that was confirmed by his family's oral tradition. In any case, the operations were ordinary and routine.[318]

The third and fourth hospitalizations took place in 1947, and the diagnosis of tuberculosis, which has been continuously rereleased in the press, must be absolutely denied. During 1947, after much effort to obtain his doctorate, he was hospitalized from March 8 to June 2 in a sanatorium in Belluno for suspected tuberculosis, and again from August 26 to September 12:[319]

The nature of the pulmonary pathology that struck him was not definitively clarified. It is certain that it was not tuberculosis. In fact, on June 3, 1947, the hospitalization registry of the sanatorium department (kept in the pneumology didactic unit, and of which I have a photocopy) recorded the results of an examination that was negative for tuberculosis: "Koch - -." A note received by family members, and kept at the curia in Belluno, contained a statement attributed to the attending physician of the time, Dr. Gottardo Gottardi, which read: "He did not have tuberculosis, rather migrating viral pneumonia, which first appeared in one lung, then moved to the other."[320]

This diagnosis was known to his family members who, despite the fear and shame that surrounded tuberculosis at the time, never kept him at a distance, even from his pregnant sister-in-law or his infant nieces. The radiological report carried out during hospitalization in 1975 only mentions the results of previous pulmonary diseases:

> Notes of diffuse emphysema. No outbreak of pulmonary thickening with characteristic activity. Small calcification morlar ilare ds. Discrete accentuation of vasal arborization to the ilreal horn. Pleuro-diaphragmatic adhesions and partial obliteration of the complementary constrophrenic sinus to ds. … Mediastinum in place, within limits. Aorto-sclerosis.[321]

However, as Lina Petri noted, the information collected from the attending physician, Antonio Da Ros, during the period in Vittorio Veneto and Rome, showed there were no consequences from the pulmonary pathology of 1947.[322]

The 1975 case history revealed yet another hospital stay in the summer of 1953 (his fifth hospitalization), due to joint rheumatism:

It was for "acute articular rheumatism, in 1953, which was

treated first at home and then for a month and a half in the hospital in Belluno" (this was his fifth hospitalization). In fact, in August of 1953, Uncle Albino stayed several days in Canale, in the house where he was born, as a guest of his brother Berto. … The rheumatism story was also resolved, according to the case history collected by Professor Caprioglio in 1975: "since then, some joint pain, especially in the rachis." In short, common back pain.[323]

In the aforementioned case history, Luciani is reported to have suffered "since then, some joint pain, especially in the rachis" and had therefore "worn an orthopedic corset occasionally, due to arthrosis of the spine."[324]

The attending physician, Doctor Da Ros, recalled three hospitalizations in Treviso in the mid-1960s, due to "a liver stone and a complication and hemorrhoids."[325] He also mentioned episodes of colic linked to this condition.[326] There were two hospitalizations in 1964, the first occurring April 7–27 and the second from August 18 to September 3.[327] They should be considered *per modum unius*, because they were related to his gallstone illness, which required cholecystectomy (sixth hospitalization). The *Diario del Vescovo* recorded a further period of illness on March 18–22, 1965.[328] From the findings we also know that in 1965 "he underwent a hemorrhoidectomy" (fifth hospitalization)[329] for a disorder that had been dragging on for twenty years.[330] In any case, these were not major diseases or treatments, as was pointed out. Regarding his two procedures in Treviso, in a handwritten note, Professor Giovanni Rama specified that he was operated on "successfully."[331]

Finally, there was an episode of retinal thrombosis in his left eye in the autumn of 1975. For about two months, the then Patriarch of Venice had been complaining about having difficulty seeing out of his left eye. He had visited Brazil on November 3–21, 1975, and after his return symptoms worsened to the point of requiring hospitalization. He was hospitalized on December 2–8 (eighth hospitalization), in the ophthalmology department in the provincial general hospital in Mestre. The department was then directed by Prof. Giovanni

Rama (1924–2007), a pioneer in Italian ophthalmology and at the forefront in introducing various surgical techniques. During his career, he carried out no less than 6,000 corneal transplants and over 52,000 surgical operations, surrounded by a group of specialists who were later to become renowned head physicians at other hospitals in the Veneto region.

Due to the family's interest,[332] a copy of the medical record of this hospitalization was received by the postulation on May 30, 2010, together with some memoirs subsequently written by Prof. Giovanni Rama and Professor Luciano Caprioglio, the cardiologist who visited the Patriarch of Venice during his hospital stay and collected the case history referred to here. The diagnosis was "occlusion of the central retinal vein of the left eye": retinal thrombosis, which, after therapeutic treatment, was resolved quickly and positively with the recovery of his vision and no after-effects.[333] Dr. Lina Petri commented:

> All the laboratory tests performed in that instance were absolutely normal (no hypertension, no diabetes, no pathology linked to altered triglyceride and cholesterol values, liver disease, kidney disease, no heart disease, no relevant pathology at the pulmonary level), all values more than normal for a subject of his age. The X-ray presenting aorto-sclerosis did not indicate to what extent, but still showed minimal vascular pathology.
>
> The examinations required in the hospital also included an oscillograph of the lower limbs, which at the time was used to assess the circulation status in his legs. This went back to his air travel to Brazil the previous month (November 3–21, 1975). In the case history, there is in fact mention of my uncle's leg problems: "On November 6, after a long journey by plane, in a sitting position, there was edema of the dorsum of the foot, without local pain, without changes in the skin color, which spontaneously regressed after two days. There was a fleeting repetition of the phenomenon after three days." However, I found no trace of his os-

cillograph results in the medical record. Professor Caprioglio reported in his objective examination, "There may be
less extensive pulsatility of the dorsal artery of the left foot.
Very slight perimallelar subedema in the left foot. No temperature changes." Translated, the foot, which had swollen
up during the flight to Brazil, still showed some very small
signs of swelling and difficulty in circulation.[334]

The prescribed therapy as explained by Lina Petri is as follows:

> The therapy established during his hospitalization was sub-
> stantially based on anticoagulant drugs to resolve the ex-
> isting retinal thrombosis and prevent the onset of others.
> These are the medications he was prescribed: *Complamin*:
> It is a haemokinetic, that is, it improves the viscosity of
> the blood, in practice it makes it more fluid and therefore
> resolves and prevents the formation of thrombus and is
> used specifically for the eyes. *Persantin*: It is an antiplatelet
> agent, antithrombotic: It prevents the platelets as they ag-
> gregate together from forming thrombus. These two drugs,
> in essence, were to treat and prevent further thrombosis at
> the same time. *CVP-duo* was similarly prescribed as well
> (against the fragility of the capillaries and retinal hemor-
> rhages). Furthermore, *Benexol B12* (a B vitamin complex)
> and *Trieffortil*, which is a specific drug for those suffering
> from arterial orthostatic hypotension were prescribed. In
> fact, Uncle Albino tended to have low blood pressure and
> this had caused him some episodes of malaise. The medi-
> cal record reads: "About six months ago [during the sum-
> mer of 1975] he had a sudden feeling of imbalance, lasting
> about three hours. The patient appeared rather pale to the
> response team."[335]

In the patient diary, there was a note from the ophthalmologist, Doctor Rama, dated March of 1978: "Repeated ophthalmoscopic checks
confirmed complete functional recovery; on the fundus there were

no signs of a previous thrombotic event."[336] The note, marking Albino Luciani's last visit five months after his death, shows how his condition remained stable 1976–1978. Lina Petri notes:

> It is clear that his clinical situation in the years 1976–1978 was always under control.[337] This was even supported by the photocopy I read of the correspondence between Professor Rama and interviewers working for writer David Yallop and, later, writer John Cornwell. These were journalists who, starting with their investigation into the sudden death of John Paul I, both managed, taking different routes, to achieve the same goal — to fatten their bank accounts with the proceeds from their book sales.

Supportive therapy was carried out with the particular goal of addressing his tendency toward arterial hypotension, using "mild cardiotonics and multivitamins."[338] From Professor Rama himself, we learned that checkups always took place two or three times a year and that, after his election to the papal throne, a visit to Rome was agreed upon in order to transfer the medical orders over to the Vatican doctors: "He let me know that he was fine, that I did not need to waste my time going to Rome. He kept postponing the appointment." Finally, the visit was set for Saturday, September 30.[339]

In conclusion, the overall analysis of the 1975 medical record painted a picture that his relatives had always supported, one "which was also confirmed by the reports released after the pope's death, both by the ophthalmologist, Professor Giovanni Rama and the attending physician Doctor Da Ros"[340] — namely, Luciani did not show any clear or evident, significant pathologies that would indicate he was a seriously ill patient. Only his episode of retinal thrombosis required attention:[341]

> I always feel uneasy in front of those who claim that at the time of the election to the papal throne Patriarch Luciani was obviously seriously ill. It is true that when my uncle addressed the sick during his General Audience on Septem-

ber 27, 1978, he stated: "The pope who speaks to you has been in the hospital eight times and had four operations," but this was part of his way of doing things. He wanted to express his sympathetic participation in the suffering of the sick people, that despite being the pope, he was like them, in that he too had experienced that "you may have one nurse or another, but they are not the same. ... It's not their service alone that you appreciate, it's the way that they serve you, the way they care for you."[342]

During his pontificate, the pope's personal physician, Dr. Antonio Da Ros, went to the Apostolic Palace three times to give the pope a routine checkup: "During his pontificate I kept in touch with Sr. Vincenza Taffarel and met with the pope three times, during which I carried out routine visits."[343] The notes from the doctor's archive, delivered to the Postulation and included in the records, preserved a copy of these autograph notes:

September 3, 1978: In Rome we joined a diocesan group from Vittorio Veneto on a visit to the pope. I met Father Diego; he told me that the pope was expecting Lydia and I for coffee at 3:30 p.m. I visited the pope. Then I walked through the Vatican Gardens with Father Diego. Mass. Returned at 8:00 p.m. ...

September 13, 1978: I left Treviso at 7:30 a.m. and went to Rome. A driver from the Vatican picked me up, and I visited the Holy Father at 9:20 a.m. At 11:00 a.m., I attended the Wednesday General Audience. At 3:30 p.m., I met with Sister Vincenza: She told me that the pope was fine. Later I met with him again and then I visited the health facility with Professor Fontana. ...

September 23, 1978: I departed for Rome and arrived there at 9:30. I visited His Holiness. Then, I met with Doctor Buzzonetti and Father Magee (see the letter dated August 24,

2009, regarding my official post as the pope's personal physician). I therefore stopped by for breakfast with the pope and his two secretaries and, on that occasion, His Holiness was presented, as already mentioned, with the contract to be sent over to Monsignor Caprio, according to the pope's wishes. In the afternoon, I accompanied the Pontiff for his taking possession of the Cathedral of St. John Lateran. From home, I called Sister Vincenza who assured me that the pope was well, despite his tiring day.

September 28, 1978: At 7:30 p.m., I called the Vatican and the pope was fine, as usual.[344]

Regarding the last medical examination carried out by Doctor Da Ros, on September 23, his deposition reads:

On September 23, I had the opportunity to visit the pope around 9:30 a.m. His health was good, as usual. On that occasion, he expressed the desire that I continue to be his personal physician and that this would be in agreement with the Vatican Health Service. I then met with Doctor Buzzonetti and Father Magee for the general arrangements. In the afternoon, I went with the pope for his taking possession of the Lateran. Back home in the evening, I called Sister Vincenza on the phone out of courtesy, and she told me that the pope's day had been tiring, but that everything was fine. Also on the evening of September 28, I had a telephone call with Sister Vincenza. Let me specify — I made a phone call to Sister Vincenza on the evening of September 28, around 7.30 p.m., and she assured me that the pope, despite having had a busy day, was fine and that there was nothing new to report.[345]

Even his brother Edoardo remembered seeing Doctor Da Ros "shortly before Albino's death," and had been assured by him that he had examined the pope and determined he was well. Edoardo also recalls having met his brother on September 2 and September 20 and finding him "neither tense nor worried, but calm and peaceful … he wasn't even tired":

> The evening before I left for Australia, we walked in the roof garden together. Albino spoke peacefully, as he always did. At other times, I had heard him say something about his health, as when he had problems with his eyes or liver. But in the Vatican, on the other hand, he told me nothing about his health problems, nor did I have any inkling. … After his death, I immediately returned from Australia. I also had the intention of understanding what had really happened. I spoke immediately with the nuns and then with the two secretaries. I verified that there had been no particular health problems in recent days, nor had anything happened that might lead one to suspect a murder.[346]

THE CAUSE
OF DEATH

D r. Renato Buzzonetti, the second physician, was the one who certified the death of the pope and drew up the death certificate. As we said, by that time he had been named Doctor Da Ros's coadjutor in Rome. Doctor Da Ros had retained his position as the pope's personal physician, despite continuing to reside in Vittorio Veneto.[347] Regarding the causes of death, Doctor Da Ros declared, "I was unable to personally ascertain his death."[348]

On October 9, the substitute of the Secretariat of State, Giuseppe Caprio, asked Doctor Buzzonetti for a detailed analysis on the medical report, which was promptly drafted and sent "in an absolutely confidential manner." The text accurately stated:

Most Reverend Excellency, I am transmitting the attached report to you in an absolutely confidential manner, making you in some way part of the professional secrecy that binds my conscience as a doctor. This report concerns the ascertainment of death of His Holiness John Paul I, of venerable memory, and the formulation of the relative clinical diagnosis.[349]

The doctor went on to analyze the causes of the pontiff's death as follows:

As far as the presumable cause of death is concerned, all the objective data presented up to now must be taken into account, in particular, the arrangement of the hypostatic spots. In this case, one must consider the incidence of "sudden death." The rapidity of the event/death appears to be supported by the circumstantial data and above all by the attitude maintained by the body, which attested that — in the transition from life to death — no symptomatology of alarm or malaise had arisen and there had been no period of agony of any importance. Being a sudden death (classifiable in the category of instant or immediate deaths), this — by definition (as is known) — is always "natural."

The most common cause of natural, sudden, and unexpected death in adults is cardiovascular disease. Among these, the most often identified specific cause is ischemic heart disease from coronary atherosclerosis.

When sudden death is called instantaneous death and occurs no later than one hour from the onset of symptoms, the cause in 80-90% of cases is circulatory arrest from cardiovascular disease. In males, an absolute prevalence (about 90%) of sudden deaths from cardiovascular causes is attributed to coronary artery disease. Indeed, some essential facts from the remote and proximate patient history were pointing towards the cardiovascular system. On September 23, these facts were communicated to me in part by Doctor Da Ros with regard to points 2 and 3 mentioned below, and in part by Father J. Magee, at the deathbed of the Holy Father. The facts in question were:

1. Sudden death running in the family (some deaths of

this kind were recorded in the pope's family: the report was generic).

2. A previous spasm (or thromboembolism) of the central artery of the retina of the left eye, which occurred years ago, which forced Cardinal Luciani to be admitted to the hospital in Mestre.

3. The (daily?) use of *Gratusminal*, an oral preparation based on mild sedatives and small doses of strophanthus (which is a cardiokinetic).

4. The episode of pain, localized in the upper third of the sternal region, which the Holy Father suffered around 7:30 p.m. on the day of his death, lasted for over five minutes and occurred while the pope was seated and intent on the recitation of Compline with Father Magee. It regressed without any therapy. In this regard, the (non-literal) testimony of Father Magee was as follows: 'The pope repeatedy brought his hand to his chest, the pain was quite strong; it was a disorder that the Holy Father had already experienced on previous occasions and that he interpreted as being "rheumatic" in nature. His Holiness decisively refused the intervention of a doctor.' The pope's secretary gave his own version of the Holy Father's interpretation of this morbid event.

It is superfluous to mention that pain, which has the aforementioned characteristics, can also be attributed to diseases other than coronary artery disease. However, there is no doubt that — in the light of the facts — this symptomatology and its recurrence constitute grounds for serious reflection.)

In conclusion: The case history, although summary; the physical examination of the body (where the edema of the lower limbs, whose onset was not very recent, was especially important); the specific circumstances of the death; the highly probative statistical criterion, all pointed to a cause of death inherent in the cardiovascular system and, in particular, in ischemic heart disease, of which myocardial infarction is the most serious clinical expression.[350]

In this report, Doctor Buzzonetti also mentioned that the primary pontifical physician, Mario Fontana, concurred with his diagnosis over the telephone, before the professor left his home to reach the Apostolic Palace on the morning of September 29. Moreover, despite the urgings of the Secretariat of State, Buzzonetti waited until Professor Fontana arrived around 8:00 a.m. Fontana, "being a good pathologist (he had been head of Pathological Anatomy at the Riuniti Hospital in Rome), examined the body and countersigned the text typed and signed by me." Finally, the document pointed out that the referring physician had communicated the text of the certificate by telephone to Fr. Romeo Panciroli, director of the Vatican Press Office, with changes highlighted in italics: "The death *presumably occurred around 11:00 p.m.* yesterday, due to sudden death *attributable* to acute myocardial infarction."[351]

The same report also discussed the hypothesis of requesting an autopsy before making a diagnosis, since "the legislation in force in the Vatican City State, in conformity with that of many states, does not allow the cause of death to be formulated with comments expressing probability, doubt, reservation, or suspicion, unless the doctor is requesting an autopsy." To this end, Doctor Buzzonetti telephoned the lawyer, Vittorio Trocchi, secretary general of the Governorate of the Vatican, who categorically excluded the possibility. The doctor then stated:

> In the cases provided for by law, the body must be placed at the disposal of the judicial authority. In this regard, before writing the diagnosis of death, the writer was authoritatively denied the practical possibility of requesting an autopsy by the lawyer, Trocchi. Therefore, the diagnosis and the cause of death necessarily had to avoid, or not include, any notion of doubt, reservation, suspicion, or probability. Based on the above considerations, I formulated the clinical diagnosis of "sudden death from acute myocardial infarc-

tion." To be exact, this term was used in the death certificate. In the press release it was worded, "sudden death attributable to acute myocardial infarction."[352]

Later in the morning, Cardinal Villot, on behalf of some cardinals, also made a request for an autopsy, but the preparation of the body and its transfer to the Clementine Hall were already underway, causing the proposal to be dropped, especially since the tribute from Italian President Sandro Pertini was scheduled for noon.[353] Doctor Buzzonetti added:

> Finally, one should remember that in the absence of any diagnosis, or in the formulation of a certain diagnostic doubt, the body should have been made available to the judicial authority of the Vatican City State. In this regard, I remember that in 1978, there was no specific legislation on medical requirements in the event of death in the territory of the Vatican City State. This gap was filled by the Decree of the Pontifical Commission of the Vatican City State no. 205, issued June 22, 1993.[354]

In any case, the doctors had not found any evidence that would have made a request for an autopsy essential. The former primary pontifical physician explained, "In this specific case, in the humble opinion of Professor Fontana and myself, there were no significant objective grounds to justify a request for an autopsy, for which the norms of Italian law had to be applied."[355] Furthermore, the doctors reasoned, "such an investigation was likely to prove insufficiently conclusive."[356] In the report, Doctor Buzzonetti highlights how his diagnosis was "judged irrefutable" by Professor Cesare Gerin, director of the Institute of Forensic Medicine at the Sapienza University in Rome. Professor Gerin had been called upon to direct the operations of the hygienic-preservative treatment of the body:[357] "The diagnosis of death was confirmed by Professor M. Fontana who — as director of the Vatican Health Service — countersigned the certificate.

Subsequently, Professor Gerin told Fontana that he considered the aforementioned diagnosis to be correct and irrefutable.[358]

On October 10, two reports signed by Doctor Buzzonetti and Professor Fontana clarified the accuracy of the reporting and scientifically justified the method.

In her report, the pope's niece, Lina Petri, underlined the hypothesis of pulmonary embolism, which was formulated at the time by Prof. Mario Alberto Dina, chair of the Department of Pathological Anatomy at Catholic University, indicating that it could have been the pope's cause of death. To support the hypothesis, Professor Dina noted the suddenness of the death, which was typical of cases where an embolus completely occludes the pulmonary artery, a death sudden enough to have prevented the pope from alarming those nearby. The primary physician attributed significance to the recurring report that the pope had swollen feet and legs in the days before his death (perhaps due to a phlebothrombosis in the lower limbs, from which the embolus that would have obstructed the pulmonary artery could have started). Finally, he stated that he had learned from the Signoracci technicians (not from the professors), that in preparing the treatment of the body for days of lying in state, "the preservative solution injected into the circulatory system at the level of the arm would have been blocked from passing from the heart to the lungs, as happens precisely in the case of a pulmonary artery that is completely occluded by an embolus."[359] However, Professor Dina never had the opportunity to read or study the clinical documentation on Pope Luciani.

In correspondence probably written in 1988, Professor Giovanni Rama noted:

> Pope Luciani tended to be hypotensive. Moreover, thrombotic events ran in his family. The most likely scenario is that he had a cardiac thrombosis (heart attack) or a cerebral thrombosis … For me there is no clinical doubt. He died from the same circulatory disorder that affected the retina of his eye. … This time it was his heart or his brain that was affected.[360]

Doctor Buzzonetti thought that the hypothesis of death due to a "pulmonary embolism from deep vein thrombosis of the lower limbs is implausible since the modest edema in the pope's legs could be explained by many other causes, such as prolonged sitting, impaired coagulation, cardiac insufficiency, etc." He also noted:

> His history of repeated short episodes of retrosternal pain, not accompanied by dyspnea (present in more than 80% of cases); and without the notes of lateral pleuritic pain, which almost always characterizes pulmonary embolism events of non-massive magnitude (present instead in more than 80% of cases); and without indications of lateral pleurisy pain, which almost always characterizes pulmonary embolism events of non-massive magnitude, as reported by John Paul I himself, all led to the attribution of the cause of death to a myocardial infarction. [It also excluded the hypothesis of] ventricular fibrillation: without efficient first aid, death occurs within four to six minutes and can be instantaneous or may be preceded by immediate warning signs such as fainting, loss of consciousness, convulsions, apnea, etc. Certainly his recurrent history of precordial pain cannot be explained by as many episodes of ventricular fibrillation.[361]

Professor Fontana similarly wrote his own report, which validated his colleague's report and supported — from a medical and scientific standpoint — the decision to exclude the use of an autopsy:

> I arrived at the papal apartments around 8:00 a.m. and went to the pontiff's bedroom where Doctor R. Buzzonetti, Cardinal Villot and other prelates were.
>
> The external examination of the corpse that I was able to perform during the final dressing of the body allowed me to exclude the presence of bruises, abrasions, or other traumatic injuries, and therefore I confirmed the diagnosis of my colleague Buzzonetti of "sudden death by acute myocardial infarction."

It is well known from the pathology that, among the many causes of sudden death, coronary artery atherosclerosis ranks first, which can precipitate tachycardia or ventricular fibrillation, or cause asystole, due to the arrest of atrioventricular conduction.

Other causes include congenital or acquired aortic stenosis, idiopathic hypertrophic subaortic stenosis, massive pulmonary embolism, subacute bacterial endocarditis, and cardiac tamponade due to an aneurysm rupture.

It has been argued by many that in these cases diagnostic clarification must necessarily rely on an autopsy. Apart from the difficulties of performing such an operation in an environment where an autopsy has never been carried out, it must be pointed out that in some cases even on the autopsy table it is not possible to highlight the very first alterations of the ischemic necrosis of the myocardium when death was sudden. ... In this regard myocardial cell death occurs long before the cytological changes are sufficiently advanced to be evident under a light microscope. Great efforts have been made to establish the histochemical and ultrastructural parameters of early cell death in order to clearly document a myocardial infarction in patients who die suddenly and immediately after an acute attack.

Considerable progress has been made with the use of the electron microscope, where ultrastructural lesions can be seen sixty minutes after the onset of ischemia. However, despite all these sophisticated techniques, the problem of identifying a truly early heart attack has not yet been solved.

In my many years spent at the Institute of Pathological Anatomy in Rome, at San Camillo Hospital and at the Military Hospital of Rome, it also occurred to me, the emeritus director of Pathological Anatomy and General Medicine of the United Hospitals of Rome, while performing autopsy investigations on subjects who died of sudden death, that the autopsies could not indisputably document ischemic myocardial lesions or serious coronary alterations.

Even on the autopsy table, we face limitations that sometimes prevent us from expressing a precise judgment on the cause of sudden death. This highlights the difficulty that a currently practicing physician may encounter when he is called to express a judgment on a case of sudden death.

The experienced physician must base his diagnostic assumption on the accounts of those who had contact with the patient during the last hours of life. He must exclude recent episodes of significant clinical importance related to other systems and, based on careful external examination of the corpse, must exclude any accidental traumatic injuries.

Reviewing the various morbid processes focuses attention on those that are most frequently the basis of immediate, natural, and unexpected death.[362]

In the days immediately preceding October 11, Doctor Buzzonetti received an unsigned note from the Secretariat of State formulating some clinical questions about the report he made. He was also asked to have the questions answered by Professors Cesare Gerin, Franco Marracino, and Pietro Fucci, "whose professional work" had been requested "for the preservative treatment of the body of John Paul I, about twenty hours after his death," and at the same time, to ask their permission to publish their opinions, or at least make the cardinals aware of them. The cardinals were gathered in the first general congregations for the election of the new pontiff and evidently wished to dispel any doubts about the accuracy of the medical report.

The Secretariat of State therefore asked the aforementioned academics the following questions:

1. Did the examination of the body make it possible to exclude traumatic injuries of any kind?
2. The doctors, who first had access to the body of the pope, collected testimony from the family members and Monsignor Noè. Did this testimony make it possi-

ble to ascertain "scientifically and on the basis of experience" the clinical diagnosis of "sudden death," understood in its correct technical sense?

3. Is "sudden death" always natural?
4. If the answer to this question is affirmative, will Professors Gerin, Fucci, and Marracino consent to have their opinions published on this matter? Alternatively, if they consider it absolutely inappropriate to provide public statements on the subject — since this request from the Secretariat of State is outside the specific mandate for which their work was requested — would they consent to communicate their authoritative opinions, in an absolutely confidential way, to the Sacred College of Cardinals?[363]

Doctor Buzzonetti, in turn, sent the Secretariat of State a document dated October 11, with a note at the bottom indicating, "Report for the Congregation of the Cardinal Fathers," and in which the doctor reported the answers provided by the academics mentioned above:

In fulfillment of the task entrusted to me this morning, today I personally consulted Prof. Cesare Gerin, Director of the Institute of Forensic Medicine at the Sapienza University in Rome, whose professional work was requested exclusively for the hygienic-preservative treatment of the body of Pope John Paul I, carried out twenty hours after his death. Responding to my specific questions, Professor Gerin stated the following:

1. The external examination of the Holy Father's body made it possible to exclude traumatic injuries of any kind.
2. According to the "information known to him," there was nothing to refute the diagnosis of "sudden death from acute myocardial infarction."

3. Even when carrying out an autopsy, in cases of very recent myocardial infarction — as in this case — it is possible to find no sign of the heart attack itself;

4. "Sudden death" in its correct technical sense, as a rule, is always "natural."

It should be noted that, in forensic medicine, the expression "sudden (or unexpected or unforeseen) death" is intended to designate a "natural" death as opposed to a "violent death" (see page 141 of the first volume of the treatise of forensic medicine by Professor C. Gerin).

Sudden death occurs in a state of well-being.
Professor Cesare Gerin, considering it absolutely inappropriate to provide public statements on the subject, since this request of the Secretariat of State is outside the specific task for which his work was requested, and also declaring himself ready to deny any news that would be divulged in his name, consents to having the above statements communicated — in an absolutely confidential manner — only to the Sacred College of Cardinals.

Professor Pietro Fucci and Professor Franco Marracino, Chairs of the Department of Forensic Medicine at the Sapienza University in Rome, both of whom directly carried out the preservation treatment on the mortal remains of His Holiness John Paul I, have authorized me to express their consent, with the considerations of the director of their institute, sharing also the strict confidentiality constraints.[364]

In transmitting the aforementioned documents to the Secretariat of State, Buzzonetti also added "the grave reservations Professor Fontana and I have should there be any further publication of the clinical information about the death of the Holy Father," which would only give rise to "new allegations and controversies."[365] This was the reason why the documents, bound by professional secrecy, remained confidential until today and have been made available for the purposes of the cause.[366]

For their part, the family members, from the very beginning, had "no doubts about his natural death." Regarding the request for an autopsy, the statement by the niece Pia Luciani is valid: "I know that it is not customary to do an autopsy on the pope, however we family members have not asked for one. We have always been sure that his death was natural."[367] In his deposition, the pope's brother, Edoardo Luciani, also agreed.[368]

In 1975, Professor Luciano Caprioglio had collected Luciani's medical history at his bedside. He was a cardiologist and the head physician of Medical Division I at the civil hospital in Mestre. Professor Rama had sought his cardiological advice. In May 2010, Professor Caprioglio delivered a copy of that medical history and made some notes on the cause of death:

> From the medical history, from the physical examination I conducted, there was no obvious systemic pathology that could be associated with this ocular disease, which, when a patient is no longer young, as is known, one must first consider the possibility of asymptomatic cardiovascular disease. I must point out, that in the years that followed, it became customary to use instrumental tests, that were not available at the time, such as the Doppler ultrasonogram of the supra-aortic trunks (one should mention that the radiologist had reported an aortosclerosis at the time), the dynamic ECG Holter, for any heart rhythm disturbances not felt by the patient, and the echocardiogram.

Moreover, on the strength of his forty-three years of hospital experience, Professor Caprioglio reached the following conclusions, which substantially agreed with the report by Doctor Buzzonetti:

> I find a nonmedical interpretation of sudden death *laughable*, but among the various possibilities that can be evoked

in the medical field (a pulmonary embolism episode from phlebothrombosis of a lower limb, cerebral stroke) heart rhythm disorder seems to me the most likely hypothesis.[369]

Caprioglio added:

> Considering the characteristics of the sudden death event which struck Pope John Paul I on September 28, 1978, it is my firm opinion that the death is to be ascribed to a death which was electrical in nature, that is, to fatal arrhythmia due to an ischemic coronary event.[370]

It is well-known that the sudden death of Pope Luciani gave rise to conspiracy theories and scandalous allegations. These flowed into the profitable waters of thriller literature.[371] Such material does not merit consideration. However, it does allow us to underline some of the clarifications that were offered in the authoritative texts of the investigation. The bad faith of David Yallop, author of the first published volume, was conspicuously censored by Professor Giovanni Rama, as seen from the autographed notes he immediately sent to Msgr. John Foley, then president of the Pontifical Commission for Social Communications and the Vatican Television Center:

> Pope Luciani tended to be hypotensive. Moreover, thrombotic events ran in his family. The most likely scenario is that he had a cardiac thrombosis (heart attack) or a cerebral thrombosis. I had written all this in my report for Y[allop]. He was absolutely professionally dishonest and extrapolated from my report whatever was convenient so that he could say things that were science fiction and did not correspond with the truth.[372]

As for the later book by John Cornwell, "in addition to the impropriety of meeting with him there was the superficiality with which he was given credentials in the Vatican offices in charge." The following is noted from the report provided by Doctor Buzzonetti, who, as he asserts, had to accept an interview with Cornwell due to pressure from Msgr. John Foley:

> The author was brought into the papal apartments, attended a private Mass with John Paul II, had at least one conversation with the pope and, finally, through Fr. Stanislaus Dziwisz, obtained permission to interview some people. After first refusing to meet him, which Monsignor E. Martinez, the substitute at the time, fully approved, I was subsequently invited by the same substitute to meet with the British journalist, and, in fact, we met on January 18, 1989. For my part, I limited myself to reporting only the news that was already universally known in the press. I kept the original tape of the interview, which indeed was reported almost literally, but it was framed by ambiguous and malignant remarks, which put me in a very bad light.
>
> The icing on this bitter cake was the interview with {Joaquín] Navarro [Valls], reported in the same book, in which he, a current Vatican employee, denied the diagnosis of death formulated at the time, which became an official document of the Holy See, and instead, presented another riskier one. This diagnostic hypothesis was mistakenly based on a presumed etiopathogenetic connection of a thrombo-embolism of the central artery of the retina of the left eye, which occurred in 1975, with a hypothesized deep vein thrombosis of the lower limbs (supposed only on the basis of a modest edema of the lower limbs).
>
> This hypothesis overlooked the elementary notion that retinal artery thrombo-embolism belongs to the systemic arterial circulation, where *oxygenated arterial blood* flows, whereas pulmonary embolism travels through the systemic venous circulation and reaches — via the right chamber of the heart — the small pulmonary circulation, where *non-oxygenated venous blood* flows in the pulmonary arteries. For lack of any reference data, it was not even hypothesized as a so-called paradoxical pulmonary embolism, the

one in which the venous embolism from the right chamber of the heart transits into the left one through an existing gap in the septum and enters the systemic arterial circulation.

When I read the book, published in 1990 with the title *A Thief in the Night*, I immediately wrote a letter of protest to the then substitute, Monsignor Cassidy, but I did not receive a reply.[373]

To conclude this examination, the report and the documentation by Doctor Buzzonetti and Professor Fontana, with comments from the renowned professors of the Institute of Forensic Medicine at the Sapienza University in Rome, who worked on the preservation of the body, remain fully valid — even with respect to the hypothesis of embolism formulated in the past and proposed more recently by Joaquín Navarro-Valls, in the context of John Cornwell's book. Although this second hypothesis seemed "suggestive and plausible" to the pope's family members, Lina Petri concluded: "However, it does not change things very much."[374]

In this regard, Pope Benedict XVI, responding to the ad hoc questionnaire in his written testimony released on June 26, 2015, stated: "From the beginning, I thought the rumors that began to circulate about a violent death of the Servant of God were nonsense. The official information for me was, and is, fully credible and convincing."[375]

THE LAST HOUR

O n September 30, the body of John Paul I was transferred to the Vatican Basilica.[376] It lay in state until October 3, while an uninterrupted stream of more than a million faithful processed to venerate it.[377] RAI broadcast the rite of translation live on Channel 1 at 6:00 p.m., showing the procession that accompanied the body of the pontiff from the Clementine Hall to the Vatican Basilica. After the Scala Regia [royal staircase] and the colonnade, the procession passed through St. Peter's Square, amidst a crowd watching in silence and waiting to pass before the body of John Paul I.

The live television broadcast also showed prayer vigils conducted by people who came from all over Italy to pay homage to him and condolences offered from around the world, including various Eastern European countries. Even Leonid Brezhnev sent a brief telegram from the Soviet Union. Recalling those events, Benedict XVI said: "The days of the pope's funeral were days of great sadness for me. That mood was matched by the pouring rain. Even nature seemed to be grieving with us."[378]

In the meantime, the Sacred College — according to the prescriptions of the apostolic constitution which regulates the period of the *Sede vacante* — had begun their meetings in view of the next conclave. During the first meeting, on September 30, arrangements were made for the funeral. The starting date of the conclave was set for October 14, and it was decided, for the time being, to suspend the Puebla Conference, which should have started on October 12.

During the second meeting, on October 2, the details of the *Novendials* were finalized. The third meeting on October 3 again dealt with the *Novendials*. It was during these meetings that the cardinals heard the answers to the ad hoc questionnaire which the Secretariat of State had formulated. The cardinals themselves had requested these answers concerning the sudden death of the pope. The questionnaire had been submitted to the professors of the Institute of Forensic Medicine of the Sapienza University in Rome who had performed the preservation treatment on the body of John Paul I.

The funeral took place in St. Peter's Square on October 4, at 4:00 p.m. The rite had the same setup as the one celebrated a few weeks earlier for Paul VI: a simple cypress-wood coffin placed on the ground, the Gospel open upon the coffin, and the paschal candle. Those present included ninety concelebrating cardinals, the representatives of 107 nations, and ten international organizations. There were over 100,000 people present despite the pouring rain.[379] The funeral was broadcast worldwide.[380] The presider was the Dean of the Sacred College, Carlo Cardinal Confalonieri. He gave the homily and mentioned the salient features of John Paul I's passage to the Chair of Peter. He asked what had motivated "the endless lines of the faithful of Rome and the whole world?" He answerd: "They moved step by step along the entire Bernini colonnade, whether under a scorching sun or pouring rain. Finally, after two or more hours of patient waiting, they would reach the Clementine Hall and the Vatican Basilica in order to see the pope one last time." Moreover, he asked, "How else can we explain the very crowded audiences on Wednesday with visitors from all over the world? How do we explain the crowds that literally filled St. Peter's Square at noon on Sunday, a time dedicated to blessing the family and joining in to recite the Angelus?"[381]

The funeral in St. Peter's Square concluded with the Litany of the Saints, followed by the supplication of the Church of Rome by the vicar, Cardinal ugo Poletti, while Patriarch Maximos V Hakim of the Melkites offered the Litany of the Eastern Churches, in Greek and Arabic. On the morning of October 4, the seventeen non-Catholic delegations present at the funeral were received, including the delegates of the Ecumenical Patriarchate of Constantinople, the Methodist World Council, and the Lutheran World Federation. Cardinal Carlo Confalonieri mentioned the favorable opinions Luciani had aroused in the various churches through the simplicity and openness to the world that he had shown during his short pontificate, and by his "desire to advance decisively on the path of unity, in full fidelity to the truth of Christ and with full docility to the inspirations of the Holy Spirit." The cardinal also commented on the deceased pontiff's desire to serve the ecumenical movement:

> We all witnessed his determination to make this aspect of his ministry one of his first priorities: his inspiration to follow the paths of simplicity, openness, and fidelity to the Lord, paths which distinguish every authentic ecumenism.[382]

In the same way, when he received the special delegations from the countries that had come to Rome for the occasion, the cardinal also mentioned the pope's "clear-eyed vision" in the way he "considered the world" — namely, as "a figure who exuded peace and inspired confidence, despite the individual and collective harshness and selfishness which too often seem to mark our age."[383]

Once the rite was over, Pope Luciani's body was brought back to the Vatican Basilica and then privately transferred to the Vatican Grottoes through the door of Santa Marta.

In keeping with tradition, the Master of Pontifical Ceremonies, Msgr. Virgilio Noè, and his private secretary, placed a silk veil over the face of the deceased; the cypress coffin was definitively closed, tied with purple silk ribbons that Cardinal Jean Villot, Msgr. Jacques Martin and the Prefect of the Papal Household, Virgilio Noè, sealed with sealing wax. In the presence of family members, the cypress coffin was placed in a lead outer coffin, the lid of which was fixed with molten tin, and the prelates again impressed the seal upon it. The official document of the entombment ends with, "*Vivas in Christo, Pater Sanctissime!*"[384] The lid of the coffin depicted the cross, the pope's coat of arms, and the inscription: "*Corpus Ioannis Pauli I P.M. vixit annos LXV menses XI dies XI.*" A third oak coffin enclosed the other two.

At 8:00 p.m. that evening, the body of John Paul I was definitively interred in a marble sarcophagus — at its ends were two reliefs of "praying angels" with outstretched wings and arms crossed over the chest. They belonged to one of the facades of the renaissance tabernacle that housed the Holy Lance, built in 1495.[385] The sarcophagus was placed next to the tomb of Pope Benedict XV under an arch in front of the tomb of Marcellus II, the pope who, at the time of the Counter-Reformation, reigned for only twenty-six days.[386] Two days later, on October 6, the future pope, Cardinal Joseph Ratzinger, commemorated John Paul I at the cathedral in Munich, pointing out some details that united Pope Luciani with Pope Marcellus II and with St. Francis of Assisi, on whose liturgical feast the burial of Pope Luciani took place:

> In the history of the popes there is a person similar to him in his destiny and who could help us to bear this better; this is Marcellus II, next to whom John Paul I has now found his final resting place. ... [Marcellus II] began immediately with actions that attracted attention and brought a breath of fresh air. He refused the ostentation of the papal coronation and began with a very simple ceremony which saved enormous sums of money which ordinarily would have been spent for such ceremonies. He decided that half of it would be used to cover papal debts and the other half would be distributed to the poor so that the day of his installation would be above all a day of joy for the poor. ... There were no special privileges for his relatives. Rather he let them know that they did not need to come to Rome. He did not meddle in the disputes of the factions, but he called all to peace, and he lived his mission, from the heart of the

Eucharist, in a manner which had long since become un-known.[387]

Resuming the comparison with the figure of Marcellus II in the testimony given for the cause, Pope Emeritus Benedict XVI concluded:

The situation of the Church in 1555 was certainly very different from that of 1978. And yet, it is evident that the good man John Paul I was a courageous man who based his life upon his faith, and who represented a sign of hope. In this sense, the man as such lives on through his message.[388]

POST SCRIPTUM

O n October 6, 1978, the then archbishop of Munich and Freis-
ing, Cardinal Joseph Ratzinger, during his homily for the Pontifical Mass of Suffrage for John Paul I, emphasized the pope's in-
alienable trait: "A light which can no longer be taken from us."[389]

In August 1977, a year before his death, when he was still the Patriarch of Venice, Albino Luciani also pointed to Cardinal Ratzinger:

> A few days ago I congratulated Cardinal Ratzinger; he has
> had the courage to proclaim loudly that "the Lord should be
> sought where Peter is."... Ratzinger appears to me to be the
> right kind of prophet. Not all those who write and speak to-
> day have the same courage. In order to go where others are
> going, some of them accept, only with cuts and restrictions,
> the Creed pronounced by Paul VI in 1968 at the closing of
> the Year of Faith. They criticize papal documents. They talk
> constantly about ecclesial communion, but never about the
> pope as a necessary reference point for those who want to
> be in true communion with the Church.

Luciani continued: "Others seem to be smugglers more than prophets; they use the post they occupy to sell, as the doctrine of the Church, what is instead their pure personal opinion.[390]

Cardinal Ratzinger also said during the suffrage liturgy for Pope Luciani, "He was buried on the day of St. Francis of Assisi, the amiable saint that he resembled so much."[391] Moreover, like St. Francis' much needed reform of the Church in his day, Luciani had taken up the right method of reform, through "passionate love for Christ. Living like him, with him, putting the Gospel into practice, staying with him as though he were present. That was his program."[392]

Consummatus in brevi, explevit tempora multa (see Wis 4:13). Given that the brief pontificate of John Paul I was not a flash in the pan, it remains to this day a sign of that continuity of hope that comes from afar and has its roots in the never forgotten treasure of an ancient Church. It is without worldly triumphs. It lives by the reflected light of Christ, close to the teaching of the early Church Fathers, which was revisited by the Second Vatican Council. From this came the priorities of a pontiff who in a short time moved the Church further along the important pathways of a return to the sources of the Gospel, a renewal of the missionary spirit, a pursuit in service to ecclesial poverty, a dialogue with the contemporary world, a spirit of collegiality in the episcopal fraternity, the search for unity with the brothers of the other Christian churches, the continuation of interreligious dialogue, and the search for peace.

The core of his openness was the proclamation of the Gospel. From the very beginning of his ministry he had emphasized proclamation as "the first duty of the entire Church," offering himself as a sign that the Bishop of Rome could be someone for everyone — especially the poor, who are "the true treasures of the Church," as he stated at the Basilica of St. John Lateran. Moreover, it is precisely in Luciani's expression of these priorities during the short course of his pontificate that we find a direct thread with the present. Thus it is in this compelling and provocative relevance that his stature and his agenda should be reconsidered. This is where we find the historical value of that inalienability evoked by Ratzinger.

There is no need, therefore, to wonder what road the Church

would have taken with him. The image that John Paul I had of the Church was that of the Sermon on the Mount, of the poor in spirit, which is neither hidden nor confused with the rationale of mystification and factions. He does not end a chapter in the history of the popes. What the Church is reliving internally from John XXIII, from the Second Vatican Council, from Paul VI, is not a parenthesis. Although the administration of Albino Luciani could not be fully developed in history, he has contributed more than anyone to bearing witness to and strengthening the plan of the Church — a Church that, together with Vatican II, went back to its sources to be faithful to the nature of its mission in the world.

Sudden death did not decree Luciani's death. He was not killed then.

He was killed post mortem by the silence of those, inside and outside the Vatican walls, who were unable to gain personal advantages in the form of worldly honors from his fleeting passage and from his clear and bare-boned evangelical witness.

He was killed post mortem by being disdainfully relegated to historical and historiographical oblivion because he could not be easily classified. He did not fit the mold. He did not line up with the ideological criteria of those who, then and now, compare actions and words with a scoreboard of values established by liberal or conservative agendas.

He was killed post mortem by greedy profitmaking from theatrical books, including certain thriller comic strips, which cleverly speculated on the captivating imagery of a violent death, relegating him to a *damnatio memoriae*. Thus what Christ said to the scribes and Pharisees about his apostles is apt: "I tell you, if they keep silent, the stones will cry out" (Lk 19:40).

This epilogue of the cause is now completed. It is offered as a contribution of systematic research and rediscovery. It is not meant to be some Stalinist rehabilitation of the fallen. It is not about asking for compensation or lodging an appeal. Rather, it is an act of profound repentance which restores to Luciano exactly what he meant *in* and *for* the Church. Therefore, it is an act of justice and peace — namely, a true act of the Church. Moreover, since the death of John

Paul I, it has been impossible to ignore his growing reputation of authentic holiness, a reputation that has not been promoted as a matter of Church policy, but one that continues to spread spontaneously and universally. The voice of the humble has broken the silence.

The stones have cried out.

APPENDIX 1

TESTIMONIAL DOCUMENT OF BENEDICT XVI

Written testimony of Pope Emeritus Benedict XVI in response to an ad hoc questionnaire, released on June 26, 2015. Portions of his answers presented below.

(Positio II, *Summarium testium – Testimonia extraprocessualia,* pp. 1192/4–1192/7.)

Benedictus XVI
Pope Emeritus
Vatican City
June 26, 2015
BEATIFICATIONIS ET CANONIZATIONIS
SERVI DEI
IOANNIS PAULI I — ALBINI LUCIANI
Summi Pontificis
(1912–1978)

I. On my knowledge of the Servant of God
1. In the summer of 1977, I spent two weeks on vacation with my

brother at the major seminary in Bressanone. I had just been consecrated a bishop in May, and in June I was welcomed into the College of Cardinals. The Diocese of Bolzano-Bressanone is part of the ecclesiastical region of Triveneto and so the Patriarch of Venice, Albino Luciani, came to visit me at the seminary in Bressanone. I felt it was an uncommonly fraternal gesture. That he had deliberately come to greet me and welcome me to Veneto that August was an expression of nobility of soul that went far beyond the norm. His cordiality, his simplicity, and the kindness he showed toward me were indelibly etched in my memory.

1. and 3. Until then, I had not yet had a chance to get to know Cardinal Luciani, and, as far as I remember, I only met him briefly before the conclave.

I am unable to provide any answers for questions **4.** and **5.**

6. When Luciani appeared in his white cassock after the election, we were all deeply impressed by his humility and his goodness. Even at meals, then, he would take his place among us. So, thanks to such direct contact, we knew immediately that we had elected the right pope.

10. On the question of the motherhood of God, I took a brief position in the first volume of my trilogy on Jesus, in the context of the interpretation of the Our Father. I believe that Pope Luciani meant to say the same thing that I affirm in the book, and that is what I have always thought.

11. In September of 1978, I went, on behalf of the pope, to the National Marian Congress in Ecuador. Shortly before, I had a brief conversation with the Holy Father who encouraged me and gave me his blessing.

12. It was clear that Pope Luciani was no towering figure when it came to physical health, and yet I found his state of health to be within the norm. I had the impression that, in this sense, his physical constitution was similar to mine.

13. On the day of the pope's death I was asleep in the archiepiscopal residence of Quito. At one point, in the middle of the night, I woke up and heard the door open and someone enter. When I turned on the light, I saw a monk in a brown robe. He looked like a mysterious messenger from the beyond, so I doubted if I was really awake. He came in and told me that he had just received news that the pope had died. At first, I could not believe it, but then I did not doubt the veracity of the information. Curiously enough, I went right back to sleep, but then the following morning I definitely learned the unthinkable news. That monk was an auxiliary bishop of Quito. He had put on his religious habit in order to communicate the news that night. At Mass, during the Prayers of the Faithful, a concelebrant prayed for the late Pope John Paul I. My lay secretary, who was present there, winced, wondering how it was possible to get confused like that. We only referred that way to Paul VI. In the end, we were all truly shocked by that news. There was no longer any doubt that it was true.

14. From the beginning, I thought the rumors that began to circulate about a violent death of the Servant of God were nonsense. The official information for me was, and is, fully credible and convincing.

15. The days of the pope's funeral were days of great sadness for me. That mood was matched by the pouring rain. Even nature seemed to be grieving with us.

16. The comparison with Marcellus II should not, of course, be forced. The situation of the Church in 1555 was certainly very different from that of 1978.

And yet, it is evident that the post-Vatican II Church was going through a great crisis and the good man that John Paul I was, a courageous man based on his faith, represented a sign of hope. In this sense, the man as such lives on through his message.

II. On His Virtues

I can only answer questions **19.-26.** in general terms. There was something special about the fact that, at both the Angelus and the Wednesday audiences, the pope most often spoke off the cuff and from the heart, thus touching people in a very direct way. As a seasoned catechist, he often called children to him during the Wednesday audiences and spoke to them about the Faith. His simplicity and his love for simple people were convincing. And yet, behind that simplicity, formation was taking place, especially of a literary type, remarkable and rich, as emerges in a fascinating way from his little book *Illustrissimi*.

III. On His *Fama sanctitatis et signorum*

27.–31. I cannot add anything to my statements in 2003; I can only confirm that I am deeply convinced of what I have said.

Benedict XVI

INTERVIEW WITH THE EYEWITNESS SR. MARGHERITA MARIN

Full text of the interview of Sister Margherita Marin, a professed religious of the Sisters of Charity or of the Holy Child Mary, as they are known. The witness was part of the team of sisters who were called to assist John Paul I at the private apartments during his pontificate, and she discovered his death. On the recommendation of the postulation, the witness was questioned in Trento, Italy, on May 12, 2009, at the Provincial Curia in the Italian Province of Triveneto.
(Positio II, Summarium Testium – Testimonia extraprocessualia, pp. 1147–1157.)

1. Did you provide evidence to the tribunal during the diocesan inquiry into the cause of the beatification and canonization of the Servant of God Albino Luciani — John Paul I?
No. I didn't testify because I wasn't called.

2. When, how, and where did you first meet the Servant of God?
At the Vatican. Two days after his election. I met John Paul I together with the other sisters of our community who were called to provide assistance at the papal apartments. Until then, I had not had the opportunity to meet him personally. But we knew about Luciani because he had Child Mary nuns with him back during his episcopate in Vittorio Veneto.

3. What other sisters of your community, besides you, made up the team that was called to assist the Holy Father John Paul I?
Sr. Vincenza Taffarel, Sr. Elena Maggi, and Sr. Cecilia Tomaselli. During the first week of his pontificate we were supported also by two other sisters of the community of the Holy Child Mary Institute in Rome who had already served in the apartments of Paul VI: Sr. Gabriella Cacciamalli and Sr. Assunta Crespani. Then only the four of us remained until the death of John Paul I.

4. Of those sisters who is still alive?
I am the only one left. I was the youngest of that group; I was thirty-seven then.

5. What tasks were you each assigned to?
I oversaw the wardrobe and the sacristy, but I also carried out other services when needed. Sister Cecilia was the cook, Sister Vincenza was a nurse, while Sister Elena coordinated our work; she was the group leader. Sister Vincenza was the oldest; she had known the Holy Father for many years. She met him in Belluno at a time when, as a young priest, he had some health problems and she assisted him as a nurse. Later, when he became a bishop, he requested a small community of the Sisters of the Holy Child Mary for the episcopal apartments, and he wanted her to assist him. Sister Vincenza also followed him to Venice and was the only one of the nuns who was with him in Venice to come to the Vatican.

6. What do you remember about those first days of the pontificate? How did he greet you nuns, and what did he say to you?

He greeted us with simplicity, without making us feel uneasy. He told us to pray, that the Lord had given him a great burden, but that, with his help and everyone's prayers, he would carry it through. The day he saw us all together for the first time he was almost apologetic; he knew that I was the youngest, and he said, "I'm sorry for taking some young nuns away." He immediately treated us with familiarity. I remember the day after our arrival I was sent, together with the secretary, Magee, to collect the vestments and to close the pope's private chapel, the one where Paul VI used to celebrate morning Mass with his secretaries, because John Paul I wanted the morning Mass to be celebrated in the private chapel inside the apartments with the sisters present together with his secretaries. "We are a family and we celebrate together," he said. On the day of the solemn Mass for the start of his pontificate, he invited the sisters who had been with him at the Patriarchate in Venice for lunch. I did not know them. The provincial superior, Sr. Maria Teresa Zambon, was there as well. Sister Vincenza told us that she had not so willingly agreed to come, because she felt she was getting too elderly, but later she was fine. She had been experiencing health problems, and I remember the Holy Father said to us, "You know, Sister Vincenza is suffering from a heart condition, and I told her not to walk too much and also to take the personal elevator if she needs it." He showed a lot of regard for us sisters.

7. Along with you sisters and the secretaries, who else assisted the Holy Father?
In addition to the two secretaries, Fr. John Magee and Fr. Diego Lorenzi, whose rooms were upstairs in the apartments, there was Angelo Gugel, who was assigned to provide personal service to the Holy Father as his papal butler.

Angelo was then living with his family outside the Vatican. He would come in the morning around eight and remained on call for the whole day. He served lunch and dinner, then after dinner he returned home. The Holy Father had known him for many years. When he was a bishop in Vittorio Veneto, he had helped Gugel secure employment in the Vatican, and after his election he immediately called him up for this service.

Each of us had her own duties to perform, so the day was full. There was also a lot to do in order to set up and arrange the apartment left by Paul VI, and we didn't have enough time to complete everything in one month. I remember a few days before the end of that month we had just begun to unpack the crates of books from Venice and place the volumes in the library. There was no time. We communicated more frequently with Father Magee. He was close to the Holy Father and gave us instructions. With Father Diego, it was less often. I heard from Sister Vincenza that he was not suitable for that office. A week before the pope died, Sister Vincenza told us that the Holy Father would soon be changing him. He was going to be replaced by a certain Father Mario, the secretary he had previously in Venice.

8. What were the schedules, the rhythm of life of the Holy Father in those thirty-four days? How did his day usually unfold?
The Holy Father got up early in the morning, around 5:00 a.m. He started the day by dedicating a lot of time to personal prayer. At about 5:30 a.m. he entered the chapel and stayed there for more than an hour and a half. He remained absorbed in prayer. Since we were always nearby, we sisters could see him praying from outside. He always prayed alone, [and] the secretaries came down later for Mass. Mass was celebrated every morning at 7:00 a.m. While the Holy Father was in the chapel, we sisters, around 6:30 a.m., recited Morning Prayer in the sitting room next to the kitchen, then we too went to the chapel for Mass. He did not give homilies during the Mass. I remember instead that sometimes, when he had to celebrate Mass somewhere else that day, he let Father Magee celebrate the Mass in his place, and he participated as a simple altar boy. He respected the Eucharistic fast, so he only had breakfast after Mass. During breakfast, Sister Vincenza was present as needed. After breakfast, he would entertain himself in his study reading the newspapers, and at around 9:00 a.m. he would go down for the audiences. He would come back up around 11:30 a.m.–12:00 p.m. Lunch was around 12:00 p.m. He had few guests; he always had lunch with his two sec-

retaries. He would retire immediately afterwards for his afternoon rest. In the afternoon, he usually stayed in the apartment. He would study and read. He walked around reading. Sometimes he also went upstairs to the roof garden. A few times, he went down to the Vatican Gardens. Cardinal Villot had once told him, "Your Holiness, if you go down to the gardens we have to close them and we can't let anyone in." The Holy Father replied, "Then, if you have to close them … I'll stay here." And so most of the time he stayed at home. In the afternoon, he usually had no appointments. He received a few people at his own request. I remember seeing Cardinal Villot and Cardinal Poletti several times; I remember a visit from the bishop of Belluno and another by the pope's brother who was leaving for Australia (both were guests for lunch, and his brother stayed overnight). Before dinner, he would recite Evening Prayer with his secretaries, often in English. Dinner was around 7:30–8:00 p.m. He didn't usually have guests in the evening; he always dined with his secretaries. He then said Night Prayer with them, and while we were still tidying up the refectory he would come by to say goodnight. Every night. I remember that he always asked us to pray for the many needs in the world. He would always ask me something about preparing the liturgy for the following day; then he wished us goodnight. He would always say to us: "Until tomorrow, sisters; if the Lord wishes, we'll all celebrate Mass together." He retired early, around 9:30 p.m.

9. During those thirty-four days, how did his awareness of the mission he had been given come across? Was he peaceful or anxious about carrying out his duties?
When I saw him, he was always calm, serene. He was full of confidence, assured. Even in prayer we could see how united he was with the Lord. He knew how to work with his collaborators and did so with great respect and humility. He would apologize for disturbing them. I never saw him show signs of impatience with anyone, ever. He instilled courage. He was friendly with everyone.

10. How was his health? Did he follow a particular diet? Did he complain of any ailments? Was he taking any medications?

I don't remember Sister Cecilia preparing different foods or special diets for him. Sister Cecilia cooked rather lightly for everyone, and the Holy Father ate what the rest of us ate. As for his health, Sister Vincenza was attentive; she knew his personal doctor, Doctor Da Ros, [and] she trusted him; they talked on the phone. The Vatican doctor, Doctor Buzzonetti, also came to the apartments, but I don't know if he visited him. Doctor Da Ros came three times for routine checkups. The first time, I think, was at the beginning, then I saw him come in mid-September, and the last time, I remember, was on September 23. Regarding his last visit, Sister Vincenza told us that the doctor determined that the Holy Father was well, very well, so much so, she said, that the doctor had also taken away his medication. However, I could not say which medication, or if he took away more than one; that was just the way she said it.

11. Did Sister Vincenza ever show concern about the pope's health?
No. I never saw her worried. If there had been anything, we would have seen her worry, but no. In fact, she was quite happy, because, the last time, the doctor told her the Holy Father was fine, so she was at peace. We knew that as a young man Luciani had some weakness in his lungs and that back in Venice he had some eye problems, but I never saw him complaining of any ailment, not even a headache, nor can I say that I noticed signs of particular tiredness or fatigue.

12. We come to the last day: Thursday, September 28. If you remember, could you give as detailed an account of that day as possible?
In the morning, he went into the chapel to pray at the usual time, and he celebrated Mass with us at seven. He normally had breakfast, and then stopped for a while to read the newspapers. Then, around nine o'clock, he went downstairs for his morning audiences. Around noon, he came back upstairs to the apartments, but I remember that he came into the kitchen, as he often did, asking us for a coffee: "Sisters, do you have any coffee? Could you make me a coffee?" He sat down to wait, took the coffee, and went to his study. He then had lunch with the secretaries. Later, he retired for his usual short afternoon rest. I don't remember exactly when he went back to his

rooms, but he stayed home that whole afternoon, he never moved from the apartments, and he received no one because he told us he was drafting a document for the bishops. However, I do not know to which bishops he was referring. I remember it well because that afternoon I was ironing in the wardrobe room with the door open, and I could see him going back and forth. He was walking around the apartment with papers in his hand that he was reading; every now and then, he would stop to make a few notes and then he would start walking again while reading and, as he walked, he would pass by where I was standing. I remember that, seeing me ironing, he also said to me: "Sister, I make you work so hard ... but you don't need to iron that shirt so well because it's hot, I sweat, and you have to change them often ... just iron the collar and the cuffs — you can't see the rest, you know." He told me this in his Venetian dialect, which he often used with us. That's how he spent the whole afternoon.

13. Do you remember if the secretaries were also in the apartments at the time?
Yes, they were home that afternoon as well, both of them.

14. Do you remember if the Holy Father fell ill that afternoon and if Father Magee called Sister Vincenza to bring some medicine to the pope?
No. I did not see this; I knew nothing about this, not even from Sister Vincenza. The Holy Father spent all that afternoon the way I said. It seems to me that he did not receive anyone — perhaps later, Cardinal Villot. He recited Evening Prayer with the two secretaries, and I remember him saying it in English. Then he went to dinner around 7:30 or 8:00 p.m. The secretaries were present at the dinner, along with Angelo, who was serving as usual, while we sisters were in the other room, as always.

15. Did you see or did you know if John Paul I felt any pain that evening, either shortly before, during or after dinner?
No. I did not see any particular indication, nor any indication from

Sister Vincenza or the secretaries, which would make me suspect anything.

16. Do you remember if Doctor Da Ros called or received a phone call from Sister Vincenza or from the pope before dinner, or around 8:45 p.m.?

I don't think the doctor called that night or was called. Of course, I can say that after dinner there was a call from Cardinal Colombo. I had already heard the Holy Father talking that morning to Father Magee about this phone call. And, after dinner, the Holy Father went to answer the phone and spoke with the cardinal of Milan. I don't remember exactly how long their conversation lasted, maybe half an hour. After, he came to us, as he always did, to say goodnight to us before retiring to his study. I remember that he asked me which Mass I had prepared for him for the following day, and I answered him: "The Mass of the Angels." He wished us a good night saying what he used to say to us every evening: "Until tomorrow, sisters; if the Lord wishes, we'll all celebrate Mass together."

There is a detail from that moment that remains imprinted in my memory: We were all together in the small living room with the door open — the door faced the door of his private study — and after he said goodnight to us, the Holy Father stood at the door of his study, turned around again and waved goodnight to us, smiling … I feel like I can still see him there at the door. It is the last image I have of him.

17. Did he retire to his rooms accompanied by his secretaries?

No. He left the way he always did; he didn't need to be accompanied. I remember that evening, when dinner was over, after Father Diego handed over the phone call from Cardinal Colombo, he left the papal apartments. He had gone out in the evening other times before. I know that the Holy Father had once told the secretaries that, if they wanted to, they could go out. And Father Diego had gone out several times. However, I don't know where he went. Father Magee, on the other hand, stayed there with us. He stopped by with us nuns to talk a little bit, to keep us company. I remember that he had the volume of the papal yearbook with him. Perhaps he had to check something. He was leafing through it and began to read the list of popes: who they were, how long they had lived, etc. … I remember that detail. He stayed with us for maybe half an hour.

Then he too retired. We usually retired around 10:00 or 10:30 p.m. Perhaps that evening could have been a little later.

18. We come to the next day: Friday the 29th. What do you remember about that early morning?
I got up as usual around 5:00 a.m., because at 5:30 a.m. the groceries we ordered arrived and the flowers were deposited just outside the elevator. That morning, I went to collect everything, and after I put it all away, I returned to pray with the other sisters. The papal apartments were so small that we could always see each other, even when we were doing different things. We were praying in the little room near the kitchen, all four of us together.

19. Can you tell me who discovered the pope's death and at what time?
Around 5:15 a.m. that morning, like every morning, Sister Vincenza had left a cup of coffee for the Holy Father in the sacristy, in front of the chapel, just outside the pope's apartment. When the Holy Father came out of his room, he would have some coffee in the sacristy before he entered the chapel to pray. That morning, however, the coffee remained there. About ten minutes later, Sister Vincenza said: "He hasn't come out yet? Why not?" I was there in the corridor. So I saw that she knocked once, then she knocked again, but he did not answer … there was still silence. Then she opened the door and walked in. I was there as she entered, but I stayed outside. I heard her say, "Your Holiness, you shouldn't pull these jokes on me."

Then she called me as she came out, shocked, so I immediately went in with her and saw him. The Holy Father was in his bed, the reading light over the headboard was on. He had two pillows under his back that propped him up a bit, his legs were outstretched, his arms were on top of the bedsheets, he was wearing pajamas, and in his hands, resting on his chest, he was clutching some typewritten pages. His head was turned a little bit to the right with a slight smile, his glasses rested on his nose, and his eyes were half-closed … he really seemed to be sleeping. I touched his hands; they were cold, I noticed, and was struck by his fingernails, which were a little dark.

20. Didn't you notice anything out of place?
No. Nothing. Nothing. Not even a crease. Nothing fell to the floor, nothing was disheveled that could suggest there had been any noticeable illness. He looked just like someone who had fallen asleep reading. Who fell asleep and stayed that way.

21. Then what did you do?
Immediately afterwards, Sister Vincenza went upstairs to call Father Magee, and I ran to call Father Diego. I knocked on his door; I called him: "Come down, the Holy Father, the Holy Father!" He woke with a start and came down. We said a prayer, then Father Magee went to call the Vatican doctor. Doctor Buzzonetti came almost immediately; I saw Cardinal Villot arrive and then Poletti.

22. Were you sisters present at the time of the doctor's report?
No, because we had left the room. Father Magee came up to us afterwards and said: "He didn't suffer, he didn't even notice it," reporting what the doctor had told him, and he also said that his sudden death had occurred around eleven o'clock at night. That's what I heard. I didn't hear anything else … there was little to say. None of us were involved in arranging the body, neither Sister Vincenza nor the rest of us; they took care of it. Angelo and others arrived later to help.

23. What do you still remember about those moments?
I remember the prelates coming and going; I remember them going back and forth in the corridor, and I felt they did not know how they were going to give the world the news that the pope, who had won everyone over in such a short time, had died like that, and so, only two hours after we nuns had found him, they put out the official news. I remember that when the Holy Father was still in his room, his niece, a young girl, came to see him. She stayed off to the side and wept with Sister Vincenza. We sisters attended the suffrage

mass celebrated by Cardinal Poletti, without the secretaries. We were called later to provide the vestments and to accompany him to the Clementine Hall. We stayed there to pray, and then we went back because we had to vacate the apartments and seal everything, according to what was established practice. I remember that Father Magee told us to take some of the Holy Father's personal effects. He gave Sister Vincenza his glasses, slippers and other objects. I took his little radio, which I still keep as a relic.

24. Do you remember if anyone instructed you to say one thing or another about the pope's death?
Father Magee told us not to say that it was the nuns, Sister Vincenza and I, who found him dead in the room, because they had decided to say that it was the secretaries who found him first.

25. Do you know who took, and what became of, the papers in his hand?
No. I cannot say who took care of them. Nor did I ask. We left him holding them; we didn't touch anything. They were typewritten sheets, or rather two or three half sheets; I am sure they were not handwritten, but I cannot say what they contained because I did not read them at that moment. Someone out in the corridor told us that they were the papers for Wednesday's audience. The study with his papers, and his room, were then sealed. They were reopened by his successor, John Paul II. I was present when the new pope cut the seals and entered the apartments.

26. After the pope's death, did you have an opportunity to meet with Sister Vincenza or the other sisters to recollect any details from that month?
Yes, we met, with Sister Vincenza a little and more with Sister Elena, who in the meantime had fallen ill with cancer. However, more than remembering details from those days, we invited each other to pray to him to intercede for us.

27. Someone later asked for information or expressed suspicion re-

garding the circumstance of the death of John Paul I?
After I returned to the community in Vittorio Veneto, I remember that Bishop Ducoli, the bishop of Belluno, called me on the phone. He was very upset and asked me to tell him how the pope had really been found — if he had fallen in some way and was on the floor. "No, your Excellency," I told him. "Look, we all saw the Holy Father in his bed, and it hadn't even been creased."

28. Do you have anything more to say about the conflicting versions regarding the pope's last hours?
How all those rumors came out, I really don't know. We were there. I can tell you, and I have told you, everything I know and have seen.

28. Is there anything else you think you could add?
I don't have anything else to add.

29. Will you allow us to transcribe what we have just recorded onto paper and then sign it?
Yes. I allow it.

Once the transcription onto paper was finished, the witness was allowed to review the testimony in order to confirm or modify it. She affixed her signature to it and her superior, Mother Costantina Kersbamer, signed it as well.

APPENDIX 2

1. Vatican City, September 10, 1978 — Letter from John Paul I addressed to Cardinal Giovanni Colombo, archbishop of Milan, regarding the appointment of a successor to the See of Venice (ArPost, *Pontificate Correspondence,* August–September 1978, folder I)

2. Vatican City, August–September 1978 — Appointment book used by John Paul I during his pontificate (Venice, ArSPV, *Fondo Luciani – Archivio proprio*, envelope IX, c.n.n., in Positio III, *Summarium documentorum*, p. 2014).

Transcription:
Visit of senior cardinals
Ottaviani
Di Jorio
<u>Audiences</u> Diplom. [Dipolmatis]=
Mission of Nations
Auxiliaries of Rome
Roman Clergy
No speeches made in Paderno
end

3. Vatican City, August–September 1978 — *Last pages of the personal appointment book he used during his pontificate* (Venice, ArSPV, *Fondo Luciani*
(*Archivio proprio*, envelope IX, agenda no. 12, in Positio III, *Summarium documentorum*, p. 2011).

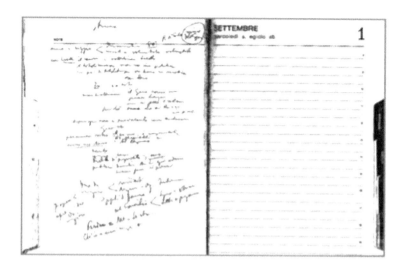

Love

I love = journey < dramatic SP. [St. Paul]

Fr [Francis] de Sales thorns of the Lord

< mist. [mysterious]: *voluntate voluptate*

with all my heart = I emphasize everything

totalitarianism does not belong in politics

a little totalitarianism is good in asceticism

with God

Ex… ex toto

let's not treat the Lord like some

poor Lazarus

to who we toss 1 [one] elem [coin]

as long as he leaves us

in peace

above all else = prevalent not exclusive

Jacob

for your love: - if not, it is s impossible

- Fr. [brothers] twins =

<u>Like myself</u> – Al Capone

tailor

I eat and drink
right of ownership
problems before Jesus we will have
they are hungry for bread
Providing some food < private
< Nations - Org. International [Bodies]
The people d. [in] hunger
at Vatican II - above = Christians
- below = pagans
7 works <
open… Providing
some
food
Forgiveness = Mt [Matthew]: If you are …
May I love you always + [more].

APPENDIX 3

CLINICAL AND DEATH-RELATED DOCUMENTATION

This clinical excursus was taken from the witness report by Dr. Lina Petri, daughter of Antonia Luciani, sister of John Paul I, which was added to the tribunal documents. Doctor Petri was the only family member to visit the body of the pontiff inside his bedroom in the apartments at the Vatican during the morning of September 29, 1978. (Positio II, Summarium testium – Testimonia extraprocessualia, XVIII, pp. 918–922.)

NOTE ON HIS HEALTH

I would now like to add a few remarks with a minimum of expertise, given that I have a medical degree but do not practice medicine.

I was able to consult the photocopy of the medical records concerning the hospitalization of my uncle Albino, Patriarch of Venice, in the Ophthalmology Department headed by Professor Giovanni Rama at the Provincial General Hospital in Mestre in 1975. There also was some correspondence and memoirs that Professor Rama wrote later, along with Prof. Luciano Caprioglio, a cardiologist who visited my uncle during his hospitalization and collected his case history. The medical records were photocopied and sent to the family at the behest of Doctor Caprioglio. …

The medical records confirm four operations, all of which were commonplace and routine. The first was in Padua at the age of eleven, for a tonsillectomy (my mother used to say that he was anxious to be discharged quickly from the hospital so he could enter the minor seminary in Feltre). The second operation was to remove his adenoids. [Note: The text of his case history contains some deletions and corrections, as if the patient first reported having been operated on in Padua at the age of eleven for adenoids and then corrected himself by attributing that first operation to his tonsils. In fact, even oral sources in his family circle are somewhat confused regarding the chronology of the two operations, but the substance does not change.] In 1964, during his episcopate in Vittorio Veneto, he underwent a cholecystectomy due to gallstones, and the following year he underwent a hemorrhoidectomy.

As can be seen, these were by no means major pathologies or interventions. Regarding the last two interventions, Professor Rama wrote a note explaining, "He was operated on successfully."

The case history then reports that he was "hospitalized in a sanatorium ward, at age thirty-three; he was infiltrated for a short period (does not remember which side). Subsequent test results were negative." In reality, there were two hospitalizations in the sanatorium during 1947, at age thirty-five, one from March 8 to June 2 and the other from August 26 to September 12. The nature of the pulmonary pathology that struck him was not definitively clarified. It is certain that it was not tuberculosis. In fact, on June 3, 1947, the hospitalization registry of the sanatorium department (kept in the pneumology didactic unit, and of which I have a photocopy) recorded the results of an examination that was negative for tuberculosis: "Koch - -." A note received by family members, and kept at the curia in Belluno, contained a statement attributed to the attending physician of the time, Dr. Gottardo Gottardi, which reads: "He did not have tuberculosis, rather migrating viral pneumonia, which first appeared in one lung, then moved to the other."

From the same medical records we learned about an "acute articular rheumatism, in 1953, which was treated first at home and then for a month and a half in the hospital in Belluno" (this was his fifth hospitalization). In fact, in August 1953, I remember that my mother always said that she was so sorry that Uncle Albino had not been able to come to Levico to baptize my brother Roberto, born on August 18, because he was not well at that time. The rheumatism story was also resolved, according to the case history collected by Professor Rama in 1975: "Since then, some joint pain, especially in the rachis." In short, common back pain.

Then we come to the eighth hospitalization in 1975. My uncle reported not seeing well out of his left eye, for about two months. A diagnosis of retinal vein thrombosis was made. …

In 1975, my uncle stayed in hospital for a week, from December 2 to 8. The diagnosis was "occlusion of the central retinal vein of the left eye" (retinal thrombosis), which, after therapeutic treatment, was resolved quickly and positively with the recovery of his vision and no aftereffects. In the patient diary, there was a note from the ophthalmologist, Doctor Rama, dated March 1978: "Repeated ophthalmoscopic checks confirmed complete functional recovery; on the fundus there were no signs of a previous thrombotic event."

Professor Rama again testified that checkups always took place two or three times a year and that he had planned to go to the Vatican himself, in September 1978, in order to transfer the medical orders over to the doctors in Rome (the meeting would have taken place "on the Saturday following the death," wrote Professor Rama).

All the laboratory tests performed in that instance were absolutely normal (no hypertension, no diabetes, no pathology linked to altered triglyceride and cholesterol values, liver disease, kidney disease, no heart disease, no relevant pathology at the pulmonary level), all values more than normal for a subject of his age. The X-ray presenting aortosclerosis did not indicate to what extent, but still showed minimal vascular pathology.

The examinations required in the hospital also included an oscillograph of the lower limbs, which at the time was used to assess the circulation status in his legs. This went back to his air travel to Brazil the previous month (November 3–21, 1975). In the case history, there is in fact mention of my uncle's leg problems:

On November 6, after a long journey by plane, in a sitting position, there was edema of the dorsum of the foot, without local pain, without changes in the skin color, which spontaneously regressed after two days. There was a fleeting repetition of the phenomenon after three days.

However, I found no trace of his oscillograph results in the medical record. Professor Caprioglio reported in his objective examination, "There may be less extensive pulsatility of the dorsal artery of the left foot. Very slight perimallelar subedema in the left foot. No temperature changes." Translated, the foot, which had swollen up during the flight to Brazil, still showed some very small signs of swelling and difficulty in circulation.

The therapy established during his hospitalization was substantially based on anticoagulant drugs to resolve the existing retinal thrombosis and prevent the onset of others. These are the medications he was prescribed: *Complamin*: It is a haemokinetic, [which] improves the viscosity of the blood, in practice it makes it more fluid and therefore resolves and prevents the formation of thrombus and is used specifically for the eyes. *Persantin*: It is an antiplatelet agent, antithrombotic: It prevents the platelets as they aggregate together from forming thrombus. These two drugs, in essence, were to treat and prevent further thrombosis at the same time. *CVP-duo* was similarly prescribed as well (against the fragility of the capillaries and retinal hemorrhages). Furthermore, *Benexol B12* (a B vitamin complex) and *Trieffortil*, which is a specific drug for those suffering from arterial orthostatic hypotension, were prescribed. In fact, Uncle Albino tended to have low blood pressure and this had caused him some episodes of malaise. The medical record reads: "About six months ago [during the summer of 1975] he had a sudden feeling of imbalance, lasting about three hours. The patient appeared rather pale to the response team."… His clinical situation in the years 1976–78 was always under control. Supportive therapy was carried out from time to time with the particular goal of addressing his tendency toward arterial hypotension, using "mild cardiotonics and multivitamins."

In one of his memos, Professor Rama stated: "Pope Luciani tended to be hypotensive. Moreover, thrombotic events ran in his family...The most likely scenario is that he had a cardiac thrombosis (heart attack)." And again: "For me there is no clinical doubt. He died from the same circulatory disorder that affected the retina of his eye. ... This time it was his heart or his brain that was affected."...

In May 2010, Professor Luciano Caprioglio noted in the margin of the copy of the medical record he delivered, which related to the hospitalization in 1975: "[My] diagnostic conclusion was verbal at the time, since I found no pathology, although I was aware of the opinion of Professor Rama who stated that in his experience subsequent cardiovascular pathology was frequently found in patients with retinal thrombosis."...

From the overall analysis of the 1975 medical record, I can verify that a picture emerged that we relatives had always supported, and which was also confirmed by the reports released after the pope's death, both by the ophthalmologist, Professor Giovanni Rama and the attending physician Doctor Da Ros: My uncle did not show any clear or evident, significant pathologies that would indicate he was a seriously ill patient. Only his episode of retinal thrombosis required attention.

DOCUMENTS RELATED TO HIS HEALTH
Doc. 1

Mestre (Venice), December 2–8, 1975 — *Documentation of the hospitalization of Patriarch Luciani on December 2–8, 1975 – Medical Records* (ArPost, *Documenti personali – documentazione clinica, folder II).*

Doc. 2

Vatican City, September 29, 1978 — *Death certificate of John Paul I written by Doctor Renato Buzzonetti, former personal physician to the pope* (ArPost, *Documenti personali – documentazione clinica*, folder II).

Transcription: Certificate of Death:

I certify that His Holiness JOHN PAUL I, ALBINO LUCIANI, born in Forno di Canale (Belluno) on October 17, 1912, died in the Vatican Apostolic Palace on September 28, 1978, at 11:00 p.m. due to "sudden death - acute myocardial infarction." Death was pronounced at 6:00 a.m. on September 29, 1978.

Vatican City, September 29, 1978
Doctor Renato Buzzonetti
Certified by the Director of Health Services (Prof. Mario Fontana)

Doc. 3

Vatican City, September 29, 1978 — *Bulletin No. 272 of the Holy See Press Office communicating the death of John Paul I* (ArPost, *Documenti personali – documentazione clinica*, folder II).

Transcription: This morning, September 29, 1978, about five-thirty, the private secretary of the pope, Rev. Fr. John Magee, when contrary to custom, he had not found the Holy Father in the chapel [of his private apartment], looked for him in his room and found him dead in bed with the light on, like one who was intent on reading. The physician who hastened to the pope's room verified the death, which took place presumably toward eleven o'clock yesterday evening, as "sudden death that could be related to acute myocardial infarction."

The venerated body will lie in state in the Clementine Hall of the Apostolic Palace.

Doc. 4

Rome, February 12, 2013 — *Summary prepared by Dr. Renato Buzzonetti for the delivery of the confidential documentation relating to the death of John Paul I, to the acts of the Cause, following a formal request sent to the Secretariat of State* (ArPost, *Documenti personali – documentazione clinica*, folder II)

Doc. 5

Vatican City, October 9, 1978 — *Letter of Dr. Renato Buzzonetti to the Most Rev. Giuseppe Caprio, substitute of the Secretariat of State, for the transmission of the documentation related to the death of the pontiff and to the previous agreements between the treating physicians* (ArPost, *Documenti personali – documentazione clinica*, folder II).

Doc. 6

Vatican City, October 9, 1978 — *Report by Dr. Buzzonetti addressed*

to the Most Rev. Giuseppe Caprio, regarding the ascertainment of death of John Paul I on the morning of September 29, 1978; medical history of the event (ArPost, *Documenti personali – documentazione clinica*, folder II).
In addition: *Report by Dr. Buzzonetti addressed to the Most Rev. Giuseppe Caprio, October 9, 1978.*

Doc. 7
Vatican City, October 10, 1978 — *Report by Dr. Buzzonetti on the ascertainment of death of the Holy Father John Paul I* (ArPost, *Documenti personali – documentazione clinica*, folder II)

Doc. 8
Vatican City, October 10–11 [?], 1978 — *Undated and unsigned note sent by the Secretariat of State to Doctor Buzzonetti in which were formulated questions to be forwarded to the professors at the Institute of Forensic Medicine of the Sapienza University in Rome who were in charge of the preservation treatment of the body of John Paul I* (ArPost, *Documenti personali – documentazione clinica*, folder II).

Doc. 9
Vatican City, October 10, 1978 — *Report by Prof. Mario Fontana, Primary Pontifical Physician, on the ascertainment of death of the Holy Father John Paul I* (ArPost, *Documenti personali – documentazione clinica*, folder II).

Doc. 10
Vatican City, October 11, 1978 — *Letter from Doctor Buzzonetti to Monsignor Caprio which reported on the confidential conversation that Doctor Buzzonetti had with Prof. Cesare Gerin, Director of the Institute of Forensic Medicine of the Sapienza University in Rome, which was then communicated exclusively to the Congregation of Cardinals* (ArPost, *Documenti personali – documentazione clinica*, folder II).

Doc. 11
Vatican City, February 24, 1988 — *Request for collaboration by*

Msgr. John Foley, then president of the Pontifical Commission for Social Communications, to Professor Giovanni Rama, head of the ophthalmology division of the hospital in Mestre, regarding Luciani's hospitalization in 1975 (ArPost, *Documenti personali – documentazione clinica,* folder II).

Doc. 12

Mestre (Venice), undated (1988) — *Professor Giovanni Rama's response to the previous request of the Pontifical Commission for Social Communications* (ArPost, *Documenti personali – documentazione clinica,* folder II).

Doc. 13

Mestre (Venice), undated (1988) — *Autograph of Prof. Giovanni Rama regarding the episode of retinal thrombosis in 1975 and the way David Yallop used the information he obtained* (ArPost, *Documenti personali – documentazione clinica,* folder II).

Transcription:

Pope Luciani did not have a retinal embolism but a thrombosis of a branch of the retinal vein of the left eye. He was hospitalized for several days (December 2–12, 1975) in order to complete his clinical testing and to monitor his treatment during the initial phase of the attack.

The test results indicated that Papa Luciani was in good general condition; he had tolerated the treatment for this episode well and was discharged and put on maintenance therapy. His vision completely recovered, and he had no further episodes.

The therapy that he was prescribed from time to time in the following years was very simple: vitamins.

Pope Luciani tended to be hypotensive. Moreover, thrombotic events ran in his family. The most likely scenario is that he had a cardiac thrombosis (heart attack) or a cerebral thrombosis. I had written all this in my report for Y[allop]. He was absolutely professionally dishonest and extrapolated from my report whatever was convenient so that he could say things that were science fiction and did not correspond with the truth.

Doc. 14

Vatican City, September 23, 1978 — *Autograph notes by Dr. Antonio Da Ros, the attending physician of John Paul I, regarding the agreements made between the Vatican Health Service and Dr. Da Ros himself for the pope's medical assistance, to be transmitted to Monsignor Caprio* (ArPost, *Documenti personali – documentazione clinica,* folder II).

Notes from my archive:

Parto alle 7.30 da Treviso, arrivo alle 8.30 a Roma; prelevato da un autista del Vaticano, vi arrivo
Saturday, Sept. 23, 1978
In quella occasione il Papa espresse il desiderio che io continuassi ad essere il Suo medico
I departed Treviso at 7:30 a.m. and arrived in Rome at 8:30. I was picked up by a Vatican driver, arrived at the Vatican at 9:30, and visited the Holy Father, as usual.
Papa da vivo, in qualità di rappresentante del Servizio Sanitario, in sostituzione del Prof. Fontana,
On that occasion, the pope expressed the desire that I should continue as his personal physician and that some points be agreed with the Vatican Health Service.
nota) e che vennero controfirmati da Mons. Magee.
Around 10:30 a.m. Father Magee, organized a meeting with Doctor Renato Buzzonetti. He had never visited the pope while he was alive, but was representing the Health Service for Professor Fontana, who was absent for health reasons.

General agreements were thus drawn up for presentation to the Holy Father, which I recorded (see note) and which were countersigned by Mons. Magee.
Erano come sempre buone. Mi tenevo in continuo contatto con Suor Vincenza Taffarel, infermiera
I presented the agreements to the pope over lunch, at which his two secretaries · --

Dott. Antonio Da Ros

Vittorio Veneto, 24/08/09

Transcription:

Saturday, Sept. 23, 1978

I departed Treviso at 7:30 a.m. and arrived in Rome at 8:30. I was picked up by a Vatican driver, arrived at the Vatican at 9:30, and visited the Holy Father, as usual.

On that occasion, the pope expressed the desire that I should continue as his personal physician and that some points be agreed with the Vatican Health Service.

Around 10:30 a.m. Father Magee organized a meeting with Doctor Renato Buzzonetti. He had never visited the pope while he was alive, but was representing the Health Service for Professor Fontana, who was absent for health reasons.

General agreements were thus drawn up for presentation to the Holy Father, which I recorded (see note) and which were countersigned by Mons. Magee.

I presented the agreements to the pope over lunch, at which his two secretaries

Doc. 15
Vittorio Veneto, August 24, 2009 — *Note by Dr. Antonio Da Ros, Luciani's attending physician in Vittorio Veneto, Venice and the Vatican, regarding the agreements made with the Vatican Health Service for assistance to the pope* (ArPost, *Documenti personali – documentazione clinica,* folder II – *pictured below*).

Doc. 16
Mestre (Venice), June 24, 2010 — *Statement by Dr. Luciano Caprioglio, former head cardiologist of Medical Division I at the Civil Hospital in Mestre, regarding the death of John Paul I* (ArPost, *Documenti personali – documentazione clinica,* folder II).

DIARY OF A PONTIFICATE
From the Conclave to the Funeral August 25–October 4, 1978

August 25: At 7:00 p.m., the first conclave after the Second Vatican Council began the *extra omnes.* In his last letter to his sister, Antonia, Albino Luciani wrote, "There is no danger for me."

August 26: On the fourth ballot, a quorum with an almost unanimous consensus was reached. He accepted his election and took the name of John Paul. At 7:20 p.m., the Cardinal Protodeacon Pericle Felici announced: "*Habemus Papam.*" At 7:30 p.m., John Paul I looked out from the central loggia to impart his apostolic blessing. The enclosure of the conclave was extended until the morning of the following day.

August 27: Nine-thirty a.m. Mass with the concelebrating conclavists and the participation of the cardinals over age eighty. *Urbi et Orbi* radio message: the six "we wish" points of his program. First Angelus: "I hope that you will help me with your prayers." Unpublished renunciation of the plural *maiestatis*. He took possession of the private apartment on the third floor of the Apostolic Palace, with his secretary, Fr. Diego Lorenzi in tow.

August 28: Cardinal Jean Villot was appointed Secretary of State and all of the official offices of the Curia were confirmed.

August 29: Msgr. Giuseppe Bosa was appointed apostolic administrator of Venice and a papal message was sent to the people of Venice. Sr. Vincenza Taffarel, the nun who had assisted him since his episcopate in Vittorio Veneto, arrived at the papal apartment to begin her service.

August 30: Address to the College of Cardinals. The speech delivered in Italian differed completely from the official written text. He addressed the cardinals in the first person: "Let us try together to give the world a show of unity." The third general conference of the Latin American episcopate, scheduled for October 12–28 in Puebla, Mexico, was confirmed. Father John Magee, former secretary of Paul VI, was confirmed as "First Secretary."

August 31: Address to the Diplomatic Corps accredited to the Holy See on the duty to build peace.

September 1: Address to the Representatives of the International Press: "If Saint Paul came back, he would be a journalist."

September 2: Meeting with family members. Meeting with the delegations of non-Catholic Churches. Letter to the emigrants from the Veneto region regarding the planned meeting in Einsiedeln, Switzerland.

September 3: Meeting and conversation with the pilgrims from Belluno, Vittorio Veneto, and Venice. Angelus: "More prayers and fewer battles." Renunciation of the coronation rite. Celebration of Mass for the Inauguration of the Ministry of the Pastor of the Universal Church. Imposition of the pallium, one-on-one greeting of the 104 cardinals who renewed their obedience. Lunch with the Sisters of the Child Mary. A team of four nuns was established to provide service in the apartments. Visit from his personal physician, Dr. Antonio Da Ros.

September 4: Address to the official delegations of the nations present for the beginning of the pontificate: "Our heart is fully open to all peoples and to all races." Private audiences with the heads of state present. Meeting with the bishops of the Triveneto region in Italy. Appointment with Cardinal Bernardin Gantin, president of the Pontifical Commission *Iustitia et Pax* and president of the Pontifical Council *Cor Unum*.

September 5: Private audience with Nikodim, Metropolitan of Leningrad and Novgorod, who died in the pope's arms. "Never in my life had I heard such beautiful words for the Church." Audience with the apostolic nuncios to Australia, Sri Lanka, and Thailand, and with two ministers from Brazil and Egypt.

September 6: First General Audience — theme: "Humility." Declined the use of the gestatorial chair. Dialogued with a boy from Malta. Called for peace in the Middle East. Angelo Gugel began service as butler in the papal apartments.

September 7: Address and conversation with the Roman clergy "with brotherly familiarity." Audience with Cardinal Vicar of Rome Ugo Poletti. Audience with three Eastern patriarchs of the Chaldean, Maronite, and Armenian Rites. Private audience with philologist Vittore Branca.

September 8: Suffrage for Metropolitan Nikodim. The Russian delegation received the future Patriarch of Moscow and All Russia, Kirill, among its members. At the pope's behest, Cardinal Johannes Willebrands was called to represent the Holy See at the metropolitan's funeral in the Soviet Union. Audience with the apostolic nuncio to Pakistan. Letter on the occasion of the 85th German *Katholikentag* in Freiburg. Cardinal Antonio Poma, president of the Italian Bishops' Conference was a guest for dinner.

September 9: No official audiences. Message of gratitude to Cardinal Silvio Oddi on his 25th anniversary of episcopal ordination.

September 10: Angelus: "God is our father; even more he is our mother." Invitation for all to join the three presidents belonging to the three monotheistic religions in praying for the Camp David talks and for peace in the Middle East.

September 11: Audiences with the archbishop of Guatemala, Cardinal Mario Casariego; the general secretary of the Synod of Bishops; and the apostolic nuncio to Spain. Carlo Pietrangeli appointed new general director of the Vatican Museums

September 12: Audiences with the Vicar of Rome Ugo Poletti and the apostolic nuncios to India and Rwanda. Initiated diplomatic relations with the Fiji Islands. Prayed at the tomb of Paul VI marking one month since his funeral.

September 13: Second General Audience — theme: "Faith." Private audience with the Delegated Metropolitans of the Orthodox Church of Cyprus. Received crates from Venice containing his personal archive and the books from his library. Visited by Doctor Da Ros. Msgr. Fortunato Marchi, treasurer of the Patriarchate of Venice, was a guest for lunch.

September 14: Met with Cardinal Eduardo Pironio, prefect of the Congregation for Religious. Audience with the bishop of Tshumbe, Congo. Letter to the seminary in Venice. Hosted his niece Pia Luciani for lunch.

September 15: Audiences with the prefect of the Congregation for Catholic Education, Gabriele Garrone; and the bishop of Accra, Ghana.

September 16: Received the president of the Republic of Somalia, General Mohamed Siad Barre. Audience with Alfonso López Trujillo, bishop coadjutor of Medellín, Colombia, and secretary general of CELAM and of the III Conference of the Latin American Bishops scheduled in Puebla, Mexico. Audience with the apostolic nuncios to Canada and Cuba.

September 17: Angelus: "School and society." In the afternoon was accompanied by Cardinal Villot for a walk in the Vatican Gardens.

September 18: Audiences with Cardinal Laurean Rugambwa, archbishop of Dar-es-Salaam, Tanzania, and with Msgr. Giovanni Cheli, Permanent Observer of the Holy See to the United Nations. Sent a telegram to the apostolic nuncio to Iran regarding the tragic earthquake there.

September 19: Audiences with Ivo Lorscheiter, bishop of Santa Maria, Brazil, and secretary of the Bishops' Conference of Brazil; and with the apostolic nuncio to Yugoslavia. Had an audience with a delegation from the Syrian Orthodox Church.

September 20: Third General Audience — theme: "Hope." Letter to the bishops of the Conferences of Argentina and Chile in reference to the dispute over the Beagle Channel. Had dinner with his brother Edoardo who stayed overnight in the apartments.

September 21: *Ad limina* visit by a group of bishops from the United States of America. Letter to U.S. President Jimmy Carter after the conclusion of the peace talks at Camp David. Audience with the Dominican Jean Jérôme Hamer, secretary of the Congregation for the Doctrine of the Faith.

September 22: Audience with the prefect of the Congregation for the Causes of Saints, Corrado Bafile; and an audience with the apostolic nuncio to Indonesia. The bishop of Belluno-Feltre, Maffeo Ducoli, was a guest for dinner.

September 23: Audiences with Cardinal Sebastiano Baggio, prefect of the Congregation for Bishops; the apostolic nuncios to Switzerland and Madagascar; and the director of *L'Osservatore Romano*, Valerio Volpini. Took possession of the Chair of the Bishop of Rome at St. John Lateran. On the way, met with the city council of Rome, led by Mayor Giulio Carlo Argan at the foot of the Capitol. Concelebrated Mass at the Lateran Basilica: "I desire only to enter into your service." Was visited by Dr. Antonio Da Ros and made general agreements with Dr. Renato Buzzonetti of the Vatican Health Service to provide assistance to the pope.

September 24: Angelus: "Not violence, but love, can do everything."

September 25: Audiences with Agnelo Rossi, prefect of the Congregation for the Evangelization of Peoples; and Cardinal José Humberto Quintero, archbishop of Caracas, Venezuela.

September 26: Letter to the seminary in Venice.

September 27: Greeting in German before the audience. Fourth General Audience — theme: "Charity." Towars the end of the audience, he called a child to join him for help in catechesis. Audience with the Patriarch of Antioch of the Melkite Greeks, Maximos V Hakim.

September 28: *Ad limina* visit of a group of bishops from the Philippines. Audiences with Cardinal Gantin and his collaborators; the apostolic nuncios of Brazil and Holland; and Gianni Crovato, editor of the newspaper *Il Gazzettino*. In the afternoon the pope remained inside the apartments. Before dinner, he met with the Secretary of State, Jean Villot. After dinner, at 9:00 p.m., he had a telephone conversation lasting about half an hour with Cardinal Giovanni Colombo, archbishop of Milan. Afterward, he retired to his rooms. He died.

September 29: At about 5:20 a.m. he was found dead in bed by Srs. Vincenza Taffarel and Margherita Marin, who were on duty at the apartments. At 6:00 a.m., Dr. Renato Buzzonetti noted his death; the canonical act of the *Recognitio cadaveris* was drafted. Vatican Radio made the announcement at 7:30 a.m. The body was then transported to the Clementine Hall. Preservative treatment began at 7:00 p.m. and was completed at 3:30 a.m. the following morning.

September 30: The body was transferred to St. Peter's Basilica, where it lay in state until October 3. Over a million faithful paid homage to him.

October 4: The funeral was celebrated. John Paul I was laid to rest in the Vatican Grottoes.

BIOGRAPHICAL CHRONOLOGY

1912 *October 17:* Albino Luciani was born in Forno di Canale (today Canale d'Agordo, province and diocese of Belluno, Italy). He was the firstborn son of Giovanni [Battista] and Bortola Tancon. The midwife baptized him at home on the same day. Giovanni's two daughters from his first marriage, Pia and Amalia, were welcomed into the new family.

1913 His father immigrated to Argentina, working as a mason near La Plata. He returned to Italy at the outbreak of World War I.

1917 *March 26:* His brother Edoardo was born, then called "Berto."

1919 *July 3:* Fr. Filippo Carli was appointed archpriest of Canale d'Agordo. *September 26:* Luciani received the Sacrament of Confirmation in the parish by the Most Reverend Giosuè Cattarossi, bishop of Feltre and Belluno. In October, Luciani entered the first grade, a year late, as his elementary school was closed during the war.

1920 *February 3:* Luciani's sister, Antonia Adele, was born, later called "Nina." The pastor inaugurated a parish bulletin. Starting in 1923, it would be entitled "Il Celentone." The young Luciani would write for it until 1935.

1923 *February 13–April 6:* Albino heard a Lenten sermon by the Capuchin Friar Remigio Braiato in Trieste, Italy. He wrote to his father, an emigrant in France, asking permission to enter the seminary. In October, Albino entered the minor seminary of Feltre for his high school studies.

1928 *February 21:* At the end of a spiritual retreat in preparation for Lent, he met the saintly Brother Leopold Mandić, who reassured him about his vocation. In October, he entered the Gregorian Seminary of Belluno for high school and theological studies.

1931 *July–September:* During summer vacation, on behalf of Fr. Filippo Carli, he compiled a catalog of the old parish library. His superiors rejected his request to enter the Society of Jesus.

1935 *June 26*: The Holy See granted him the faculty to waive the canonical age required for entering the priesthood. *July 7:* He was ordained to the priesthood by Bishop Giosuè Cattarossi in the church of San Pietro in Belluno. *July 8:* He celebrated his first Mass in the archpriest's Church of Forno di Canale. *July 9:* He was appointed an associate pastor with Father Augusto Bramezza, the new pastor in Canale. *December 18:* He was appointed an associate pastor with Msgr. Luigi Cappello, archdeacon of Agordo, a position he held until 1937.

1936 *October 27*: He was appointed a religion professor at the Institute and Vocational Training School at the Royal Institute of Mining of Agordo for the entire 1936–37 academic year.

1937 In July, he was appointed vice-rector of the Gregorian Seminary of Belluno, at the behest of its new rector, Msgr. Angelo Santin. Luciani was entrusted with teaching dogmatic theology and other disciplines, a commitment he maintained until 1958.

1940 *June 10:* Italy entered the war. The bimonthly periodical *Amici del Seminario Gregoriano* [Friends of the Gregorian Seminary] was published in the diocese, with Luciani's support and collaboration.

1941 *March 27*: By indult of Pius XII, Luciani was allowed to take the *ad lauream* examination at the Pontifical Gregorian University in Rome without having to attend courses. *April 5:* He began his collaboration with *L'Amico del Popolo* [The Friend of the People] (until April 14, 1956).

1942 *October 17:* He earned a Licentiate in Sacred Theology, *magna cum laude*, with a thesis on Trials by Ordeal. He enrolled in the doctoral program, but the war prevented his traveling to Rome.

1943 *July 19:* Mussolini and Hitler met at Villa Gaggia, near Belluno. Father Albino commented in dialect: "We are in the hands of two madmen." He began activities working with the youth.

1944 *August 20–21:* There was a Nazi reprisal in the Biois valley. The partisans kidnapped some men from Canale to shoot them. Thanks to the intervention of Father Albino, they were freed.

1947 *February 17–27:* Luciani was in Rome for his doctoral exams. He received his degree *magna cum laude*, defending his thesis on the origin of the human soul according to Antonio Rosmini. His supervisors were Fr. Charles Boyer, SI, and Fr. Maurice Flick, SI. *March 8–June 3:* Luciani was admitted to the San Gervasio Hospital of Belluno for suspected tuberculosis, which later turned out to be migratory viral pneumonia. *July 1:* Luciani was appointed episcopal pro chancellor and secretary of the Inter-Diocesan Synod of Belluno and Feltre (October 28–30, 1947). *December 16:* Pius XII appointed him as a secret supernumerary chamberlain. Msgr. Giovanni Battista Montini, substitute of the Secretariat of State, signed the note of appointment.

1948 *February 2:* He was appointed pro-vicar general of the Diocese of Belluno. He began working on behalf of the diocesan catechetical office. *March 2:* His mother, Bortola Tancon, died. In autumn, the diocese launched a catechetical year, led by Luciani.

1949 *May 15:* Luciani was appointed pro-delegate general for the *sede vacante* of Belluno by Bishop Girolamo Bortignon. In December he published his booklet "Catechetica in Briciole" [Catachism in Crumbs] dedicating it to the memory of his mother, his "first catechism teacher."

1950 *April 4:* Luciani officially received his doctorate in theology. *June 13:* Girolamo Bortignon, secretary of the Triveneto Episcopal

Conference (CET), notified him of his appointment as a member of the commission for the regional text of the catechism.

1952 *January 9:* His father Giovanni died.

1954 *February 6:* He was appointed Vicar General of the Diocese of Belluno.

1955 *October 21:* He started a film forum at the cinema of the former Salesian Institute in Belluno. *October 24:* Bishop Gioacchino Muccin proposed Luciani as a candidate for the episcopate in a letter addressed to the prefect of the Sacred Congregation of the Consistory.

1956 *June 30:* He was appointed canon of the Cathedral of Belluno. *July 6:* He went to Borca di Cadore, Italy, where he attended a conference of theology teachers of the seminaries of the Italian Region of Veneto with Cardinal Angelo Roncalli and Bishops Bortignon and Muccin.

1957 *January 10–14:* He was approved as a candidate for the episcopate based upon the positive vote of the members of the mixed General Congregation. *July 15:* Met with Patriarch Roncalli in Calalzo di Cadore.

1958 *October 28:* Angelo Roncalli was elected pope. *December 15*: Luciani was elected bishop of Vittorio Veneto. *December 21:* He had a special audience with John XXIII. *December 27:* Luciani received episcopal consecration from John XXIII in St. Peter's Basilica. He met with the pope in the afternoon.

1959 *January 1:* Celebrated a Pontifical Mass in the Cathedral of Belluno. *January 11:* He was officially installed in the Diocese of Vittorio Veneto. *January 16:* He celebrated a Pontifical Mass on the feast of St. Titian. *January 25:* John XXIII announced the Roman Synod, the Ecumenical Council, and the updating of the Code of Canon Law. *August 25:* Luciani sent his *votum* in preparation for the council. *October 10:* He began his first pastoral visitation. *October 16:* He joined with other bishops in presenting the pope a postulatory letter asking to promulgate St. Bernardine of Siena as a Doctor of the Church.

1960 *December 23:* He celebrated Mass for the workers of the Zoppas Corporation during the long trade-union dispute. He supported a solidarity fund.

1961 *May 11–12:* Luciani was in Rome for the canonization of St. Bertilla Boscardin; John XXIII received the bishops of Venice. *May 20:* At the CET meeting, Luciani was responsible for the commission on catechism and the commission on the discipline of the clergy.

1962 *May 11:* The director of the Diocesan Administrative Office, Fr. Guerrino Cescon, admitted to the bishop that there was a severe cash shortage which was the start of the "Antoniutti case" crisis. *May 16–17:* In Rome, Luciani reported to the Congregation of the Council on the case and sent a report to the pope's secretary, Msgr. Loris Capovilla. *June 29:* Luciani explained the difficult situation to the diocesan clergy. *October 8*: He left to attend the Second Vatican Council together with Bishop Muccin. *October 11:* The council began. *November 16:* He had an audience with John XXIII, who spoke to him about the pilgrimage to Loreto and Assisi and about the council. *November 24:* Another meeting with the pope in the Vatican Gardens. In December, he returned to Vittorio Veneto with Msgr. Charles Msakila and sent the first *Fidei Donum* missionary of the Diocese of Vittorio Veneto to Gitega, Diocese of Ngozi in Burundi.

1963 *June 3:* John XXIII died. *June 17:* Went with Bishop Muccin to Rome to participate in the last day of the *novendiale*. *June 21:* Paul VI was elected. *September 25:* Bishop Giuseppe Dalvit, of São Mateus, Brazil, arrived in Vittorio Veneto. *September 28:* Luciani was in Rome for the second session of Vatican II. *October 7:* He presented his *animadversiones* regarding the *De Ecclesia*.

1964 *June 2:* He began his second pastoral visit. *July 23–30:* He participated in a pilgrimage to Lourdes with sick Italian priests. *September 14–21:* He was in Rome for the third session of the Second Vatican Council.

1965 *January 21:* He celebrated Mass using the new rite for the first time. *March 23:* He established the Diocesan Missionary Commission. *July 14:* Fr. Guerrino Cescon was convicted for the financial scandal of 1962. *September 14–December 8:* He was in Rome for the fourth session of Vatican II until its closure.

1966 *January 16:* He celebrated a Pontifical Mass with Archbishop Giuseppe Zaffonato, of Udine, Italy, to invoke "a renewed wind of

Pentecost" after the Second Vatican Council. *February 26:* He held a conference on religious freedom in Belluno. *June 21–23:* He attended the first General Assembly of the Italian Bishops' Conference (CEI). In July, Luciani published an essay on the diocesan priest in the light of Vatican II. *July 31:* He published a letter to priests on the laity in the light of the Second Vatican Council. *August 16–September 2:* He made a trip to Burundi. In November, the Piave River in Italy flooded, inundating countryside and villages alike. In the following days, Luciani visited various disaster sites. He visited the victims in Treviso with Italy's President Saragat and in Oderzo with the prime minister, the Honorable Aldo Moro.

1967 *January 23:* He established the Diocesan Pastoral Council. *September 8:* Luciani wrote his "*Letter to Priests on the Year of Faith*" which was published with the title, "*Less Than a Syllabus,*" and later, "*A Little Syllabus.*" *September 12–15:* The schism of the parish of Montaner, Italy, occurred; the faithful rejected their new pastor, Fr. Pietro Varnier, leading to the formal closure of the parish with an exception made for December 24. *November 7–9:* At the CET meeting, Luciani reported on the relationships between culture, theology, and spirituality and on the role of theologians in the light of Vatican II. At the end of November, he was commissioned by the Vatican to make an apostolic visit to the Capuchin friaries in the Province of Bressanone and the Capuchin friaries in Trento.

1968 *February 19–24*: During the General Assembly of the CEI in Rome, he introduced one of the working groups to his own text on the spiritual life of the laity. *April 8:* He spoke in front of Catholic doctors in Conegliano, explaining the state of theological studies on birth control. He compiled a dossier on conjugal fruitfulness, which would be delivered to Paul VI. *July 29:* He wrote a letter to the diocesan priests, "*I just read the Encyclical Humanae Vitae.*"

1969 *April 14–19:* In Rome, he was elected to the CEI Commission for the Doctrine of the Faith and Catechesis. *September 17:* The Patriarch of Venice, Giovanni Urbani, died suddenly. *December 15:* Luciani was appointed Patriarch of Venice.

1970 *January 10:* Had an audience with Paul VI. *January 14:* The bishops of the Triveneto gathered in Vittorio Veneto to elect Luciani president of the CET. *February 8:* Luciani entered Venice. *February 27:* He began collaborating with *Il Gazzettino. October 25:* He began his pastoral visits to the parishes.

1971 *January 20:* The board of directors of Banco San Marco had an audience with Paul VI. *January 27–29:* Luciani was in Paris for the twinning between the Church of Saint-Eustache and the Basilica of the Madonna della Salute in Venice. *March 5:* Luciani had an audience with the pope on the twentieth anniversary of the Cini Foundation. He began collaborating with the magazine *Il Messaggero di Sant'Antonio. June 6:* During the SAVA dispute [Veneto Aluminum Joint-Stock Company], he disseminated his letter *"Where is your brother?"* in the diocese. *June 12–14:* He visited Basel and Mariastein, Switzerland. On his return, he visited Annecy, tracing the footsteps of St. Francis de Sales. *June 29–July 6:* He was in Lourdes with the Triveneto branch of the Italian National Union for Transporting the Sick to Lourdes and International Shrines (UNITALSI). *September 30–November 6:* He was in Rome to participate, by pontifical appointment, in the Synod of Bishops on Ministerial Priesthood and on Justice in the World. *December 29:* He mediated for the Banco di San Marco.

1972 *March:* The Vatican Bank sold its shares of the Catholic Bank of Veneto to the Banco Ambrosiano. *June 12–17:* He was in Rome for the 9th Assembly of the Italian Bishops' Conference (CEI) and was elected vice-president. He was elected president of the board of directors of the CEI. *September 16:* Paul VI, on a pastoral visit to Venice, imposed the papal stole on Luciani in front of the faithful. In the afternoon, he concelebrated Mass with the pope in Udine. *October 7:* He presented his proposal for the pastoral care of the working world.

1973 *January 18:* Paul VI created him a cardinal. *February 22:* He talked with the Honorable Giulio Andreotti about saving the Banco di San Marco. *March 2:* He attended the consistory in Rome. *March 5:* He received the cardinal's berretta and gave a thank you speech. *June 11–16:* At the General Assembly of the CEI he was chosen to be one of the representatives of the Italian episcopate at the 1974 Synod of Bishops.

1974 *February 21:* The CEI issued the notification, "Faced with the Referendum." *March 9:* The patriarch met with representatives of the Italian Catholic Federation of University Students (FUCI). He asked them not to take a public position as an association on the issues of the referendum. *March 28: L'Osservatore Romano* published one of his articles: "*St. Thomas and Divorce.*" *April 17:* The student community of San Trovaso was closed and its FUCI assistant withdrawn.

1975 *May 18–20:* Luciani went to Germany for the millennium of the Cathedral of Mainz. He took part in the Day of the Italian Worker Abroad. *June 2–7:* At the General Assembly of the CEI, he resigned from the post of vice president. *June 7:* He had a private audience with Paul VI. *July 20–26:* He attended the UNITALSI regional pilgrimage to Lourdes. *September 18–21:* He made the pilgrimage to Rome for the Holy Year. *October 1:* He made a pilgrimage to Pompeii. *October 4:* The weekly *La Voce di San Marco* closed. He started the publication of *Gente Veneta* and entrusted it to his secretary, Fr. Mario Senigaglia. *November 3–21:* He was in Brazil to visit the communities of Italian emigrants in the Diocese of Santa Maria in Rio Grande do Sul. He also met some *fidei donum* priests in Brazil. *November 10:* He received an honorary degree from the Federal University of Santa Maria; as a *lectio doctoralis* he delivered a lecture on prudence. *December 2–8:* He was hospitalized for a retinal thrombosis in his left eye.

1976 In January, he published *Illustrissimi,* his collection of imaginary letters. *January 22:* He began his second pastoral visitation. *February 14:* He authorized pastors to divest themselves of valuables and set an example for them by selling a pectoral cross and a ring; the beneficiary was the Don Orione Center in Chirignago, Italy. *May 17–21:* He was in Rome for the General Assembly of the CEI; on May 20, he met with the pope. *September 10–13:* He was in Split (Yugoslavia) as the representative of the CEI for the millennium of the Marian shrine in Croatia.

1977 *May 9–14:* He attended the General Assembly of the CEI and was elected as the representative of the Italian episcopate for the Synod of Bishops. *July 9–12:* He made a pilgrimage to Fátima on the seventieth anniversary of the apparitions and met with Sister Lucia in Coimbra (July 11). *September 18:* Vittorio Cini died. In his will, he designated the Patriarch of Venice as his successor in leading the Cini Foundation. *September 29–October 30:* The Synod of Bishops met on the topic: "Catechesis in Our Time."

1978 *February 28–March 3:* He preached for Lent in Canale d'Agordo. *June 24–27:* He held pastoral meetings of the diocese on the topic "Evangelization and Ministries: Being in the Church, Today, at the Service of Our Brothers and Sisters and the World." *June 29:* He celebrated the patronal feast in Agordo. *July 24–August 5:* A rest at the Lido of Venice, at the Stella Maris Heliotherapy Institute. *August 6:* Paul VI died. *August 10:* Luciani left for the conclave. *August 12:* He participated in the pope's funeral. *August 16:* He celebrated Mass in the Basilica of San Marco in Piazza Venezia, Rome. *August 25:* The conclave began. *August 26:* He was elected pope. *September 28:* He died.

HISTORY OF THE CAUSE OF CANONIZATION

Immediately after John Paul I's death on September 28, 1978, his home diocese began receiving requests for his canonization from every part of the world. The then bishop of Belluno-Feltre, Maffeo Ducoli, declared that he had "received thousands of requests to introduce his cause … all kept in the archives of the Curia in Belluno." Without any formality, with an initiative that started from the grassroots level, a petition began, which caught the interest of several countries at an international level, including Switzerland, France, Canada, and the United States.

Later, on June 9, 1990, the Most Reverend Serafim Fernandes de Araújo, archbishop of Belo Horizonte, Brazil, personally presented a request for the introduction of the cause to Pope John Paul II, with a petition signed by the entire Bishops' Conference of Brazil. The 226 signatory bishops highlighted the reasons that had led them to the petition in solidarity, having considered the virtuous *habitus* of the Bishop of Rome, Albino Luciani, who showed himself to be "a typical synthesis of the man of God, who was filled with humanity and at the same time, filled with Christ." As such, he was "an apostle of the Second Vatican Council, whose teachings he correctly explained with crystalline lucidity and whose directives he rightly put into practice." In conclusion, the Brazilian bishops stated, "It is our deepest conviction that we are interpreting the favorable judgment of many other brothers in the episcopate, and translating the very lively aspiration of the faithful of the Church in Brazil, as well as that of Catholics all over the world." Even the then bishop of Belluno advocated the opening of the cause. However, as he recalled in his deposition during the proceedings, "the Congregation for the Causes of Saints replied that they considered it premature to introduce the cause of John Paul I because causes were already underway for other popes of the 20th century, namely Pius IX, Pius XII, John XXIII, and Paul VI, in addition to Pius X, who had already been canonized." Thus the bishop of Belluno did not consider that it would be "more appropriate to send the Episcopal Conference of Triveneto a collegial request for the introduction of the cause." It was only during the ministry of the Most Reverend Vincenzo Savio, (Salesian) bishop of Belluno-Feltre (February 18, 2001–March 31, 2004), that it became possible to launch a diocesan inquiry into the heroicity of the life and virtues of John Paul I and his reputation for holiness.

On April 26, 2003, Bishop Savio formally requested permission from Cardinal Camillo Ruini, then Vicar of Rome, to introduce the process, not at the Vicariate of Rome, the natural seat for competence, but in his home Diocese of Belluno-Feltre. He offered the following reasons: "The Servant of God's stayed very briefly in the Diocese of Rome; his pontificate lasted just over a month. On the other hand, most of his life took place — and, consequently, his teaching was expressed — first in this diocese, in the neighboring Diocese of Vittorio Veneto, then, finally in the Patriarchate of Venice." The bishop, informing his diocese about the initiative he had taken, fully explained the reasons that led him to take this step (prompted by the more than 300,000 petition signatures that were received) and to formulate the request that the cause be prepared in Luciani's home diocese:

It was here that Albino Luciani lived his childhood, received his seminary formation, and served as a priest and as the Vicar General of the Diocese of Belluno until he was forty-six. Moreover, his commitments, first as bishop and later as patriarch, always kept him in his home region of Venice, except for the thirty-three days of his pontificate.

Alongside these reasons, he also offered the possibility "of deepening the context of the faith of his family and local area in which Albino Luciani had grown up."

On June 17, 2003, the Congregation for the Causes of Saints granted the *nihil obstat,* and on November 23, 2003, twenty-five years after the death of John Paul I, the process was solemnly and formally opened at the cathedral-basilica in Belluno. The opening session of the diocesan inquiry was presided over, in a very exceptional way, by the then prefect of the Congregation of the Causes of the Saints, Cardinal José Saraiva Martins. He emphasized how this event offered an opportunity to learn more about the person and work of Albino Luciani, "so that one day we can invoke this great man of the Church as Blessed, a man who went from the local Church of Belluno to the universal Church as the Bishop of Rome." The postulator general of the Salesians, Fr. Pasquale Liberatore, was appointed as the postulator of the cause. After his death in October 2003, the bishop appointed Msgr. Giorgio Lise. In 2004, he was replaced by Fr. Enrico dal Covolo who had already taken over for Father Liberatore as the postulator general of the Salesians.

The *Inquisitio Dioecesana* began its work on November 22, 2003. Only three years later, on November 10, 2006, the work was completed. It was divided into 203 sessions, during which 167 witnesses were examined in the episcopal sees of Belluno, Vittorio Veneto, Venice, and Rome. All of the interviews were conducted in person except for one. Nine of the witnesses were *ex officio*; and there were three historical experts as well.

Once the Congregation for the Causes of Saints received the investigation documents, however, it became clear that there were some gaps in the archival documentation compiled by the Historical Commission. In particular, reference was made to the documentary material at the Patriarchal See of Venice and the congregation told the Bishop of Belluno-Feltre to set up a new ad hoc one. In March 2008, the Most Rev. Giuseppe Andrich, bishop of Belluno, instituted the tribunal for the *Inquisitio Diocesana Suppletiva* in order to complete the work carried out by the Historical Commission. I was entrusted with the task of carrying out this investigation, in particular, at the Historical Archives of the Patriarchate of Venice and at the Archives of the Episcopal Conference of Triveneto. On June 13, 2008, the Congregation for the Causes of Saints issued the formal Decree of Validity for the Diocesan Acts of the Cause, which applied to both the main and supplementary diocesan investigations carried out by the ecclesiastical tribunal of Belluno-Feltre.

Thus the Roman phase of the process began. On June 27, Fr. Cristoforo Bove was appointed as the relator of the cause. The task of drafting the *positio* was entrusted to me. When Father Bove passed away on November 5, 2010, the cause was assigned to Fr. Vincenzo Criscuolo, the general relator of the Congregation for the Causes of Saints. He continued the work already begun, requesting the appropriate investigations and the necessary further acquisitions, regarding both the documentary and testimonial parts. Moreover, the late opening of the cause had compromised the acquisition of valuable eyewitness testimony, and led as well to a certain dispersion of documentary material, for which careful research was required.

During the study of the procedural documentation, various archives needed to be consulted again, including the Pievanal Archive in Canale d'Agordo, the Archdeacon Historical Archives-Library in Agordo, the Episcopal Archive in Belluno, the Diocesan Archive in Vittorio Veneto, the Archives of the Cini Foundation in Venice, as well as the archives of the Congregation for the Clergy, the Congregation for Bishops, and the Secretariat of State. Furthermore, the acquisition of additional testimony was arranged, which had not been sought among the texts examined by the tribunal during the *Inquisitio Dioecesana*. Therefore, between 2008 and 2015, the extra-tribunal depositions of twenty-one witnesses were also entered into the record, with particular focus on the period of the pontificate and the death of John Paul I. Of these depositions, the testimony of Pope

Benedict XVI was of quite exceptional importance because of its historical *unicum*. Under the guidance of the relator, the drafting of the *positio* was then started. It was also compiled in part by the theologian Davide Fiocco, while the historian Mauro Velati contributed to the *Biographia ex Documentis*. On October 16, 2015, the gishop of Belluno-Feltre appointed Cardinal Beniamino Stella, a native of the Diocese of Vicenza, as the new postulator of the cause. Years ago, Albino Luciani himself had helped him get accepted into the Pontifical Ecclesiastical Academy.

In addition to the drafting of the ritual acts, in the light of the new documentary acquisitions, considerable effort went into retrieving and critically transcribing various yet-unpublished texts and making an inventory of all the publications of the Servant of God that were included in the *positio* and his dossier. These had to be arranged according to established criteria, which included the entire body of documentary and testimonial evidence needed to show the Servant of God's heroicity of life, virtues, and his reputation of holiness. The Roman phase, conducted in recent years by the general Relator of the Congregation for the Causes of Saints, was characterized, as usual, by the research needed in order complete the acquisition of the writings of the Servant of God. This was done by making a historical-scientific study, by examining all the documentary and testimonial sources with the relative critical evaluation, and finally laying out and assembling the *positio*, which was composed in five volumes, totaling more than 3,600 pages. The *positio* was delivered to the congregation, on October 17, 2016, thus launching the final judicial examination which was to be carried out by the judging bodies of the congregation. They were called to vote in two examination sessions. One was the Congress of Theological Consultors and the other was the Ordinary Session of Cardinals and Bishops. The Congress of Theological Consultors expressed its unanimous positive vote on June 1, 2017. On November 7 of that year, the Ordinary Session of Cardinals and Bishops gave the same response. Approved by Pope Francis, the decree for the proclamation of his heroic virtues was promulgated on November 9, 2017.

SELECTED BIBLIOGRAPHY

Only the archival sources cited in the text and pertinent to the subject matter are listed here. They were consulted as part of the research carried out for the cause of canonization of John Paul I. In the course of this research, almost seventy archives were consulted in thirty different locations. Particularly important were the institutional archives preserved in the places where Albino Luciani stayed and the private institutions and sources related to him. Moreover, only his published writings, volumes, and articles, which are cited in the text, and related to the last days of his life, are reported. In addition, the list of thriller literature that flourished surrounding the death of Pope Luciani has been excluded, except for passing mention, for example, of the books of David Yallop and John Cornwell.

SOURCES
A) ARCHIVES
Agordo, Archdiocesan Library and Archive

Belluno, Episcopal Archive
Belluno, Archive of "L'Amico del Popolo" (Friend of the People)
Bologna, Private Archive of Monsignor Claudio Righi
Canale d'Agordo, Parish Archive
Canale d'Agordo, John Paul I Foundation Archive
Canale d'Agordo, Private Archive of the Luciani family
Milan, Private Archives of Fr. Bartolomeo Sorge, SI
Rome, Private Archive of Renato Buzzonetti
Rome, Archive of 30Giorni nella Chiesa e nel mondo
Rome, Private Archive of Giancarlo Zizola
Rome, Private Archive of Sr. Giulia Scardanzan
Rome, Augustinian General Archive
Rome-Belluno, Archive of the Postulation
Santa Giustina, Italy, Archive of the Pope Luciani Center of Spirituality
Vatican City, Vatican Secret Archive
Vatican City (at the John Paul I Foundation), Private Archive Albino Luciani
Vatican City, Archive of the Secretariat of State
Vatican City, Archive of the Congregation for Bishops - File no. 3 (Prot. 967/69) - Vacancy and Provision for the See of Venice
Venice, Historical Archive of the Patriarchate of Venice
    – Luciani Fund
    – Private Archive [not fund ordered]
Venice, Private Archive of Monsignor Mario Senigaglia
Venice, Cini Foundation Archive
Vittorio Veneto, Diocesan Archive – Teachers

B) ACTS RELATIVE TO THE CAUSE OF BEATIFICATION AND CANONIZATION OF JOHN PAUL I

Congregatio de Causis Sanctorum, Bellunensis-Feltrensis Beatificationis et Canonizationis Servi Dei Ioannis Pauli I (Albini Luciani) (1912–1978). Positio super vita, virtutibus et fama sanctitatis, edited by D. Fiocco, S. Falasca and M. Velati, vols. I-V, Belluno 2016.

C) OFFICIAL DOCUMENTS OF THE HOLY SEE
Vatican City, *Acta Apostolicae Sedis*

D) PUBLISHED WRITINGS BY ALBINO LUCIANI

Illustrissimi, Messaggero, 1976.

Opera omnia, vols. I-IX, Messaggero, 1988–89.

 Volume I (1988), *Catechetica in briciole*, pp. 15–80.

  – *L'origine dell'anima umana secondo Antonio Rosmini. Esposizione e critica*, pp. 81–226 (text from the second edition, Messaggero, 1958).

  – *Illustrissimi. Lettere del patriarca*, Messaggero, 1976, pp. 229–436.

 Volume II (1988), Vittorio Veneto, 1959–62. *Discorsi, scritti, articoli.* [Speeches, writings, articles]

 Volume III (1988), Vittorio Veneto, 1963–66. *Discorsi, scritti, articoli.*

 Volume IV (1988), Vittorio Veneto, 1967–69. *Discorsi, scritti, articoli.*

 Volume V (1989), Venice, 1970–72. *Discorsi, scritti, articoli.*

 Volume VI (1989), Venice, 1973–74. *Discorsi, scritti, articoli.*

 Volume VII (1989), Venice, 1975–76. *Discorsi, scritti, articoli.*

 Volume VIII (1989), Venice, 1977–78. *Discorsi, scritti, articoli.*

 Volume IX (1989), Rome, August–September 1978.

  – *Belluno*, March 5, 1923–December 27, 1957, pp. 355–475.

  – *Dall'epistolario,* June 20, 1935–September 26, 1978, pp. 476–506.

  – *Indice onomastico*, pp. 515–553.

  – *Indice analitico*, pp. 555–604.

Insegnamenti di Giovanni Paolo I, Libreria Editrice Vaticana, 1979.

E) DEGREE AND DOCTORAL THESES

De Luca, F. *La dottrina sociale della Chiesa nel magistero di Albino Luciani*, assignment for bachelor's degree, supervising professor, P. Doni, Facoltà Teologica dell'Italia settentrionale, Padua campus, 1989–90.

Falasca, S. *Sermo humilis e referenze letterarie negli scritti di pa-*

pa Luciani: il caso di Illustrissimi, doctorate in Italian studies, XXIV cycle, Tor Vergata University of Rome, coordinating professor A. Gareffi, 2011–12.

Fontanive, C. *Preparazione scolastica e culturale di Albino Luciani–Giovanni Paolo I*, University of Padua, 1996–97.

Luciani, P. *Albino Luciani Patriarca di Venezia (1970–1978), Doctorate in Humanities Tradizione e contemporaneità*, cycle XXVIII, S.S.D. MSTO/07, Catholic University of the Sacred Heart, Milan 2014–15.

F) BOOKS

Andreotti, G. *A ogni morte di Papa. I Papi che ho conosciuto*, Rizzoli, 1980.

Bassotto, C. *Il mio cuore e ancora a Venezia*, Tipolitografia Adriatica, 1990.

Biffi, G. *Memorie e digressioni di un italiano cardinale*, Cantagalli, 2007.

Bizzarri, L. *Il Papa del sorriso. Giovanni Paolo, il Primo*, Rai-Eri, 2009.

Cornwell, J. *Un ladro nella notte. La morte di Papa Giovanni Paolo I*, Pironti, 1990.

D'orazi, L. *Impegno all'umiltà. La vita di Papa Luciani*, Logos, 1987.

De Rosa, G. *La storia che non passa. Diario politico 1968–1989*, edited by S. Demofonti, Rubbettino, 1999.

———. *Mio fratello Albino, ricordi e memorie della sorella di Papa Luciani*, 30Giorni Press, 2003.

Falasca, S., D. Fiocco, and M. Velati. *Albino Luciani Giovanni Paolo I. Biografia ex documentis - Dagli atti del processo canonico*, Tipi Press, 2018.

Ferrighetto, G. *"Mi chiamerò Giovanni Paolo!" Papa Albino Luciani nelle parole di papa Karol Wojtyła*, De Bastiani, 2008.

Fiocco D., ed. *Albino Luciani. Semplicità e umiltà*, Messaggero, 2019.

———. *Papa Luciani. Briciole di attualità*, Tipi Press, 2020.

Kummer, R. *Albino Luciani. Papa Giovanni Paolo I. Una vita per la Chiesa*, Messaggero, 2009.

Lai, B. *Il "mio" Vaticano. Diario tra pontefici e cardinali*, Rubbettino, 2006.

———. *Il Papa non eletto. Giuseppe Siri, cardinale di Santa Romana Chiesa*, Laterza, 1993.

Luciani, P. *Un prete di montagna. Gli anni bellunesi di Albino Luciani (1912– 1958)*, Messaggero, 2003.

Marcucci E. and C. Napoli. *Giovanni Paolo I. Papa per 33 giorni*, Cappelli, 1978.

Martin, J. *Oltre il portone di bronzo. Dagli appunti segreti di un cardinale vissuto a fianco di sei Papi*, Paoline, 1996.

Melloni, A. *Il Conclave. Storia dell'elezione del Papa*, Il Mulino, 2005.

Nicolini, G. *Trentatre giorni, un pontificato*, Po Institute of Graphic Arts, 1983.

———. *Papa Luciani*, Velar, 1995.

Pancheri, F. S. *Il breve sorriso di Papa Luciani*, Ripetta 124, 1979.

Preziosi, A. *Indimenticabile. I 33 giorni di papa Luciani*, Cantagalli, 2019.

Roncalli, M. *Giovanni Paolo I. Albino Luciani*, San Paolo, 2012.

Scopelliti N. and F. Taffarel, *Lo stupore di Dio. Vita di papa Luciani*, Ares, 2006.

———. *Luciani, la polvere del Signore*, Conegliano Graphic Arts, 2009

Sorge, B. *La traversata. La Chiesa dal Concilio Vaticano II a oggi*, Mondadori, 2010.

Tornielli, A. and A. Zangrando. *Papa Luciani. Il sorriso del santo*, Piemme, 2003.

Yallop, D. *In nome di Dio. La morte di Papa Luciani*, Pironti, 1985.

G) ARTICLES AND STUDIES

Acerbi, A. "*La Chiesa del Vaticano II (1958-1978),*" in *Storia della Chiesa*, XXV/1, edited by M. Guasco, E. Guerriero and F. Traniello, Paoline, 1994, pp. 101–117.

Alberigo, G. "*Papa Luciani,*" in *Jesus. Duemila anni di attualità*, V, Saie, 1979, pp. 1109–1111.

———. "*Grande sacerdote per tutti i cristiani,*" in *Corriere della Sera*, August 8, 1978, p. 3.

———. "*Un sorriso che ha fatto storia,*" in *Humilitas*, 1 (1984) 2, p. 9.

Alzati, C. *Giovanni Paolo I. Una svolta decisiva per il pontificato romano di fine Novecento,* in *DVAM,* pp. 505–508.

Andreotti, G. "*Il Papa breve,*" in *30giorni,* 21 (2003) 8/9, pp. 24–25.

Bertoli, G. "*Il periodo veneziano e romano di Luciani: anni non facili per la Chiesa e il mondo,*" in *Humilitas,* 10 (1993) 1, pp. 7–8.

Bortignon, G. "*Commemorazione. La gioia di credere nel destino dell'uomo,*" in *Humilitas,* 4 (1987) 2, pp. 7–8.

Branca, V. "*Lo stupore di Dio,*" in *30giorni,* 16 (1998) 7/8.

———. "*Non poteva essere popolare chi andava controcorrente,*" in *Humilitas,* 5 (1988) 4, pp. 7–8.

Brunelli, L. *L'ultimo mistero di papa Luciani,* in *Il Sabato,* 52 (December 29, 1990), pp. 48–52.

———. and T. Ricci, "'*Il Signore gli ha voluto bene.*' *Un buon parroco per Roma,*" in *30giorni,* 10 (1992) 3, pp. 56–60.

———. "*Intervista alla sorella di Giovanni Paolo I,*" in *Humilitas,* 10 (1993) 1, pp. 1–3, 18–19; 10 (1993) 2, pp. 3–4.

Buonasorte, N. "*L'enigma Luciani e il Conclave,*" in *DVAM,* pp. 491–503.

Busa, R. "*Riflettendo, come in uno specchio, la luce del Signore,*" in *30giorni,* 22 (2004) 9, pp. 90–92.

———. "*Intervista a don Carlo Bolzan. Com'era composto il bagaglio del Papa da Venezia a Roma e viceversa,*" in *Humilitas,* 10 (1993) 2, pp. 9–10, 17–19.

Caprile, G. "*Il mese di pontificato di Giovanni Paolo I,*" in *La Civiltà Cattolica,* 129 (1978) 3079, pp. 63–71.

———. "*Il Conclave e la elezione del nuovo Pontefice,*" in *La Civiltà Cattolica,* 129 (1978) 3078, pp. 521–525.

Cardinale, G. "*Papi umili e fedeli. Intervista al card. Bernardin Gantin, decano emerito del Sacro Collegio,*" in *30giorni,* 16 (1998) 9, pp. 28–29.

Colombo, G. "*Messaggio dell'arcivescovo per la morte del papa Giovanni Paolo I – Milano, 29 settembre 1978,*" in *Rivista Diocesana Milanese,* 69 (1978), pp. 764–765.

Cracco, G. "*Modelli di papi e idee sul papato,*" in *DVAM,* pp. 443–472.

———. "*Dal Veneto al mondo: davvero,*" in *DVAM,* pp. 11–20.

Dametto, I. "*Suor Vincenza e il suo Papa*," in *Humilitas*, 3 (1986) 2, pp. 1–3.

De Rosa, G. "*Quale Papa?, in ID., Erudizione e pietà dei Papi del Concilio. Giovanni XXIII – Paolo VI – Giovanni Paolo I*," Sangermano, 1985, pp. 137–141.

———. "*Una scelta di fede*," ivi, pp. 143–147.

———. "*Si e spenta una luce ma non la speranza*," ivi, pp. 149–151.

———. "*Il momento dello Spirito*," ivi, pp. 153–157.

Ducoli, M. "*Con occhi semplici*," in *30giorni*, 22 (2004) 5 p. 89.

Falasca, S. *Un'umanità non di facciata. Intervista con il cardinale Aloisio Lorscheider*, in *30giorni*, 16 (1998) 7/8, pp. 24–28.

———. "*Un'intuizione confermata. Intervista al cardinale Paulo Evaristo Arns*," in *30giorni*, 16 (1998) 7/8, p. 32.

———. "*La sua pazienza ci aspetta. Luciani e la confessione*," in *30giorni*, 21 (2003) 3, pp. 72–78.

———. "'*Mai sentito cose cosi belle.' Intervista con Miguel Arranz*," in *30giorni*, 24 (2006) 6, pp. 58–64.

———. "*Quell'incontro a Fatima. Intervista con Mario Senigaglia*," in *30giorni*, 25 (2007) 1, pp. 72–77.

———. "*Il 'Pontefice' di Giovanni Paolo I. In ricordo del cardinale Aloisio Lorscheider*," in *30giorni*, 25 (2007) 12, pp. 60–61.

———. "*Papa Luciani e la Fondazione Giorgio Cini, in Lettera da San Giorgio*," XI, 21 (September 2009–February 2010), pp. 19–21.

———. "*Sermo humilis e referenze letterarie negli scritti di papa Luciani: il caso di Illustrissimi*," in *Dolomiti. Rivista di cultura e attualità della provincia di Belluno*, 35 (2012) 6, pp. 14–21.

———. "*Papa Roncalli a Luciani: 'Il vescovo parli semplice.' Nei quaderni del futuro Giovanni Paolo I un inedito dell'udienza del '58*," in *Avvenire*, June 5, 2013.

———. "*La povertà secondo Luciani. Un inedito del 1970*," in *Avvenire*, August 26, 2015, p. 3.

———. "*Albino Luciani, un Papa 'apostolo del Concilio,'*"in *Avvenire*, August 25, 2016, p. 3.

———. "*La sola ricchezza del Cristo povero*," in *Le Tre Venezie*, 135 (2016), pp. 6–14.

———. "*La scelta teologica del Sermo humilis*," in *Le Tre Venezie*, 135

(2016), pp. 44–49.

———. *"Albino Luciani e la Fondazione Giorgio Cini,"* in *Le Tre Venezie,* 135 (2016), pp. 72–75.

———. *"Il Conclave: unconsensounanime,"* in *Le Tre Venezie,* 135 (2016), pp. 76–79.

———. *"Giovanni Paolo I e Francesco apostoli della misericordia,"* in *Avvenire,* January 9, 2016, p. 3.

———. *"L'anelito alla pace e Carter nel Luciani ancora segreto,"* in *Avvenire,* August 26, 2017, p. 3.

———. *"Il Sermo humilis di Albino Luciani,"* in *Avvenire,* August 26, 2018, p. 15.

———. *"La piccola speranza di Peguy per Luciani,"* in *Avvenire,* August 2, 2019, p. 15.

———. *"Il Papa letterato,"* in *L'Osservatore Romano,* September 28, 2019, p. 11.

Farusi, F. *"Cercavano un Papa buon pastore,"* in *Il Sabato,* August 28, 1993, cited in *Humilitas,* 12 (1995) 3, p. 10.

Fiocci, D. *"Nel segno di Rosmini: gli studi accademici,"* in *Le Tre Venezie,* 135 (2016), p. 43.

———. *"Le priorità di Giovanni Paolo I Vescovo di Roma,"* in *Le Tre Venezie,* 135 (2016), pp. 80–84.

———. *"La collegialità episcopale in Albino Luciani. Storia di una ricerca teologica attraverso scritti editi e inediti,"* in *Studia Patavina,* 64 (2017) pp. 499–512.

"Giovanni Paolo I," in *Enciclopedia dei Papi,* III, Institute of the Italian Encyclopedia 2000.

La Bella, G. *"Luciani e la povertà,"* in *DVAM,* pp. 397–410.

Lanzani, V. *"Il sepolcro di Giovanni Paolo I,"* in *Roma sacra. Guida alle chiese della Città eterna,* 26–27 (2003), p. 115.

Lorenzi, D. *"Era stato un giorno di lavoro e di preghiera come gli altri. Poi ...,"* in *Il Gazzettino,* 219 (September 28, 1979) 5.

———. *"Giovanni Paolo I nel ricordo di don Diego Lorenzi,"* in *Messaggi di Don Orione. Quaderni di storia e spiritualità,* 3 (2000), pp. 57–74.

Lorscheider, A. *"Trentatre giorni indimenticabili ...,"* in *30giorni,* 21 (2003) 7, pp. 66–67.

Luciani, P. (Patrizia) *"Albino Luciani, gli anni Settanta e un difficile ecumenismo,"* in *Studia Patavina*, 65 (2018) 3, pp. 529–542.

Luciani, P. (Pia) *"Ricordi dei familiari. Con amabile fermezza,"* in *Le Tre Venezie*, 135 (2016), p. 97.

Magee, J. *"Un pontificato breve, ricco e spiritualmente completo,"* in *Humilitas*, 7 (1990) 2, pp. 1–2.

———. *"Testimonianza di mons. Magee. Conferenza tenuta a Venezia il 30 maggio 1989 presso la Scuola di san Rocco,"* in *Humilitas*, 7 (1990) 3, pp. 3–4.

Malacaria, D. *"Il segreto di Fátima,"* in *30giorni*, 25 (2007) 6, pp. 90–91.

Mazzorana, G. *"Mons. Gioacchino Muccin: 'Giovanni Paolo I aveva una ricchezza culturale, pastorale e spirituale non comune,'"* in *Humilitas*, 4 (1985) 2, pp. 1–2.

Melloni, A. *"Luciani e il 1978,"* in *DVAM*, pp. 483–490.

Mondin, B. *"Giovanni Paolo I – 1978,"* in *Nuovo dizionario enciclopedico dei Papi. Storia e insegnamenti*, Città Nuova, 2006, pp. 582–588.

Montanelli, I. *"33 giorni di sorprese,"* in *Humilitas*, 12 (1995) 3, pp. 4–5.

Morozzo Della Rocca, R. *"I 'voti' dei vescovi italiani per il Concilio,"* in *Le deuxieme Concile du Vatican (1959–1965). Actes du colloque international de Rome (28–30 mai 1986)*, École Française de Rome, 1989, pp. 119–137.

Muccin, G. *"Ritratto di Albino Luciani,"* in *Rivista diocesana di Belluno e di Feltre*, 61 (1980), pp. 305–319.

———. *"Giovanni Paolo I,"* in *Gli ultimi papi. Testimonianze*, Urbaniana University Press, 1980, pp. 137–160.

Niero, A. *"L'applicazione del Concilio Vaticano II durante il patriarcato di Albino Luciani,"* in *Humilitas*, 8 (1991) 3, pp. 7–8.

Noe, V. *"Il cardinale Virgilio Noe ricorda Giovanni Paolo I,"* in *Humilitas*, 9 (1992) 3, p. 9.

Ossola, C. *"Il sermo humilis di Albino Luciani,"* in *Avvenire*, September 21, 2008, p. 5.

Pancheri, F. S. *"Un Papa inedito,* in *Il magistero di Albino Luciani. Scritti e discorsi,"* edited by A. Cattabiani, *Messaggero*, 1979, pp.

9–41.

Parolin, P. *"Luciani, immagine viva del buon Pastore,"* in *Avvenire*, September 3, 2013, p. 15.

Pattaro, G. *"Papa Luciani nel ricordo di don Germano,"* in *Appunti di teologia. Notiziario del Centro Pattaro di Venezia*, 21 (2008) 4, pp. 1–5; 22 (2009) 1, pp. 2–5.

Pegrari, M. *"La finanza bianca e il vescovo Luciani,"* in *DVAM*, pp. 411–440.

Ponzi, M. *"Visita al conclave,"* in *L'Osservatore Romano*, 194 (August 25, 1978), p. 3.

Ratzinger, J. *"Anche il 'mostrare' ha il suo significato,"* in *30giorni*, 16 (1998) 7/8, p. 29.

———. *"Omelia del pontificale in suffragio di papa Giovanni Paolo I. Duomo di Monaco, 6 ottobre 1978,"* in *Bollettino dell'arcidiocesi di Monaco e Frisinga*, 26 (1978), p. 3.

Ricci, T. *"Quell'estate in compagnia di tre Papi,"* in *30giorni*, 6 (1988) 6, pp. 8–17.

———. *"Il fascino di quei 33 giorni,"* in *30giorni*, 10 (1992) 3, pp. 50–55.

Ruozzi, F. *"'Un papa più mostrato che dato?' Albino Luciani e le fonti televisive,"* in *DVAM*, pp. 509–560.

Sartori, L. *"L'ermeneutica del magistero nella Chiesa cattolica,"* in *Il Regno*. Attualità, 22 (1977), pp. 521–523.

Senigaglia, M. *"Quasi un diario. Uno stile pastorale che demitizza il passato,"* in *Humilitas*, 3 (1986) 2, pp. 7–8.

Serafini, L. *"Il museo Albino Luciani,"* in *Le Tre Venezie*, 135 (2016), p. 30.

Taffarel, F. Mons. *"Carraro: 'Quando occorre, sa essere forte e deciso,'"* in *Humilitas*, 1 (1984) 2, pp. 5–6.

Thiandoum, H. *"Tre papi e un orientamento fondamentale comune,"* in *30giorni*, 16 (1998) 7/8, pp. 30–33.

Valente, G. *"'La politica di Dio e resistere ai superbi, ma dare la grazia agli umili' (Albino Luciani),"* in *30giorni*, 16 (1998) 7/8, pp. 23–24.

Velati, M. *"Il patriarca Albino Luciani a Venezia,"* in *Le Tre Venezie*, 135 (2016).

Vian, G. *"Albino Luciani: dalla memoria alla storia,"* in *DVAM*, pp. 21–31.

Zagonel, M. *"A Vittorio Veneto nel solco del Concilio,"* in *Le Tre Venezie*, 135 (2016), pp. 50–59.

Zambarbieri, A. *"Albino Luciani tra 'vecchia' e 'nuova' teologia*, in *DVAM*, pp. 311–354.

Zizola, G. *"Rapporto Luciani. Morte di un povero Cristo,"* in *Epoca*, September 28, 1988, p. 169.

———. *"Perché non ci credo,"* in *Panorama*, June 18, 1984, p. 120.

———. *"Luciani e i media,"* in *DVAM*, pp. 307–310.

NOTES

1. Cf. ArPost, *Copia delle note riservate del Dipartimento di Stato americano, agosto-settembre 1978, Nota dell'ambasciata di Roma alla Segreteria di Stato degli USA del 26 agosto 1978*, no. E1.

2. Cf. Positio IV, *Biographia ex documentis*, p. 2880.

3. Cf. Positio III, *Summarium documentorum*, p. 2005.

4. Unpublished homily by Cardinal Eduardo Francisco Pironio given in the Cathedral of Vittorio Veneto, Italy, on February 25, 1979 (ArPost, Transcription from magnetic recording); cf. Positio IV, *Biographia ex documentis*, p. 2883.

5. Cf. D. Fiocco, "*La Pieve di Canale d'Agordo. Vivacità culturale ed ecclesiale*," *Le Tre Venezie*, 135 (2016), pp. 15–20. A partial *excursus* of Luciani's vast repertoire of humanistic-literary and artistic studies, combined with his competence in the disciplines which he acquired and taught in the area of traditional ecclesiastical education, can be found in the degree thesis by C. Fontanive, *Preparazione scolastica e culturale di Albino Luciani – Giovanni Paolo I,* University of Padua, 1996–1997, and in Patrizia Luciani, "*Un prete di montagna. Gli anni bellunesi di Albino Luciani (1912–1958),*" Messaggero, 2003. For the significance of his magisterium supported by a strong speculative capacity and a keen sensibility in reworking the terms found in his vast

readings, cf. F. S. Pancheri, *Un Papa inedito, in Il magistero di Albino Luciani. Scritti e discorsi*, edited by A. Cattabiani, Messaggero, 1979, pp. 9–41.

6. Cf. Paul VI, *Motu proprio Ingravescentem aetatem*, II, 2, in *AAS*, 62 (1970) 12, p. 811.

7. It was established that, when *sede vacante*, the Vatican Secretary of State and those in charge of the Vatican dicasteries would lose their offices, with the exception of the camerlengo of the Roman Church, the major penitentiary, and the vicar general for the Diocese of Rome [cf. Paul VI, *Constitutio apostolica Regimini Ecclesiae Universae, Proemium* and 2, §5, in *AAS*, 59 (1967) 14, pp. 889–891].

8. Cf. N. Buonasorte, "*L'enigma Luciani e il Conclave*," *DVAM*, pp. 493–495; F. Ruozzi, "'*Un papa più mostrato che dato?' Albino Luciani e le fonti televisive*," ibid., p. 533.

9. Cf. M. Roncalli, *Giovanni Paolo I. Albino Luciani*, San Paolo, 2012, pp. 547–548; G. Andreotti, *A ogni morte di Papa. I Papi che ho conosciuto*, Rizzoli, 1980, pp. 159–160; N. Buonasorte, "*L'enigma Luciani e il Conclave*," p. 500; G. Albergio, "*Per un rinnovamento del servizio papale nella Chiesa alla fine del xxxx secolo (agosto 1978)*," *L'officina bolognese, 1953–2003*, EDB, 2004, pp. 199–213.

10. Cf. *Attività del Sacro Collegio*, in *L'Osservatore Romano*, August 20, 1978, p. 1; M. Ponzi, "*Visita al Conclave*," *L'Osservatore Romano*, 194 (August 25, 1978), p. 7; G. Caprile, "*Il Conclave e l'elezione del nuovo Pontefice*," *La Civiltà Cattolica*, 129 (1978) 3078, p. 521; F. Ruozzi, "*Un papa più mostrato che dato?*", p. 532.

11. Cf. the documentary film *Giovanni Paolo I: Il Papa del sorriso*, edited by L. Bizzarri for the series *La grande storia* of RaiTre, in consultation with S. Falasca.

12. Cf. Positio IV, *Biographia ex documentis*, pp. 2855–2861. Cf. M. Velati, "*I patriarca Albino Luciani a Venezia*," *Le Tre Venezie*, 135 (2016), pp. 60–65.

13. Cf. Positio II, *Depositiones testium*, T. CII, § 1657, p. 787.

14. Cf. Ibid., T. CLVIII, § 2274, p. 1022.

15. Cf. Positio II, *Testimonia extraprocessualia*, T. XI, pp. 1131–1132.

16. Cf. ArPost, *Lettera del patriarca Luciani a don Giuseppe Gu-*

mirato, abate di Malcontenta, con le risultanze della seconda visita pastorale, 19 agosto 1978 (Positio III, *Summarium documentorum,* no. 190); *Governo della diocese,* envelope 5, *Lettera del patriarca Luciani a don Vittorio Dinon del 16 agosto 1978,* c.n.n.; Positio V, *Inquisitio dioecesana suppletiva,* p. 896.

17. Cf. *Agenda del 1978,* envelope XXIV, agenda no. 10.

18. A. Luciani, *"Un grande Papa per un tempo difficile, 8 agosto 1978,"* in *OpOm,* VIII, p. 579.

19. Some authors have fantasized about omens, making it a case of *vaticinium ex eventu* following the conversation, which took place in Coimbra in July of 1977, between Luciani and the Fátima seer Sr. Lucia dos Santos. According to these authors, the seer would have predicted the pontificate and its brevity [cf. R. Kummer, *"Albino Luciani. Papa Giovanni Paolo I. Una vita per la Chiesa,"* Messaggero, 2009, pp. 666–669, 676–678, 685; D. Malacaria, *"Il segreto di Fátima,"* *30giorni,* 6 (2007), pp. 90–91]. Luciani's brother Edoardo referred to that meeting on several occasions (Positio II, *Depositiones testium,* T. XVII, § 349). His niece Lina Petri decidedly downplayed its weight and meaning: "My uncle told me about that episode while we were talking in general about the problems of the Church" (Positio II, *Testimonia extraprocessualia,* T. XVIII). Father Mario Senigaglia, an assiduous and trusted collaborator of Patriarch Luciani in Venice, after a detailed report on the meeting in Fátima, definitively clarified the matter: "Never, not even once, did I suspect that mysterious 'prophetic revelations' were made by Sister Lucia to Patriarch Luciani" [Positio II, *Testimonia extraprocessualia,* T. XIX; cf. S. Falasca, *"Quell'incontro a Fatima. Intervista con Mario Senigaglia,"* *30giorni,* 1 (2007), pp. 72–77]. Finally, it was Cardinal Giuseppe Caprio, substitute of the Secretariat of State at the time, who ensured that "from the dispositions he gave and the plans he made for the future, everything leads to the belief that he did not expect things would end so soon" (Positio II, *Documenta testimonialia,* no. 2, pp. 1194–1197).

All that remains for the records is what Luciano wrote, which was publicly confirmed during the Angelus on Sunday August 27: "Yesterday morning I went to the Sistine Chapel to vote quietly. I would never have imagined what was about to happen" (John Paul I,

Testo del discorso pronunciato a braccio prima dell'Angelus di dome-nica 27 agosto 1978, in Positio III, *Summarium documentorum*, no. 237, p. 2034).

20. G. Nicolini, *Trentatré giorni, un pontificato*, Istituto padano di arti grafiche, 1979, p. 15.

21. Cf. G. Andreotti, *A ogni morte di Papa*, p. 156.

22. S. Falasco, "*Un'umanità non di facciata. Intervista con il cardinale Aloísio Lorscheider*," *30giorni*, 7/8 (1998), p. 25. S. Falasca, "*Mio fratello Albino, ricordi e memorie della sorella di Papa Luciani*," *30giorni*, 2003, pp. 92–96. Each reconstruction by Vaticanists and historians, given the obligation of confidentiality and the secrecy of the acts of the conclave, remains a more or less plausible interpreta-tion, which refers to the classical criteria of the dynamics of politics (extensive review in M. Roncalli, pp. 536–560. Cf. also the review by R. Kummer, "*Albino Luciani*," pp. 669–675, which refers to the re-constructions of A. Greeley, *Der Weisse Rauch. Die Hintergründe der Papstwahlen 1978*, Styria, 1979, and that of B. Lai, *I segreti del Vatica-no da Pio XII a papa Wojtyła*, Laterza, 1984).

23. F. Farusi, "*Cercavano un Papa buon pastore*," *Il Sabato*, Au-gust 28, 1993, cited in *Humilitas*, 3 (1995), p. 10. The pastoral char-acteristics that would have guided the sacred college are also high-lighted in a confidential note of the American Consulate in Milan to the Embassy in Rome, to the U.S. Secretariat of State, which cites as a source a confidential conversation with Cardinal Giovanni Co-lombo, without prejudice to the confidentiality of the details of the Conclave. (ArPost, *Copie delle note riservate del Dipartimento di Sta-to americano, agosto-settembre 1978, Nota riservata del Consolato americano di Milano all'ambasciata di Roma, alla Segreteria di Stato degli USA e ad altri consolati italiani del 18 settembre 1978*, no. A60).

24. Cf. G. De Rosa, *La storia che non passa. Diario politico 1968–1989*, edited by S. Demofonti, Rubbettino, 1999, p. 239; G. Andreotti, "*A ogni morte di Papa*," p. 149; N. Buonasorte, "*L'enigma Luciani e il Conclave*," p. 500; M. Roncalli, "*Giovanni Paolo I*," p. 552.

25. H. Thiandoum, "*Tre papi e un orientamento fondamentale comune*," *30giorni*, 16 (1998) 7/8, p. 32.

26. G. De Rosa, *Una scelta di fede*, in Id., *Erudizione e pietà dei*

Papi del Concilio. Giovanni XXIII – Paolo VI – Giovanni Paolo I, San-germano, 1985, p. 147.

27. Cf. *"Omelia del card. Giovanni Colombo pronunciata il 31 agosto 1978 nel duomo di Milano per la celebrazione di ringraziamen-to per il nuovo papa,"* Rivista diocesana Milanese, 69 (1978), pp. 655–658.

28. Cf. A. Melloni, *Luciani e il 1978*, in *DVAM*, pp. 483–490.

29. Cf. G. Muccin, *"Ritratto di Albino Luciani,"* Rivista diocesana di Belluno e di Feltre, 61 (1980), pp. 305–319; G. Muccin, *Giovanni Paolo I," Gli ultimi papi. Testimonianze*, edited by A. Rossi, Urbaniana University Press, 1980, pp. 137–160.

30. G. Caprile, *"Il Conclave e l'elezione del nuovo Pontefice,"* p. 524.

31. Cf. ArPost, *Copie delle note riservate del Dipartimento di Stato americano, agosto-settembre 1978, Nota della Segreteria di Stato degli USA all'ambasciata americana di Roma del 26 agosto 1978*, no. E3.

32. Cf. ArILS, Fondo Giulio Andreotti, *"Andreotti: scelta illumi-nata,"* Il Mattino, August 28, 1978, envelope 98 Vatican 1, c.n.n.: pre-senting the opinions of Piccoli, Zaccagnini, Rumor, Saragat, Nenni, and Romita.

33. ArPost, *Copie delle note riservate del Dipartimento di Stato americano, agosto-settembre 1978, Nota dell'ambasciata americana a Mosca alla Segreteria di Stato degli USA e ad altre ambasciate del 2 settembre 1978*, no. E35.

34. Rome, ArILS, Fondo Giulio Andreotti, *Dispaccio riservatissi-mo no. 2274 dell'ambasciata italiana di Mosca al ministero degli Este-ri dell'8 settembre 1978*, envelope 98 Vat. 1, no. 4/D. Giuseppe Wal-ter Maccotta was Italy's Ambassador to Moscow from 1977 to 1981. The confirmation of the officials of the Vatican Secretariat of State was immediately recognized by diplomats as a sign of continuity in international relations, with particular attention paid to the detente between the two world blocs, to disarmament, to negotiations in the Middle East, and to reconciliation in Lebanon.

35. Positio II, *Depositiones testium*, T. CXI, § 1839, p. 850. Cf. *Summarium testium*, T. CXLVII, § 2177, p. 980.

36. Cf. ibid.

37. As Giorgio Cracco observed, evoking Luciani then became an opportunity to "speak against" (against the Roman Curia, against the inaction of ecclesial structures, etc.), or it was the expression of a "gratifying and extemporaneous myth, which would have had the task of freeing humanity from unspecified fears and oppression." It was a media *fiction* in the face of scant historiographical interest for which Luciani received "only slight attention," cf. G. Cracco, *"Dal Veneto al mondo: davvero,"* DVAM, pp. 12–13. Cf. also Patrizia Luciani, *"Albino Luciani Patriarca di Venezia (1970–1978),"* PhD in Humanities. *Tradizione e contemporaneità*, cycle XXVIII, S.S.D. MSTO / 07, Università Cattolica del Sacro Cuore, Milan, 2014/2015, pp. 3–10.

38. The six "we wish": "We wish to continue to put into effect the heritage of the Second Vatican Council. Its wise norms should be followed out and perfected. … We wish to preserve the integrity of the great discipline of the Church … both in the exercise of the evangelical virtues and in service to the poor, the humble, the defenseless. … We wish to remind the entire Church that its first duty is that of evangelization … to announce … salvation. … We wish to continue the ecumenical thrust … [dedicating] attention to everything that would favor union. … We wish to pursue with patience but firmness that serene and constructive dialogue that Paul VI had at the base of his plan and program for pastoral action. … We wish finally to express our support for all the laudable, worthy initiatives that can safeguard and increase peace in our troubled world." (John Paul I, *"Urbi et Orbi"* radio message, August 27, 1978, text given in Positio III, *Summarium documentorum*, pp. 2027–2033).

39. Cf. D. Fiocco, *"Le priorità di Giovanni Paolo I vescovo di Roma,"* Le Tre Venezie, 135 (2016), pp. 80–84.

40. John Paul I, *Udienza generale: la speranza, 20 settembre 1978,* in Positio III, *Summarium documentorum*, no. 266, pp. 2104–2105. The citation is reported here according to the transcription of the spoken text, which differs from the official one in *Insegnamenti di Giovanni Paolo I*, Libreria Editrice Vaticana, 1979, pp. 71–75. Considering the innovative significance of Luciano's language, a section has been included in the *positio*, which presents a philological reconstruction of all the writings and speeches he made during his pontif-

icate. In order to adhere respectfully to the texts actually spoken by John Paul I, it was necessary to conduct an examination by verifying the differences found in the official and unofficial texts with respect to the recordings of the time.

41. Positio III, *Summarium documentorum*, no. 266, p. 2015.

42. John Paul I, *"Urbi et orbi" radio message, August 27, 1978*, in Positio III, *Summarium documentorum*, no. 236, pp. 2028–2030.

43. Ecumenical commitment is woven throughout his entire pontificate. It was a significant indicator of his desire to foster unity with the sister Churches of the East, which already in his homily of September 3, addressing his greetings to all the people, after the cardinals, he mentioned the patriarchs of the Eastern Churches, a mention that was expunged from the official text (Giovanni Paolo I, *Omelia per la Santa messa d'inizio del ministero di Pastore della Chiesa universale, 3 settembre 1978*, in Positio III, *Summarium documentorum*, no. 252, pp. 2059–2065). On September 2, he held subsequent audiences in the private library with the delegates of numerous non-Catholic denominations who were then present for the celebration on September 3. The pope expressed the need to further the dialogue between the Christian communities that had been initiated by the council and to continue to pray for the unity desired by Christ; cf. *Il Papa auspica progressi ecumenici*, in *L'Osservatore Romano*, 202 (September 3, 1978), p. 2. The morning of September 5 was also dedicated to audiences with the delegations of the non-Catholic churches and communities gathered in Rome. In the midst of these audiences came the sudden death of the Prelate of the Russian Orthodox Church, Nikodim (1929–1978), Metropolitan of Leningrad and Novgorod, Patriarchal Exarch for Western Europe and president of the Office of the Patriarchate of Moscow for relations between the Orthodox churches and the other churches. For the audience and the death of the Metropolitan, cf. Positio II, *Testimonia extraprocessualia*, T. XIII, pp. 1139–1143; cf. S. FALASCA, *"Mai avevo sentito cose così belle." Intervista con Miguel Arranz*, in *30Giorni*, 24 (2006) 6, pp. 58–64.

44. Cf. Giovanni Paolo I, *Allocuzione al Corpo diplomatico accreditato presso la Santa Sede, 31 agosto 1978*, in Positio III, *Summarium*

documentorum, no. 242, p. 2030; cf. *AAS*, 70 (1978) 10, pp. 705–708; *Pace e progresso per tutti popoli*, in *L'Osservatore Romano*, 200 (September 1, 1978), pp. 1–2. In continuity with John XXIII and Paul VI, the pope illustrated the contribution that the Church could make in building a humanity founded on brotherhood: at the international level, collaborating in the search for the best solutions for peace, justice, development, disarmament, and humanitarian aid, and at the pastoral level, collaborating in the formation of the consciences of the faithful and of all people of good will.

45. Giovanni Paolo I, *Allocuzione ai membri delle Delegazioni ufficiali presenti alla celebrazione per l'inizio del pontificato, 4 settembre 1978*, in Positio III, *Summarium documentorum*, no. 253, pp. 2065–2066,

46. Cf. C. Ossola, "*Il sermo humilis di Albino Luciani*," *Avvenire*, September 21, 2008, p. 5. Cf. S. Falasca, "*La scelta teologica del sermo humilis*," *Le Tre Venezie*, 135 (2016), pp. 44–49.

47. Positio II, *Depositiones testium*, T. CLVIII, § 2274, p. 1022.

48. As Luciani's secretary, Fr. Diego Lorenzi, a member of the Don Orione Fathers, succeeded Fr. Mario Senigaglia who held this office in the Patriarchate in Venice from May of 1970 until October 3, 1976. Previously, this office was held by seven priests in succession: Fr. Ausilio da Rif (December 1958–January 1959); Fr. Vittorio Battistin (January–April 1959); Fr. Piergiorgio da Canal (February 1959–July 1961); Fr. Paolo Carrer (August 1961–July 1963); Fr. Arrigo Gobbo (July 1963–June 1967); and Fr. Francesco Taffarel (June 1967–May 1970). Moreover, Luciani, from the last three years of his episcopate in Vittorio Veneto, up until the Vatican, had also availed himself of the help of Fr. Carlo Bolzan, a retired military chaplain (cf. Positio IV, *Biographia ex documentis*, p. 2397).

49. Cf. Positio II, *Depositiones testium*, T. CLVIII, § 2274, p. 1022.

50. Ibid.

51. Ibid. Maffeo Ducoli (1918–2012) was bishop of Belluno-Feltre from 1975 to 1996.

52. Cf. ibid., T. IX, § 142, pp. 314–315; *L'Amico del Popolo*, 34 (January 28, 1978), p. 7; *Humilitas*, 2 (1987), p. 3; M. Ducoli, *Con occhi semplici*, in *30giorni*, 5 (2004), p. 89; cf. Positio II, *Depositiones*

testium, T. CLVIII, § 2274, p. 1022.

53. The unpublished text continues: "Thank Fr. General for me and recommend me to the prayers of your brothers, whom I bless with all my heart. I, Paulus PP. I" (Rome, Augustinian General Archives, *Lettera di Giovanni Paolo I a padre Gioele Schiavella vicario generale dell'Ordine agostiniano del 28 agosto 1978*, c.n.n.). The other letter also shows Luciani's gentle and constant attention toward the humblest people: "Dear Father, thank you for your best wishes, your prayers, and the kind things you said about the new, poor pope. I am very grateful for all the attention you have given me in these days and I heartily bless you together with your brothers (including Franceschino!) And the good Sisters. I, Paulus PP. I" (Rome, Augustinian General Archives, *Lettera di Giovanni Paolo I al priore padre Prosper Grech del 28 agosto 1978*, c.n.n.). Franceschino was the elderly lay brother who tidied up the rooms of the college.

54. Cf. Positio II, *Depositiones testium*, T. CXX, §§ 1950–1951, pp. 888–889.

55. Cf. Positio II, *Testimonia extraprocessualia*, T. XIV; T. XV, p. 1147.

56. During the diocesan process (2003–06), Sister Margherita, the only survivor of the group of four nuns who were part of the papal apartments team, was not questioned (she was contacted by me later, cf. Positio II, *Testimonia extraprocessualia*, T. XV, pp. 1147–1157; cf. also, in Appendix 3, *Storia della Causa di canonizzazione*). In fact, the only sisters among the witnesses questioned during the diocesan investigation were Srs. Celestina Tellatin and Federica Minato. They had been part of the religious community serving the patriarchal apartments in Venice. They came to the Vatican only for lunch on Sunday, September 3, 1978 (cf. Positio II, *Depositiones testium*, T. CLXII, pp. 1041–1042 and CLXIII, pp. 1043–1044). After appropriate research began during the Roman phase of the cause, it was Sr. Giulia Scardanzan, the superior of the General House on Via Paolo VI in Rome, who reconstructed for the first time the circumstances highlighted here (cf. Positio II, *Testimonia extraprocessualia*, T. XIV, pp. 1144–1147). Marco Roncalli lists the names of the religious as Vincenza, Clorinda, Assunta, and Gabriella. However, they are the four

who worked only in the first week of the pontificate (cf. M. Roncalli, *Giovanni Paolo I*, p. 616).

57. Positio II, *Testimonia extraprocessualia*, TXIV, p. 1150.

58. Ibid.

59. Cf. J. Martin, *Oltre il portone di bronzo: dagli appunti segreti di un cardinale vissuto a fianco di sei Papi*, Paoline, 1996, p. 146.

60. Positio II, *Testimonia extraprocessualia*, T. XV, no. 6, p. 1150.

61. Positio II, *Depositiones testium*, T. CXX, § 1951, p. 889.

62. Ibid, T. CLV, § 2249, p. 1009.

63. Cf. Positio IV, *Biographia ex documentis*, p. 2897

64. Cf. Positio II, *Testimonia extraprocessualia*, T. XV, no. 6, p. 1149.

65. Cf. Positio II, *Depositiones testium*, T. XXVI, § 490, pp. 432–433.

66. Ibid, T. CLXI, § 2307, p. 1039.

67. Cf. Positio II, *Testimonia extraprocessualia*, T. XVI, no. 18, p. 1154.

68. Ibid., no. 7, p. 1150.

69. Fr. Mario Senigaglia stated, "The pope contacted me through Sister Vincenza and Fr. Diego Lorenzi, asking me to send him his notes and notebooks, and I took care to send them to him" (cf. Positio II, *Depositiones testium*, T. CV, § 1740, p. 819). According to the witness Carlo Vian, on August 29 Msgr. Giuseppe Bosa, together with Carlo Vian, Camillo Bassotto, and Sister Vincenza, were to come to Rome bringing the pope's personal effects that were immediately needed (cf. ibid., T. CXXX, §§ 2041, 2046, pp. 927–929).

70. Cf. Positio V, *Inquisitio dioecesana suppletiva*, Luciani Fund-Private Archive, pp. 3258–3283. I reconstructed the composition archive-library and the route it traveled based on the data I acquired during a survey of the material stored at ArSPV, which I conducted from March 25 to April 4, 2008, during the supplementary investigations related to the cause.

71. Cf. S. Falasca, *La biblioteca ex libris Albino Luciani*, in EAD., *Sermo humilis e referenze letterarie negli scritti di papa Luciani: il caso di Illustrissimi*, Doctorate in Italian Studies, XXIV cycle, University of Rome Tor Vergata, coordinating prof. A. Gareffi, 2011–2012, p.

243. Albino Luciani's personal library in Venice did not have a catalog, so it is not possible to establish the total number of volumes. On his death, the books and papers from his archive-library were returned to Venice at the end of October 1978. Fr. Diego Lorenzi records the crates with the books and papers from the papal apartments were sealed on October 17, 1978 (cf. Positio III, *Summarium documentorum*, p. 1999).

72. Cf. Positio II, *Depositiones testium*, T. VI, § 106, p. 303; T. CLVIII, § 2275, p. 1023; R. Busa, *Riflettendo, come in uno specchio, la luce del Signore*, in *30giorni*, 9 (2004), pp. 90–92; Id., *Come era composto il bagaglio del Papa da Venezia a Roma e viceversa*, in *Humilitas*, 2 (1993) 9, pp. 10–19. The move did not take place on September 8, as reported by M. Roncalli, *Giovanni Paolo I*, p. 591 and p. 616, which is based upon a controversial volume by Camillo Bassotto (*Il mio cuore è ancora a Venezia*, Tipolitografia Adriatica, 1990).

73. Cf. Positio II, *Testimonia extraprocessualia*, T. VIII, no. 1, p. 1090. Father Lorenzi's version is different: "The Vatican Secretariat of State sent me a priest from Ireland, Father Magee. He had been Monsignor Macchi's assistant secretary since 1974 (Positio II, *Depositiones testium*, T. CLVIII, § 2275, p. 1024). In addition, Father Magee continued secretarial service with John Paul II until February 7, 1982. He then served as Master of Pontifical Ceremonies until February 17, 1987, when he was appointed the bishop of Cloyne. John Paul II consecrated him as a bishop on March 17, 1987.

74. Cf. ibid., cf. Positio II, *Testimonia extraprocessualia*, T. II, pp. 1066–1067.

75. Cf. Positio IV, *Biographia ex documentis*, p. 2898.

76. Positio II, *Testimonia extraprocessualia* , T. XV, no. 7, p. 1150.

77. In this sense, statements from the household members were in agreement. His niece Pia Luciani said: "My father asked my uncle directly why he had chosen that secretary. He replied that it was the father general of the Orione Movement who sent him, pointing out the difficulties of finding a job for him, due to personal problems … and my uncle decided to keep him temporarily in the Patriarchate." Positio II, *Depositiones testium*, T. XXVI, § 493, p. 434; cf. T. XXXIX, § 720, p. 519; cf. Positio II, *Testimonia extraprocessualia*, T. VI, attach-

ment 5, pp. 1086–1087; T. XVIII, p. 1173; T. XII, p. 1173.

78. Positio II, *Testimonia extraprocessualia*, T. VI, pp. 1086–1087; cf. T. XV, no. 7, p. 1150; cf. Positio II, *Documenta testimonialia*, no. 7, pp. 1206–1207. Cf. M. RONCALLI, *Giovanni Paolo*, p. 618, n102 (a note from 1983 by Bishop Loris Capovilla).

79. Positio II, *Testimonia extraprocessualia*, T. VI, attachment 5, pp. 1086–1087.

80. Disharmony that also transpired outside the Apostolic Palace, cf. G. Zizola, *Rapporto Luciani. Morte di un povero Cristo*, in "Epoca," September 28, 1988, p. 169; Id., *Perché non ci credo*, in *Panorama*, June 18, 1984, p. 120.

81. Cf. P. Mattei, *È la preghiera la chiave di volta della vita cristiana*, in *30giorni*, 1/2 (2012), p. 58.

82. Positio II, *Testimonia extraprocessualia*, T. IX, p. 1123, *Allegato: lettera di mons. Pasquale Macchi a Giovanni Paolo I del 10 settembre 1978*. According to Giancarlo Zizola, on September 14 Monsignor Macchi would have already returned to Rome, "after sorting out the truckloads of stuff exported after the death of Paul VI" (G. Zizola, *Rapporto Luciani*, p. 169).

83. Positio II, *Testimonia extraprocessualia*, T. XV, no. 7, p. 1150.

84. Positio II, *Depositiones testium*, T. XXVI, § 518, p. 433.

85. Positio II, *Testimonia extraprocessualia*, T. XII, p. 1136.

86. Positio II, *Depositiones testium*, T. CLVIII, § 2261, pp. 1015–1016. In the last months of his episcopal ministry in Vittorio Veneto, Luciani had also asked his niece Pia to be his secretary.

87. Positio III, *Summarium documentorum, Lettera autografa di mons. Luciani al segretario Arrigo Gobbo*, p. 1482 (ArDVV, *Vescovo Albino Luciani – Corrispondenza 1958–1970*, c.n.n.).

88. Positio II, *Depositiones testium*, T. CLVIII, § 2261, p. 1016.

89. Positio II, *Testimonia extraprocessualia*, T. XVIII, p. 1173.

90. Cf. Positio II, *Depositiones testium*, T. CLXV, § 2335, p. 1051; T. CLXI, § 2303–2304, pp. 1037–1039. Gugel then continued his service with John Paul II (cf. T. XXVI, § 492, p. 434) and, when needed, with Benedict XVI.

91. Ibid., T. CLXI, § 2303, p. 1038.

92. Cf. Positio IV, *Biographia ex documentis*, pp. 2900–2901.

93. During his period in Venice, he had the Jesuit Leandro Tiveron. Cf. S. Falasca, *La sua pazienza ci aspetta. Luciani e la confessione*, in *30giorni*, 21 (2003) 3, pp. 72–78. Cf. Positio IV, *Biographia ex documentis*, p. 2900.

94. Positio II, *Testimonia extraprocessualia*, T. XII, p. 1136.

95. The description given by Sr. Margherita Marin (Positio II, *Testimonia extraprocessualia*, T. XV, no. 8, pp. 1150–1151) seemed more accurate. Magee, on the other hand, seemed to reconstruct a typical day of the pope in a personal way, sometimes yielding to *pro domo sua* variations: "The Holy Father's day began around 4:30 a.m. At 5:10 a.m., he would come out of his bedroom to get a cup of coffee, which Sister Vincenza left outside the door every morning. At 5:30 a.m., I was always at the chapel door to welcome the Holy Father and offer him holy water before entering the chapel. After we had recited Morning Prayer together, the Holy Father read aloud a passage from the *Imitation of Christ* each morning, and then made a commentary to help us in our meditation. At 7:00 a.m., he celebrated Mass with the secretaries and in the presence of the sisters and a few guests" (ibid., T. VIII, no. 8, p. 1151).

96. Cf. Positio II, *Depositiones testium*, T. CLXI, § 2308, p. 1040. Cf. Positio II, *Testimonia extraprocessualia*, T. VIII, no. 2, pp. 1094–1095.

97. Positio II, *Testimonia extraprocessualia*, T. XV, no. 8, p. 1151.

98. Cf. Positio IV, *Biographia ex documentis*, p. 2902; cf. Positio II, *Testimonia extraprocessualia*, T. VIII, no. 5, p. 1093 (Msgr. Magee himself). Cf. ibid., T. IV, p. 1071 (Cardinal Julian Herranz Casado).

99. Cf. Positio II, *Depositiones testium*, T. CLXI, § 2307, p. 1039.

100. Msgr. John Magee scheduled audiences from 10:00 a.m. to 12:30 p.m. (cf. Positio II, *Testimonia extraprocessualia*, T. VIII, no. 8); papal butler Angelo Gugel from 11:00 a.m. to 1:00 p.m. (cf. *Depositiones testium*, T. CLXI, § 2307, p. 1039).

101. Cf. Positio IV, *Biographia ex documentis*, pp. 2092–2093; cf. Positio II, *Testimonia extraprocessualia*, T. VIII, no. 7, p. 1094.

102. Cf. *Conferenza di mons. Magee tenuta a Canale d'Agordo il 27 settembre 2008*, in Positio II, *Testimonia extraprocessualia*, T. VIII, attachment 1, p. 1107. On the same occasion the prelate recounted

that, going up to the roof garden on a windy afternoon, he brought some files with documents, as was his custom. After half an hour, the secretary was informed that pages written in a language other than Italian were falling from the sky: "So I looked down and there were four or five levels of roofs and I don't know how many pages were stuck in the rain gutters at each level."

103. Again, Monsignor Magee had them scheduled at 5:00 p.m. (Positio II, *Testimonia extraprocessualia,* T. VIII, no. 8, p. 1094), while Angelo Gugel had them scheduled from 6:00 p.m. to 7:00 p.m. (Positio II, *Depositiones testium,* T. CLXI, § 2307, p. 1039).

104. Cf. Positio II, *Testimonia extraprocessualia*, T. VIII, no. 8, p. 1095.

105. Cf. ibid., no. 6, p. 1093.

106. Ibid., T. XV, no. 8. Cf. Positio II, *Depositiones testium,* T. CLXV, § 2336, p. 1051; G. Nicolini, *Trentatré giorni*, p. 137.

107. Positio II, *Depositiones testium,* T. CLXV, § 2235, p. 1002.

108. A mission that should have detained him in Australia from September 21 to October 4. Cf. Belluno, Archives and Protocol Office of the Chamber of Commerce of Belluno, *Registro delle delibere di Giunta, Verbale di Giunta del 9 agosto 1978 con cui si autorizza il cav. Edoardo Luciani a effettuare la missione in Australia, per manifestazioni dal 21 settembre al 4 ottobre 1978*, resolution no. 151, nos. 169–193.

109. Cf. Positio II, *Depositiones testium,* T. XVII, § 349, p. 379.

110. Cf. ibid., T. XXVI, § 493, p. 435. On the relationship of trust with Cardinal Villot cf. Positio IV, *Biographia ex documentis,* p. 2907.

111. Positio II, *Depositiones testium,* T. XVII, § 349, p. 379. Cf. Positio I, *Informatio,* p. 48.

112. Cf. Positio II, *Depositiones testium,* T. XVII, § 348, p. 379.

113. Cf. *Il Papa auspica progressi ecumenici. Incontro di Giovanni Paolo I con i suoi familiari,* in *L'Osservatore Romano,* 202 (September 3, 1978), p. 2. Since the agenda of Cardinal Albino Luciani had for some time listed a meeting with the Venetians who emigrated to Einsiedeln in Switzerland, he wrote an autographed message in his own hand, entrusting it to his brother Edoardo: "Dear emigrants, I had greatly desired to be with you in Einsiedeln on September 10. This

would have been to honor Our Lady at one of her famous shrines, but also to be among you, who remind me that my father, my mother, and my sister were, like you, emigrants to Switzerland. However, the Lord unexpectedly placed me on another path. My heart will be present with you, along with my apostolic blessing, which I impart to all of you, to your families, and upon your work" (*Autografo di papa Giovanni Paolo I agli emigranti veneti ad Einsiedeln in Svizzera, 2 settembre 1978,* in Positio III, *Summarium documentorum,* no. 247, p. 2051). The letter, dated September 2, 1978, was published by G. Nicolini, *Trentatré giorni,* p. 100, where it was revealed that the autograph was entrusted to his brother Edoardo, a detail confirmed by Edoardo himself. The autograph was reproduced and transcribed in *Humilitas,* 8 (1991) 1, p. 4.

114. Positio II, *Depositiones testium,* T. I, § 24. p. 278. Cf. L. Petri, "*State tranquilli come sto tranquillo io,*" in *Le Tre Venezie,* 135 (2016), pp. 98–99.

115. Cf. *Nostre informazioni,* in *L'Osservatore Romano,* 212 (September 15, 1978), p. 1. His cousin Silvio Luciani and members of his family.

116. Cf. Positio IV, *Biographia ex documentis,* p. 2904.

117. Cf. Positio II, *Depositiones testium,* T. XXVI, § 492, p. 434.

118. The autograph note, taken from the appointment book used by John Paul I during his pontificate, is reproduced and transcribed in Positio III, *Summarium documentorum,* no. 235, sheet no. 3, p. 2015; cf. Appendix 2. The only ring that John Paul I wore during the entire pontificate was the one given to all the bishops who had participated in the Second Vatican Council.

119. Cf. Positio II, *Depositiones testium,* T. LIV, § 987, p. 592. Cf. Ibid., T. XXVI, § 493, p. 434.

120. Ibid., T. LVI, p. 603; T. LIV, § 987, p. 592. Cf. ArPost, *Documenti personali – documentazione clinica, Testimonianza del dott. Antonio Da Ros circa gli accordi intercorsi con il Servizio Sanitario del Vaticano per l'assistenza medica al Papa, 24 agosto 2009,* folder II (Positio III, *Summarium documentorum,* no. 112, p. 1380). Cf. Positio II, *Depositiones testium,* T. CLVIII, § 2276, p. 1025.

121. Regarding the ecumenical meeting of John Paul I with Met-

ropolitan Nikodim, one of the most significant personalities in the history of ecumenism, cf. the testimony *de visu* of the Jesuit Miguel Arranz in Positio II, *Testimonia extraprocessualia,* T. XIII, pp. 1139–1143.

122. Cf. Positio II, *Testimonia extraprocessualia,* T. XI, p. 1133. Cf. *Bollettino dell'archidiocesi di Bologna,* 9 (1978), pp. 356–357: reports the cardinal's homily at the suffrage celebration on September 30, 1978. He also remembered the Piperno family on September 26, writing a letter to the widow Maria Piperno and daughter Linda (cf. OpOm IX, p. 506; cf. ArBL, *Lettere autografe di Albino Luciani, Lettera di Giovanni Paolo I del 26 settembre 1978 a Maria e Linda Piperno,* section D. rep. I/G, envelope 57/6/269, c.n.n.).

123. The conference was scheduled for October 12–28.

124. Positio IV, *Biographia ex documentis,* p. 2906.

125. Cf. *Nostre informazioni,* in *L'Osservatore Romano,* 220 (September 24, 1978) 2.

126. Positio III, *Summarium documentorum,* no. 235, sheet no. 3, p. 2015.

127. Cf. Positio II, *Depositiones testium,* T. IX, § 142, p. 315; cf. M. Ducoli, *Con occhi semplici,* in *30giorni,* 5 (2004), p. 89.

128. Cf. V. Branca, *Lo stupore di Dio,* in *30giorni,* 7/8 (1998) 41. Cf. *Nostre informazioni,* in *L'Osservatore Romano,* 206 (September 8, 1978), p. 1.

129. Positio II, *Documenta testimonialia,* no. 5. Cf. S. Falasca, *Papa Luciani e la Fondazione Giorgio Cini,* in *"Lettera da San Giorgio,"* XI, 21 (September 2009–February 2010), pp. 19–21.

130. Of the audiences mentioned in the press, one was with Lino Marconato, director of the Bank of San Marco in Venice, a credit institution that Patriarch Luciani had taken an active interest in protecting in 1972 (M. Roncalli, *Giovanni Paolo I,* p. 637); however, the source and other evidence are missing. The same applies to another audience with Fr. Germano Pattaro (cf. G. Zizola, *Rapporto Luciani*). Regarding Father Pattaro's visit to the Vatican — as reported by Camillo Bassotto in his controversial book (1990) and taken up by M. Roncalli, *Giovanni Paolo I,* pp. 617–618, 627–628 — Fr. Diego Lorenzi's tribunal testimony was drastic: "What Camillo Bassotto recount-

ed in his book *Il mio cuore è ancora a Venezia,* about Pattaro having a personal meeting with Pope Luciani, I can affirm that it was all invented" (Positio II, *Depositiones testium*, T. CLVIII, § 2268, p. 1020). Cf. also G. Bertoli, *Il periodo veneziano e romano di Luciani: anni non facili per la Chiesa e il mondo*, in *Humilitas*, 1 (1993), pp. 7–8. Bassotto claimed his information was based on private material from a prelate who allegedly collected certain details and confidences that Luciani expressed during his pontificate; the author never wanted to reveal the identity of the prelate because of a specific promise he made to his source. M. Roncalli in *Giovanni Paolo I*, p. 591 — supported by the testimony of Cardinal Loris Capovilla — identifies him as Fr. Carlo Bolzan, who died on December 30, 1994. G. Zizola, in *Rapporto Luciani*, reported that a meeting between John Paul I and Father Pattaro took place on September 13: "The Pope made an urgent call to him. He had been marginalized in Venice and now the pope wanted him at his side. Luciani asked him to help him." Cf. G. Pattaro, *Papa Luciani nel ricordo di don Pattaro,* in "*Appunti di teologia. Notiziario del Centro Pattaro di Venezia*," 21 (2008) 4, pp. 1–5. The journalist, who died in 2011, told me that he had met the priest from Venice after his audience with the pope. Luciani's written remarks about Pattaro, however, are negative (cf. Positio III, *Summarium documentorum*, no. 162, p. 1512).

131. Cf. Positio III, *Summarium documentorum*, no. 235, folder no. 3, p. 2021. On *Lex Ecclesiae Fundamentalis*, cf. G. Alberigo, *Legge e Vangelo. Discussione su una legge fondamentale per la Chiesa,* Paideia, 1972, pp. 487–657.

132. Positio II, *Testimonia extraprocessualia*, T. II, p. 1067.

133. Cf. Positio I, *Informatio*, pp. 86–89.

134. Positio II, *Depositiones testium*, T. CLXI, §§ 2305–2306, p. 1039.

135. Ibid., T. CLXV, § 2327, p. 1048.

136. Ibid., T. CLVIII, § 2275, p. 1024.

137. Cf. Ibid., T. CLXV, § 2337, p. 1052.

138. Positio II, *Testimonia extraprocessualia*, T. XV, no. 9, p. 1151; cf. Positio I, *Informatio*, p. 89.

139. Positio II, *Documenta testimonialia*, no. 2, p. 1213.

140. Positio II, *Testimonia extraprocessualia*, T. I, p. 1066.

141. Positio IV, *Biographia ex documentis*, pp. 2908–2911.

142. Positio II, *Documenta testimonialia*, no. 2, p. 1213.

143. Ibid., no. 5, p. 1214; cf. Positio IV, *Biographia ex documentis*, p. 2912. Regarding the audience on September 23, Cardinal Sebastiano Baggio emphasized qualities of clarity and pragmatism he observed in John Paul I.

144. John Paul I, *Lettera ai vescovi delle Conferenze episcopali dell'Argentina e del Cile in riferimento alla disputa sul canale di Beagle, 20 settembre 1978*, in Positio III, *Summarium documentorum*, no. 267, pp. 2111–2112; cf. *AAS*, 70 (1978) 11, p. 762. G. Nicoloni, *Trentatré giorni*, pp. 148–149, fixes the date of the letter as September 23, the date on which *L'Osservatore Romano* released news about the appeal of the presidents of the episcopal conferences involved.

145. John Paul I, *Udienza generale: l'umiltà, 6 settembre 1978*, in Positio III, *Summarium documentorum*, no. 255, p. 2072; cf. *Insegnamenti di Giovanni Paolo I*, Libreria Editrice Vaticana, 1979, pp. 49–53.

146. Cf. ArPost, *Copie delle note riservate del Dipartimento di Stato Americano, agosto–settembre 1978, Nota confidenziale dell'ambasciata americana di Roma alla Segreteria di Stato degli USA del 6 settembre 1978*, no. A37.

147. This is the well-known speech given before the Angelus in which Pope Luciani says: "God is our father; even more he is our mother." There are two rough drafts of this speech handwritten by John Paul I in his personal appointment book, which attest, among other things, to the care he used to take in preparing all his speeches, even those delivered off the cuff (cf. Positio III, *Summarium documentorum*, no. 234, pp. 2003–2006).

148. *Per un accordo di giustizia e di pace*, in *L'Osservatore Romano*, 206 (September 8, 1978), p. 1.

149. Cf. ArPost, *Copie delle note riservate del Dipartimento di Stato Americano, agosto–settembre 1978, Nota secreta dell'ambasciata americana di Roma alla Segreteria di Stato degli USA del 18 settembre 1978*, no. A59. Ibid., *Nota secreta della Segreteria di Stato degli USA all'ambasciata americana di Roma del 18 settembre 1978*, no. A62. The date of September 17 is inferred from the pope's letter of

reply. On the dispute and the results of the summit, cf. G. Rulli, *Sulla via della pace per il Medio Oriente*, in *La Civiltà Cattolica*, 129 (1978) 3079, pp. 82–92.

150. ArPost, *Copie delle note riservate del Dipartimento di Stato Americano, agosto–settembre 1978, Nota confidenziale dell'ambasciata americana di Roma alla Segreteria di Stato degli USA del 27 settembre 1978*, no. A69 (the English text is reported and transcribed in Positio IV, *Biographia ex documentis,* p. 2957). There is some uncertainty in the dispatch with regard to the date of the presidential letter. In the transcription of the papal text, it is shown as September 17, while in the accompanying text it is shown as September 18, as it is in the aforementioned dispatches (it could however refer to the date of delivery). The diplomatic note features the presence of the pope's signature, unusual for this kind of message. Cf. S. Falasca, *L'anelito alla pace e la lettera a Carter nel Luciani ancora segreto*, in *Avvenire*, August 26, 2017, p. 3.

151. Signs of this focus could be seen in his numerous audiences with the representatives of the Eastern Churches. On Thursday, September 7, he met with three Eastern patriarchs: Chaldean Patriarch Paul II Cheikho of Babylon; Armenian Patriarch Hemaiagh Pierre XVII Ghedighian of Cilicia; and Maronite Patriarch Antoine Pierre Khoraiche, of Antioch [cf. *Nostre informa*, in *L'Osservatore Romano*, 206 (September 8, 1978), p. 1]. On Wednesday, September 13, he met with Metropolitans Chrysostomos of Kition and Chrysostomos of Paphos, delegates of the Orthodox Church of Cyprus [cf. *Nostre informa*, in *L'Osservatore Romano*, 211 (September 14, 1978), p. 1]. On Tuesday, September 19, he met with the delegation of the Syrian Orthodox Church, led by the archbishop of Mosul Mar Gregorios Saliba and the archbishop for Scandinavia and the British Isles, Mar Timotheos Aboodi [cf. *Nostre informa*, in *L'Osservatore Romano*, 216 (September 20 , 1978), p. 1]. On Wednesday, September 27, he met with the Melkite Greek Patriarch Maximos V Hakim of Antioch, accompanied by Archbishop Joseph Tawil, who also attended his final general audience [cf. *Nostre informa*, in *L'Osservatore Romano*, 223 (September 28, 1978), p. 1].

152. G. Nicolini, *Trentatré giorni*, p. 117. Cf. M. Roncalli, *Giovan-*

ni Paolo I, p. 612, with reference to an article by A. Montonati, *Papa Luciani voleva andare a Beirut*, in *Famiglia Cristiana*, November 5, 1978.

153. Cf. John Paul I, *Allocuzione ai vescovi della XII regione pastorale degli Stati Uniti d'America, in occasione della visita* ad limina, *21 settembre 1978*, in Positio III, *Summarium documentorum,* no. 268, pp. 2112–2114; *AAS*, 70 (1978) 10, pp. 765–767; *L'Osservatore Romano*, 218 (September 22, 1978), p. 1; cf. Positio IV, *Biographia ex documentis*, p. 2914.

154. Monday, September 11, the audience with Cardinal Mario Casariego, archbishop of Guatemala [*Nostre informazioni*, in *L'Osservatore Romano*, 209 (September 11–12, 1978), p. 1]; Thursday, September 14, with Albert Tshomba Yungu, bishop of Tshumbe, Congo [*Nostre informazioni*, in *L'Osservatore Romano*, 212 (September 15, 1978), p. 1]; on Friday, September 15, he received Dominic Kodwo Andoh, bishop of Accra, Ghana [*Nostre informazioni*, in *L'Osservatore Romano*, 213 (September 16, 1978), p. 1]; on Saturday, September 16, Alfonso López Trujillo, coadjutor of Medellín, Colombia, and secretary general of the Latin American Episcopal Council (CELAM) and of the Third Conference of the Latin American Episcopate scheduled in Puebla, Mexico [*Nostre informazioni*, in *L'Osservatore Romano*, 214 (September 17, 1978) p.1; Monday, September 18, Cardinal Laurean Rugambwa, archbishop of Dar-es-Salaam, Tanzania [*Nostre informazioni*, in *L'Osservatore Romano*, 215 (September 18–19, 1978) p.1]; Tuesday, September 19, the secretary of the Brazilian Bishops' Conference, Ivo Lorscheiter, bishop of Santa Maria, Brazil [*Nostre informazioni*, in *L'Osservatore Romano*, 216 (September 20, 1978), p. 1]; Monday, September 25, Cardinal José Humberto Quintero, archbishop of Caracas, Venezuela [*Nostre informazioni*, in *L'Osservatore Romano*, 221 (September 25– 26, 1978), p. 1]

155. Cf. Positio III, *Summarium documentorum*, no. 235, sheet no. 2, p. 2014.

156. Cf. ibid., no. 235, sheet no. 3, p. 2015.

157. On September 6, Ireneo Ali Amantillo was appointed bishop of the new diocese of Tandag in the Philippines [*AAS*, 70 (1978) 11, p. 776]. G. Nicolini, *Trentatré giorni*, p. 125 — on the basis of *Nos-*

tre informazioni, in *L'Osservatore Romano*, 210 (September 13, 1978), p. 1 — fixes the date as September 12. When there is divergence in the dating of appointments, the *Acta Apostolicae Sedis* is the official source. It records September 8 as the day Giovanni Cheli was appointed Permanent Observer of the Holy See to the United Nations, and the day Didier-Léon Marchand was appointed bishop of Valence, France [*AAS*, 70 (1978) 11, p. 776]. This was followed, on September 18, by the appointment of Rémy Augustin as bishop of Port-de-Paix, Haiti, and François Colimon as his coadjutor. On September 19, Adam Dyczkowski was appointed auxiliary bishop of Wrocław, Poland. On September 20, Jacques André Marie Jullien was appointed bishop of Beauvais-Noyon-Senlis, France. On September 21, Jerzy Stroba was appointed archbishop of Poznań, Poland. On September 23, Javier Azagra Labiano was appointed bishop of Cartagena, Spain, and finally, on September 25, Augusto César Alves Ferreira da Silva was appointed bishop of Portalegre-Castelo Branco, Portugal. The Apostolic Brief registered the appointment of Donato Squicciarini as archbishop and apostolic nuncio to Burundi on August 31 [*AAS*, 70 (1978) 11, p. 755].

158. Cf. Positio III, *Summarium documentorum*, no. 235, sheet nos. 2, 6, pp. 2015, 2018.

159. Cf. Positio II, *Depositiones testium*, T. CIII, § 1690, p. 796.

160. Cf. *Lettera di nomina dell'Amministratore apostolico di Venezia mons. Giuseppe Bosa*, in Positio III, *Summarium documentorum*, no. 239, p. 2034. Cf. "*Rivista diocesana del patriarcato di Venezia*," 63 (1978) 5, p. 358. Cf. Positio II, *Depositiones testium*, T. CLVIII, § 2275; T. CXXX, § 2046; Positio II, *Documenta testimonialia*, no. 5, p. 1200.

161. Cf. A. Luciani, *Lettera alla diocesi sulla nomina di tre vicari episcopali, 27 luglio 1978*, in *OpOm*, VIII, pp. 564–566.

162. Cf. John Paul I, *Messaggio ai veneziani, 29 agosto 1978*, in Positio III, *Sum- marium documentorum*, no. 240, p. 2036; *Primo messaggio del Papa ai veneziani*, in "*Rivista diocesana del patriarcato di Venezia*," 63 (1978) 5, p. 381.

163. Cf. John Paul I, *Lettera del Papa per l'apertura dell'anno scolastico del Seminario di Venezia, 15 settembre 1978*, in Positio III, *Summarium documentorum*, no. 263, p. 2096.

164. According to statements by Msgr. Ettore Malnati, a theologian and the vicar of culture and the laity in the Diocese of Trieste, the candidate was Monsignor Macchi. However, Macchi would have asked John Paul I to leave him free to fulfill the testamentary wishes of Paul VI. According to Malnati, the pope would also have consulted Cardinal Colombo, first in writing and then by telephone, on the evening of September 28 (Positio II, *Testimonia extraprocessualia*, T. IX, p. 1123, and attachment). The hypothesis is credited in the biography of Marco Roncalli, in which the author reports a conversation he had with Malnati (M. Roncalli, *Giovanni Paolo I*, pp. 615, 621).

165. There is no trace of what Vatican expert Giancarlo Zizola claimed (Rome, Private Archives Giancarlo Zizola, *Corrispondenza, Appunti "A colloquio con Luciani,"* sheet 7) and what was taken up by M. Roncalli, *Giovanni Paolo I*, p. 619 [which quotes G. Vian, *Sposa e pastore. Oltre vent'anni di Chiesa veneziana (1978–2000)*, Servitium, 2001, p. 19], for which Luciani would have wanted to consult the entire Venetian presbytery in order to facilitate the new patriarch's being welcomed at the Lagoon. According to Cardinal Sebastiano Baggio, neither of the hypothesis would have been opposed to, or would have suggested, Archbishop Battisti of Udine, Italy. Another hoped-for candidacy at the time, dictated by the wishes of some in Venice, was that of Loris Capovilla, the then Papal Delegate to Loreto, Italy. Yet another, constantly endorsed by the press, was the completely unlikely candidacy of Cardinal Baggio himself (G. Zizola, *Perché non ci credo*, cited, p. 121): "I learned from my informant in the Congregation of Bishops that Baggio had a very tough fight with the new pope. … One of the reasons for the conflict was the choice of Luciani's successor in Venice. The list included Archbishop Capovilla, Father Sorge, and the abbot of the Abbey of Praglia, Father Visentin. Baggio objected. Luciani at one point turned to the cardinal, who insisted on pushing his own candidate, and addressed him: 'Your Eminence, would you like to go to Venice then?'" (G. Zizola, *Rapporto Luciani*, p. 169). Fr. Pelagio Visentin, OSB, was not abbot, but a monk of the Abbey of Praglia.

166. Cf. the notes reported by Bartolomeo Sorge in Positio II, *Testimonia extraprocessualia*, T. XII, pp. 1133–1139.

167. ArCV, *Vacanza e provvista della Sede di Venezia (anno 1978), Nota ex audientia Summi Pontificis del card. Baggio del 30 agosto 1978*, c.n.n.; cf. Positio IV, *Biographia ex documentis*, p. 2019.

168. ArCV, *Vacanza e provvista della Sede di Venezia (anno 1978), Informativa di padre Pedro Arrupe, S.I., risposta a prot. 54/62, del 31 agosto 1978*, c.n.n.; cf. Positio IV, *Biographia ex documentis*, p. 2919.

169. ArCV, *Vacanza e provvista della Sede di Venezia (anno 1978), Nota dattiloscritta del card. Sebastiano Baggio del 31 agosto 1978 in merito al colloquio con il card. Ugo Poletti*, c.n.n.; *ivi, Minuta autografa del card. Sebastiano Baggio del 31 agosto 1978 in merito al colloquio con il card. Ugo Poletti*, c.n.n.; cf. Positio IV, *Biographia ex documentis*, p. 2919.

170. ArCV, *Vacanza e provvista della Sede di Venezia (anno 1978), Lettera dattiloscritta di padre Paolo Dezza del 2 settembre 1978*, c.n.n.; cf. Positio IV, *Biographia ex documentis*, pp. 2919–2920.

171. Cf. ArCV, *Vacanza e provvista della Sede di Venezia (anno 1978), Nota autografa di padre Agostino Mayer del 4 settembre 1978*, c.n.n.; cf. Positio IV, *Biographia ex documentis*, p. 2920.

172. ArCV, *Vacanza e provvista della Sede di Venezia (anno 1978), Parere del card. Antonio Poma del 4 settembre 1978*, c.n.n.; cf. Positio IV, *Biographia ex documentis*, p. 2920.

173. Ibid.

174. ArPost, *Documenti autografi – corrispondenza, Lettera di Giovanni Paolo I al card. Giovanni Colombo, 10 settembre 1978*, folder I, c.n.n; cf. Positio II, *Testimonia extraprocessualia*, T. X, pp. 1124–1127; cf. the autograph in Appendix 2.

175. Fr. Angelo Viganò, a Salesian, was ordained a priest in Treviglio, Italy, in 1950. He graduated in literature and philosophy from the Catholic University in Milan. From 1960 to 1966, he served as the director of the Sant'Ambrogio Institute in Milan. From 1966 to 1975, he was director of the Salesian Catechetical Center in Leumann-Turin and collaborated in the drafting of the basic document for the renewal of catechesis in Italy.

176. ArCV, *Vacanza e provvista della Sede di Venezia (anno 1978), Nota autografa del card. Baggio del 27 settembre 1978 sul colloquio con don Angelo Viganò*, c.n.n.; at the bottom it is noted: "September

28. Read to Cardinal Villot." Cf. Positio IV, *Biographia ex documentis*, p. 2921. Fr. Luigi Ricceri was the rector major of the Salesians before Fr. Egidio Viganò, brother of Father Angelo.

177. At the bottom of the document are noted the three: "Viganò, Cé, Ablondi," of which the successor John Paul II finally chose was Marco Cé [ArCV, *Vacanza e provvista della Sede di Venezia (anno 1978), Nota dattiloscritta del card. Baggio del 28 ottobre 1978 per l'udienza con il Papa,* c.n.n.; cf. Positio IV, *Biographia ex documentis*, p. 2921].

178. Cf. Positio II, *Depositiones testium*, T. CLVIII, § 2276, p. 1025.

179. Positio II, *Testimonia extraprocessualia*, T. XV, no. 12, p. 1152.

180. Ibid., no. 4, p. 1149.

181. The witness was questioned in Trento, Italy, on May 12, 2009, at the Provincial Curia in the Italian Province of Triveneto belonging to the Sisters of Charity or of the Holy Child Mary, as they are known. Her provincial superior, Mother Constantina Kersbamer, was also present.

182. Cf. *AAS*, 70 (1978) 10, pp. 768–769; Positio III, *Summarium documentorum, Discorsi, insegnamenti e documenti del pontificato,* p. 2140.

183. Cardinal Bernardin Gantin of Benin (1922–2008) was already president of the Pontifical Commission *Iustitia et Pax*, when on September 4 he was also appointed president of the Pontifical Council *Cor Unum*, established by Paul VI in 1971. This was the only appointment to the heads of the Vatican dicasteries made by John Paul I. The particular esteem expressed by the pope toward the cardinal from Africa was confirmed by the deposition of Edoardo Luciani who recalled a confidential conversation he had with his brother during his pontificate: "I remember that he spoke to me about Cardinal Gantin in a positive way, particularly about a sermon of his that he considered original" (cf. Positio II, *Depositiones testium*, T XVII, § 349, p. 379).

184. Cf. *Nostre informazioni*, in *L'Osservatore Romano*, 224 (September 29, 1978), p. 1. In this last audience granted to a dicastery

head, Luciani also asked the African cardinal to stand in for him in honoring a promise he had made, before being elected pope, to visit the parish of Piombino Dese in the province of Padua, Italy (cf. Positio IV, *Biographia ex documentis*, p. 2912).

185. Cf. G. Cardinale, *Papi umili e fedeli. Intervista al card. Bernardin Gantin, decano emerito del Sacro Collegio*, in *30giorni*, 16 (1998) 9, pp. 28–29.

186. Cf. Positio II, *Testimonia extraprocessualia*, T. XV, no. 12, p. 1152.

187. Ibid. In describing the same circumstance, the Irish secretary John Magee notes that John Paul I was "reading documents sent by the Secretariat of State" (cf. ibid., T. VIII, no. 10, p. 1094).

188. Ibid., no. 12, pp. 1152–1153.

189. Cf. ibid., no. 13, p. 1153.

190. Cf. ibid., no. 14.

191. Ibid., no. 16.

192. Cf. ibid., no. 16, p. 1154.

193. Ibid.

194. Cf. Positio II, *Depositiones testium*, T. CLVIII, § 2276, pp. 1025–1026.

195. Cf. Positio II, *Testimonia extraprocessualia*, T. VIII, no. 10, pp. 1095–1096.

196. Ibid., p. 1096.

197. Positio II, *Testimonia extraprocessualia*, T. VIII, attachment, p. 1108.

198. Ibid.

199. Ibid., attachment p. 1108.

200. Positio II, *Depositiones testium*, T. CLVIII, § 2276, p. 1026.

201. Ibid. Cf. also D. LORENZI, *Giovanni Paolo I nel ricordo di don Diego Lorenzi*, in *Messaggi di Don Orione. Quaderni di storia e spiritualità*, 102 (2000) 3, p. 66.

202. This is the *Rai Due Giallo* television program, edited and hosted by Enzo Tortora. Regarding the chest pains, he explained that the pope had not considered it appropriate to call the doctors. The witness reiterated this version in his memoir published in ibid., pp. 57–75. The pope's niece, Lina Petri, commented on this: "Father Di-

ego's 'revelation' dates back to the end of the eighties (among other things, this took place at my mother's house in Levico. She was sitting next to Father Diego and had to hear this 'wonderful' news on live TV!) that on the evening of September 28 her uncle felt chest pains but did not want to call the doctor" (Positio II, *Testimonia extraprocessualia*, T. XVIII, p. 1176).

203. Cf. T. Ricci, *Quell'estate in compagnia di tre Papi*, in *30giorni*, 6 (1988) 8/9, p. 8–17. Starting in 1988 and throughout the pontificate of Pope John Paul II, the international monthly *30Giorni nella Chiesa e nel mondo* was practically the only magazine in the publishing landscape that repeatedly published insights into the person and work of Albino Luciani.

204. Positio II, *Testimonia extraprocessualia*, T. XV, no. 15, p. 1153. The witness also adds that any concern on the part of Sister Vincenza would have been noticed by her sisters (cf. ibid., no. 11, p. 1152).

205. Cf. Positio II, *Depositiones testium*, T. CLVIII, § p. 1025. At the conclusion of his deposition before the diocesan tribunal on June 6, 2005, Doctor Da Ros issued a certificate signed by Fr. Diego Lorenzi, dated February 11, 1990, attesting to his medical service in Venice and the Vatican (cf. ibid., T. LIV, attachment, pp. 595–596).

206. Ibid., T. LIV, § 987, p. 592.

207. ArPost, *Documenti personali – documentazione clinica, Appunti del medico curante dott. Antonio Da Ros, relativi ai contatti con il Papa e alle visite occorse durante il pontificato [s.d.]*, folder II (Positio III, *Summarium documentorum, Documentazione "de morte,"* p. 1383).

208. The meeting of the pope's brother Edoardo, his sister, Antonia, and other family members with Sr. Vincenza Taffarel took place on the evening of October 2, at the Institute of the Holy Child Mary, next to St. Peter's Square, where the nun was temporarily staying (cf. Positio II, *Testimonia extraprocessualia*, T. XV, p. 1175).

209. Ibid., T. XVIII, p. 1176. Edoardo Luciani himself, meeting his brother several times at the Vatican, stated in his deposition: "At other times I had heard him say something about his health, as when he had problems with his eyes or liver. But in the Vatican, on the oth-

er hand, he told me nothing about his health problems, nor did I have any inkling" (Positio II, *Depositiones testium,* T. XVII, § 350, p. 380).

210. Ibid., T. XXVI, § 494, p. 435; cf. also the deposition of Edoardo Luciani (ibid., T. XVII, § 350, p. 380).

211. Dr. Renato Buzzonetti (1924–2017), primary pontifical physician for John Paul II and Benedict XVI, became emeritus on June 15, 2009. During the pontificate of Paul VI up to the pontificate of John Paul I he had been an assistant to Professor Mario Fontana, then director of the Vatican Health Service and primary pontifical physician.

212. Positio II, *Testimonia extraprocessualia*, T. XX, p. 1187.

213. The doctor was probably referring to Evening Prayer, celebrated before supper, as referenced by the other texts.

214. ArPost, *Documenti personali – documentazione clinica*, folder II, *Relazione del dott. Buzzonetti indirizzata a mons. Giuseppe Caprio con data 9 ottobre 1978, in merito alla constatazione del decesso di Giovanni Paolo I la mattina del 29 settembre 1978; anamnesi medica sull'evento*, c.n.n.; cf. Positio III, *Summarium documentorum, Documentazione* "de morte," p. 1358. On February 28, 2013, he released the signed report regarding the death of John Paul I, providing an attachment with the relative documentation that had been reported in volume III of the Positio, pp. 1354–1369, cf. Appendix 3.

215. Positio II, *Testimonia extraprocessualia*, T. XX, p. 1190.

216. Ibid., p. 1186; on p. 1190, he states, "The copies of these writings, which are still in my possession, were delivered by me to Fr. Vincenzo Criscuolo of the Congregation for the Causes of the Saints on February 12, 2013."

217. As already explained in this regard, cf. Positio IV, *Biographia ex documentis*, p. 2921; cf. Positio II, *Depositiones testium*, T. CLVIII, § 2276, p. 1026.

218. Cf. Positio II, *Testimonia extraprocessualia*, T. XV, no. 14, p. 1153.

219. Ibid., T. VIII, attachment, p. 1096.

220. D. Lorenzi, *Giovanni Paolo I nel ricordo*, p. 66; cf. Positio II, *Depositiones testium*, T. CLVIII, § 2276, p. 1026.

221. Cf. ibid.

222. Positio II, *Testimonia extraprocessualia*, T. VIII, attachment, p. 1109.

223. Cf. ibid., T. VIII, no. 10, pp. 1096–97; T. XV, no. 16, p. 1153.

224. Cf. above regarding the documentation concerning the designation of the Patriarch of Venice.

225. Cf. Father Lorenzi: "And so the pope was able to explain to him what was important to him: that is, that Cardinal Colombo speak with Father Viganò and insist that he accept the appointment" (Positio II, *Depositiones testium*, T. CLVIII, § 2276, p. 1026).

226. Cf. Positio II, *Testimonia extraprocessualia*, T. X, pp. 1124–1129.

227. G. Colombo, *Messaggio dell'arcivescovo per la morte del papa Giovanni Paolo I – Milano, 29 settembre 1978* in "Rivista Diocesana Milanese," 69 (1978), pp. 764–765. Cf. also the testimony of the archbishop emeritus of Bologna, Giacomo Biffi, who, on the morning of September 29, gave Cardinal Colombo the news of the death of John Paul I (Positio II, *Testimonia extraprocessualia*, T. III, p. 1068).

228. "The following morning I was supposed to leave for Veneto to celebrate a wedding and so I used that moment of calm to prepare some notes for the homily" (D. Lorenzi, *Giovanni Paolo I nel ricordo*, p. 67); cf. what was stated by Angelo Gugel in Positio II, *Depositiones testium*, T. CLXI, § 2303, p. 1038.

229. Sister Margherita stated that Father Lorenzi was present at dinner, but that after passing the phone call from Cardinal Colombo over to the pope, he left the papal apartments and returned after midnight (cf. Positio II, *Testimonia extraprocessualia*, VIII, attachment, p. 1111). The pope's niece Amalia Luciani believes that he went out with friends that evening (cf. Positio II, *Depositiones testium*, T. XXXIX, § 722, p. 520). His other niece, Lina Petri, subscribed to the same version. She had heard it from Msgr. Giulio Nicolini, according to whom "everyone knew that on the evening of September 28, when the pope died, Father Diego was not in the Vatican, but out with friends" (Positio II, *Testimonia extraprocessualia*, T. XVIII, pp. 1175–1176).

230. Ibid., T. XV, no. 17, p. 1154.

231. ArPost, *Documenti personali – documentazione clinica*, Ver-

bale del colloquio con Angelo Gugel del 28 ottobre 2012, c.n.n.

232. Cf. Positio II, *Depositiones testium*, T. CLXI, § 2303, p. 1038.

233. "Around 9:00 p.m., the pope, having finished dinner, met me as I came out of the study and spoke to me personally, saying: 'Good night, Angelo.' Those were his last words to me" (ibid.).

234. Positio II, *Testimonia extraprocessualia*, T. XV, no. 17, p. 1154.

235. Ibid., T. VIII, attachment, p. 1109.

236. Cf. ibid., p. 1104.

237. Ibid., p. 1110. Dr. Buzzonetti also confirms the presence of the bell in his report: "The light was on from the lamp placed above the headboard of his bed. The bell was hanging a few centimeters above the Holy Father's head" (ArPost, *Documenti personali – documentazione clinica, Relazione del dott. Buzzonetti indirizzata a mons. Giuseppe Caprio con data 9 ottobre 1978, in merito alla constatazione del decesso di Giovanni Paolo I la mattina del 29 settembre 1978; anamnesi medica sull'evento*, folder II; cf. Positio III, *Summarium documentorum*, no. 101, pp. 1358–1361).

238. Positio II, *Testimonia extraprocessualia*, T. VIII, no. 10, p. 1097.

239. Ibid.

240. The stories of the secretaries, Magee and Fr. Diego Lorenzi — no strangers to contradictions over the years — have tended to be reworked to sound more like apologues. This was probably dictated by the fact that the men felt accused of the events that later occurred. It is therefore not surprising that in their narratives they tended to portray themselves as indefatigable secretaries, but they often disagree and contradict each other. For example, take the interview given by Lorenzi to *Il Gazzettino* on September 28, 1979, where he claimed to have spent the evening preparing a homily for a wedding he was planning to celebrate in his hometown (cf. D. Lorenzi, "*Era stato un giorno di lavoro e di preghiera come gli altri. Poi*," in *Il Gazzettino*, 219 [September 28, 1979], p. 5). Now, compare it with what Magee said: "Father Diego had already left because he often went out in the evening from his accommodations in the Vatican; leaving me alone with the Holy Father ... he came back to his room after mid-

night ... I don't want to criticize him, but he said ..." (cf. Positio II, *Testimonia extraprocessualia*, T. VIII, attachment, p. 1111). Regarding Magee, there was also the account of his adventurous retreat to England to escape journalists: "the morning after the pope's funeral, I was feeling ill ... my superior came in and told me: ... 'This morning there was someone from the Vatican pointing you out as the pope's murderer.' ... I asked someone from the Secretariat of State to book a flight for me and I left Italy. ... So, I went to England, to my sister in Liverpool. ... On the front page it read: 'Doubts about the death of Pope Luciani. Interpol is looking for the secretary, Magee' and there was my picture with the word WANTED. ... I stayed ten days at home, then I returned to Rome" (ibid., pp. 1112–1114). Two notes from the following morning's account are symptomatic: "Things were going badly for me ... I too was accused of killing him with a cup of coffee" (ibid.).

241. Positio II, *Depositiones testium*, T. CLVIII, § 2276, p. 1026.

242. Cf. D. Lorenzi, *Era stato un giorno*, p. 5.

243. Positio II, *Testimonia extraprocessualia*, T. XV, no. 17, p. 1154.

244. Ibid.

245. Ibid., T. XV, no. 28, p. 1157.

246. Ibid., nos. 18–19, p. 1154.

247. Ibid., no. 20, p. 1155.

248. Cf. ibid. Four days before his death, the pope had invited the bishop of Belluno-Feltre for dinner in the papal apartments on September 24 (cf. Positio II, *Depositiones testium*, T. IX, § 142, p. 315).

249. Cf. Positio II, *Testimonia extraprocessualia*, T. XX, pp. 1186–1187.

250. Cf. ibid., T. XV, no. 27, p. 1156: "It was then said that the pope had not even gone to bed and had died earlier" (ibid., T. VIII, p. 1113). One of the most repeated rumors, circulating even among prelates, was that the pope was found dead on the floor, cf. *"Luciani si abbatte sul pavimento della sua stanza da letto morendo solo"* [G. Valente, *"La politica di Dio è resistere ai superbi e dare grazia agli umili." Albino Luciani*, in *30giorni*, 7/8 (1998), p. 23]. This claim was endorsed by the then Prime Minister, Giulio Andreotti, as was also

reported by Andreotti himself in A. Tornielli and A. Zangrando, *Papa Luciani, il sorriso del santo*, Piemme, 2003, p. 152. In the conversation I had with the senator on this matter on February 22, 2009, he reported that he had received this information from one of the cardinals, without naming him, who was part of the delegation that accompanied Pope John Paul II on January 25, 1979, as he departed for the CELAM Conference in Puebla, Mexico.

251. Therefore it seems we cannot rely on what was reported by the Irish secretary, who stated that "all four nuns in the house" had gathered outside the door of his room to call him (cf. Positio II, *Testimonia extraprocessualia*, T. VIII, no. 10, p. 1097).

252. Cf. ibid., T. XV, no. 21, p. 1155; cf. also Magee's testimony that Father Diego at the time was "still asleep" (ibid., p. 1097) and he told one of the nuns "to go to Father Diego and wake him up and tell him what had happened" (ibid., attachment, p. 1112).

253. Ibid., T. XV, p. 1155.

254. Ibid., attachment, pp. 1111–1112. At the time of the pope's death, the camerlengo, Cardinal Jean Villot, was also serving as the Vatican Secretary of State.

255. Ibid., T. XX, p. 1186.

256. Ibid., T. XX. p. 1185; ArPost, *Documenti personali – documentazione clinica, Lettera del dott. Renato Buzzonetti, in data 9 ottobre 1978, al Sostituto della Segreteria di Stato mons. Giuseppe Caprio, per la trasmissione della documentazione relativa alla morte di Giovanni Paolo I e ai pregressi accordi intercorsi tra i medici curanti*, folder II, c.n.n.

257. Cf. autograph notes of Dr. Antonio Da Ros, regarding the agreements between the Vatican Health Service, and by Doctor Da Ros himself for medical assistance to the pope, to be transmitted to Monsignor Caprio, in which we read: "Doctor Da Ros, physician to the pope. Dr. Renato Buzzonetti shall be appointed, for urgent needs and to assist at audiences and ceremonies. Professor Fontana cannot be asked to provide this service because of a question of delicacy" (Positio III, *Summarium documentorum, Documentazione* "de morte," p. 1381–1382).

258. On January 9, 2013, the relator of the cause, Fr. Vincenzo

Criscuolo, OFM, conducted an interview with Doctor Buzzonetti at which I was present. Buzzonetti explained: "I considered the proposal risky, and I was not at all enthusiastic, I did not like this diarchy. On the afternoon of September 23, I was thinking about the answer I would have to give, and that I was very loath to give, because I would be taking the responsibility to work, doubled-up, with a doctor who lived in Vittorio Veneto. I had already done this with Fontana, for Paul VI, but we were in the same hospital ward in Rome. Moreover, from the way Doctor Da Ros spoke, I could tell he had a different medical approach than mine. Still, I had to obey those who asked me for this service, not only as a Vatican employee, but also as a Christian. I talked about it with my wife, who told me 'Be brave, accept'" (ArPost, *Documenti personali – documentazione clinica, Verbale del colloquio con il dott. Renato Buzzonetti in data 9 gennaio 2013*, folder II, c.n.n.).

259. ArPost, *Documenti personali – documentazione clinica, Lettera del dott. Renato Buzzonetti, in data 9 ottobre 1978, al Sostituto della Segreteria di Stato mons. Giuseppe Caprio, per la trasmissione della documentazione relativa alla morte di Giovanni Paolo I e ai pregressi accordi intercorsi tra i medici curanti*, folder II, c.n.n.

260. Cf. Positio II, *Testimonia extraprocessualia*, T. XX, pp. 1185–1186.

261. Ibid.

262. ArPost, *Documenti personali – documentazione clinica, Relazione del dott. Buzzonetti indirizzata a mons. Giuseppe Caprio con data 9 ottobre 1978, in merito alla constatazione del decesso di Giovanni Paolo I la mattina del 29 settembre 1978; anamnesi medica sull'evento*, folder II, c.n.n.; cf. Positio III, *Summarium documentorum, Documentazione* "de morte," pp. 1358–1359.

263. Positio II, *Testimonia extraprocessualia*, T. XV, no. 22, p. 1155.

264. Ibid., T. XX, p. 1187.

265. Ibid.

266. Ibid., p. 1186.

267. D. Lorenzi, *Giovanni Paolo I nel ricordo*, p. 67.

268. Positio II, *Depositiones testium*, T. CLVIII, § 2276, p. 1025.

"September 29, 1978, 6:30 a.m. Father Diego phoned me to say the pope was dead" (ArPost, *Documenti personali – documentazione clinica, Appunti del dott. Antonio Da Ros, medico curante del Servo di Dio, relativi ai contatti con il Papa e alle visite occorse durante il pontificato*, folder II, c.n.n.; cf. Positio III, *Summarium documentorum*, no. 114, p. 1383).

269. Positio II, *Depositiones testium*, T. XXVI, § 494, p. 435.

270. Ibid.

271. According to Magee (Positio II, *Testimonia extraprocessualia*, T. VIII, attachment, p. 1113), the butler, Angelo Gugel, would also have collaborated in the dressing. Instead he stated, "The following morning I learned of the pope's death while I was leaving San Paolo to go to work," which would have begun at 8:00 a.m. (Positio II, *Depositiones testium*, T. CLXI, § 2303, p. 1037).

272. ArPost, *Documenti personali – documentazione clinica, Relazione del dott. Buzzonetti indirizzata a mons. Giuseppe Caprio con data 9 ottobre 1978, in merito alla constatazione del decesso di Giovanni Paolo I la mattina del 29 settembre 1978; anamnesi medica sull'evento*, folder II, c.n.n.; cf. Positio III, *Summarium documentorum*, p. 1358.

273. Positio II, *Testimonia extraprocessualia*, T. XV, no. 25, p. 1156.

274. Ibid., T. XX, p. 1187.

275. Cf. D. Lorenzi, *Giovanni Paolo I nel ricordo*, p. 67.

276. Cf. Positio III, *Summarium documentorum*, p. 2002.

277. Cf. S. Falasca, *Sermo humilis*, p. 53, note 1. Citation from John Paul II, General Audience, Wednesday, October 25, 1978.

278. Cf. Positio III, *Summarium documentorum*, pp. 1999–2139.

279. Positio II, *Testimonia extraprocessualia*, T. XV, no. 25, p. 1156.

280. Cf. Positio IV, *Biographia ex documentis*, p. 2975; Positio III, *Summarium documentorum*, pp. 1999–2026.

281. Cf. ArPost, *Documenti pontificato, Biglietto del card. Pietro Parolin del 28 maggio 2015*, c.n.n.

282. Cf. Positio II, *Testimonia extraprocessualia*, T. XV, no. 23, p. 1155.

283. Fanciful conjecture about the concealment of the glasses and other personal objects at the time of death stems from the well-known novel on Luciani's death by D. Yallop, *In God's Name*, published in 1984.

284. Fr. Francesco Taffarel, who died on October 1, 2014, was given the glasses by Sr. Vincenza Taffarel and kept them at his rectory in Tarzo in the Diocese of Vittorio Veneto until November 6, 2009, when he gave them to me. To be clear, the postulation wanted this personal object to be kept in the museum dedicated to the memory of John Paul I in his hometown of Canale d'Agordo (cf. the certificate attached to the delivery of the object in ArPost, *Documentazione oggetti personali*, c.n.n.). Cf. L. Serafini, *Il museo Albino Luciani*, in *Le Tre Venezie*, 135 (2016), p. 30.

285. Cf. Positio II, *Testimonia extraprocessualia*, T. XV, no. 21. The testimony given by Fr. Diego Lorenzi seems unlikely: "Doctor Da Ros and his wife came directly to the Vatican to visit the body and attended the Mass of Suffrage which was celebrated in the private chapel by Monsignor Magee" (Positio II, *Depositiones testium*, T. CLVIII, § 2276, p. 1025). Having to leave Vittorio Veneto without notice and therefore without a plane ticket, the doctor could not reach the Vatican until around noon, as Doctor Da Ros stated in his interview recorded on July 16, 2009, in which he added that he had seen the body reposing in the Clementine Hall and then assisted at its preservation treatment which started at around 7:00 p.m. (ArPost, *Documenti personali – documentazione clinica*, *Verbale del colloquio con il dott. Da Ros del 16 luglio 2009*, c.n.n.).

286. Cf. *Ioannis Pauli I obitus et funebria*, in *AAS*, 70 (1978) 12, pp. 798–800.

287. Cf. Positio II, *Testimonia extraprocessualia*, T. XV, no. 23, p. 1155.

288. Cf. ibid., T. VIII, attachment, p. 1113.

289. ArPost, *Documenti personali – documentazione clinica*, *Bollettino n. 272 della Sala stampa della Santa Sede in cui viene divulgata la versione ufficiale del ritrovamento del Servo di Dio morto da parte del segretario particolare e l'imputazione del decesso all'infarto miocardico acuto*, folder II, c.n.n.; cf. Positio III, *Summarium documen-*

torum, p. 1335.

290. Cf. Positio II, *Testimonia extraprocessualia*, T. XV, no. 24, p. 1156.

291. Ibid., T. XVIII, p. 1174.

292. Ibid., p. 1175.

293. Positio II, *Depositiones testium*, T. XXVI, § 494, p. 435.

294. Cf. ibid., T. CLXV, § 2336, p. 1051.

295. Cf. F. Ruozzi, *"Un papa più mostrato che dato?"*, p. 547.

296. Cf. Positio II, *Testimonia extraprocessualia*, T. VIII, allegato, p. 1113; cf. F. Farusi, *Cercavano un Papa buon pastore*, cited, p. 10. There was also deceptive journalism about the cup of coffee that had gone cold. It started on October 5, 1978, with an item by Vatican expert Giancarlo Zizola on "what I thought had really happened that sad night in the papal apartments" (cf. G. Zizola, *Luciani e i media*, in *DVAM*, pp. 307–310).

297. Positio II, *Depositiones testium*, T. XXVI, § 494, p. 435.

298. The statement that at that time read "his niece, Lina Petri, worked in the Vatican Press Office" was not true (D. Lorenzi, *Giovanni Paolo I nel ricordo*, p. 67).

299. Positio II, *Testimonia extraprocessualia*, T. XV, no. 23, p. 1155.

300. Ibid., T. XVIII, p. 1174.

301. Cf. J. Cornwell, *Un ladro nella notte. La morte di papa Giovanni Paolo I*, Pironti, 1990, p. 407: The author wrote "torn sleeves," misrepresenting Lina Petri's statement describing them as "wrinkled."

302. Also, another detail of the niece's story concerning the position of the lifeless body ("they had placed him on the bed": Positio II, *Testimonia extraprocessualia*, T. VIII, attachment, p. 1113) gave rise to various fanciful suppositions disseminated by the press, now completely dispelled by the eyewitness testimonies of Sr. Margherita Marin and Doctor Buzzonetti.

303. Cf. Positio IV, *Biographia ex documentis*, p. 2978.

304. Cf. Positio III, *Summarium documentorum*, p. 2051; *AAS*, 70 (1978) 11, pp. 760–761; *L'Osservatore Romano*, 220 (September 24, 1978), p. 2. This is how then Cardinal Ratzinger, speaking in 1998,

recalled the events: "At the time, his death was a severe blow to my heart. I could not understand why that good person had so quickly been taken from us and from the pontifical throne. I was reminded of a phrase that had been coined for Pope Marcellus II, who also died suddenly: 'shown, not given.' In the meantime, however, it has become increasingly clear to me that even 'being shown' has its meaning" (cf. J. Ratzinger, *Anche il "mostrare" ha il suo significato*, in *30giorni*, 7/8 [1998], p. 29; Positio II, *Documenta testimonialia*, no. 2.2, p. 1217).

305. Positio II, *Testimonia extraprocessualia*, T. XXI, no. 13, pp. 1192–1193; cf. Positio I, *Preanotatio relatoris generalis*, p. III; S. Falasca, *La povertà secondo Luciani. Un inedito del 1970*, in *Avvenire*, August 26, 2015, p. 3.

306. Cf. Positio II, *Testimonia extraprocessualia*, T. XV, no. 23, p. 1155.

307. Ibid., T. XX, p. 1189.

308. ArPost, *Documenti personali – documentazione clinica, Relazione in data 10 ottobre 1978 del prof. Mario Fontana, archiatra pontificio, sulla constatazione del decesso di papa Giovanni Paolo I*, folder II, c.n.n.; Positio III, *Summarium documentorum*, pp. 1636–1637.

309. Cf. Positio II, *Depositiones testium*, T. CLXI, § 2303, p. 1037; cf. Positio II, *Testimonia extraprocessualia*, T. XV, no. 23, p. 1155.

310. Cf. Positio II, *Testimonia extraprocessualia*, T. XVIII, p. 1174.

311. Positio II, *Documenta testimonalia*, p. 1195.

312. Cesare Gerin (1906–1996), was an authoritative professor who was internationally renowned for his studies in various important areas of forensic medicine. Since 1950, he had been the Department Chair and Director of the Institute of Forensic Medicine and Insurance at the Sapienza University in Rome. The year he died, the department was named after him.

313. Cf. Positio IV, *Biographia ex documentis*, p. 2297; Positio II, *Testimonia extraprocessualia*, T. X, p. 1189.

314. Positio II, *Testimonia extraprocessualia*, T. XVIII, p. 1176; cf. Edoardo Luciani himself stated in his deposition: "Sister Vincenza confirmed to me that he was better off there than he was in Venice" (Positio II, *Depositiones testium*, T. XVII, § 350, p. 380).

315. Positio II, *Testimonia extraprocessualia*, T. XVIII, p. 1176.

316. Cf. Positio III, *Summarium documentorum*, nos. 84–96, pp. 1337–1352. The section regarding the health of John Paul I refers to data from his medical records.

317. ArPost, *Documenti personali – documentazione clinica, Documentazione del ricovero del Servo di Dio nei giorni 2–8 dicembre 1975 – Notizie anamnestiche,* folder II, c.n.n.; cf. Positio III, *Summarium documentorum*, no. 91, pp. 1344–1346.

318. Cf. Positio II, *Testimonia extraprocessualia*, T. XVIII, p. 1178.

319. ArPost, *Documenti personali – documentazione clinica, Estratto dal registro dei ricoveri nell'anno 1947 presso il reparto sanatoriale di pneumatologia di Belluno per il ricovero del Servo di Dio,* folder II, c.n.n.; Positio III, *Summarium documentorum*, no. 86, p. 1340.

320. Positio II, *Testimonia extraprocessualia*, T. XVIII, p. 1178. Cf. Belluno, Episcopal Archive, *Documenti riguardanti S. E. Mons. Albino Luciani – Periodo Bellunese 1935–1958*, date missing (1947), *Dichiarazione del dott. Gottardo Gottardi circa la malattia polmonare che afflisse il Servo di Dio nel 1947*, section. D. unit I/G, envelope 56/1, no. 20; Positio III, *Summarium documentorum*, no. 85, p. 1339.

321. ArPost, *Documenti personali – documentazione clinica, Documentazione del ricovero del patriarca Luciani nei giorni 2–8 dicembre 1975 – Referto dell'esame radiologico*, folder II, c.n.n.; Positio III, *Summarium documentorum*, no. 93, p. 1347.

322. Cf. Positio II, *Testimonia extraprocessualia*, T. XVIII, p. 1178.

323. Ibid. The pope's niece Lina Petri again: "I remember that my mother [Antonia] always said that she was so sorry that Uncle Albino was too ill at the time to come to Levico to baptize my brother Roberto, who was born on August 18." (cf. ArPost, *Documenti personali – documentazione clinica*, folder II; cf. Positio III, *Summarium documentorum*, no. 84, pp. 1337–1338).

324. ArPost, *Documenti personali – documentazione clinica, Documentazione del ricovero del Servo di Dio nei giorni 2–8 dicembre 1975 – Notizie anamnestiche,* folder II, c.n.n.; cf. Positio III, *Summarium documentorum*, no. 91, pp. 1344–1346.

325. Positio II, *Depositiones testium*, T. LIV, § 986, p. 591.

326. Cf. ibid., § 988, p. 592.

327. Cf. *"Bollettino ecclesiastico della diocesi di Vittorio Veneto,"* 52 (1964) 5, p. 199; 52 (1964) 6, p. 267; ArPost, *Documenti personali – documentazione clinica, Nota spese Spedalità gratuita nel Nosocomio dal 7 aprile al 27 aprile 1964 del 31 dicembre 1964*, prot. 5398.

328. Cf. *"Bollettino ecclesiastico della diocesi di Vittorio Veneto,"* 53 (1965) 3, p. 174.

329. Positio II, *Testimonia extraprocessualia*, T. XVIII, p. 1179 (Positio III, *Summarium documentorum*, no. 84). This agrees with what he wrote on April 3, 1964, found in the Capovilla archive: "I am about to enter the clinic to undergo an operation for liver stones" (Positio II, *Testimonia extraprocessualia*, T. VI, attachment 3.2, p. 1083). Cf. Positio II, *Depositiones testium*, T. I, § 38; T. XXVI, § 513; T. LXVII, § 1282).

330. Cf. Positio II, *Depositiones testium*, T. XV, § 264; T. XX, § 393.

331. ArPost, *Documenti personali – documentazione clinica, Appunti olografi del prof. Giovanni Rama, primario di Oculistica, in risposta alle domande formulate da mons. Foley*, 1988, folder II, c.n.n.; cf. Positio III, *Summarium documentorum*, no. 109, pp. 1374–1376.

332. ArPost, *Documenti personali – documentazione clinica, Nulla osta a firma della nipote Pia Luciani in data 10 maggio 2010 per la consegna della documentazione clinica relativa al ricovero del Servo di Dio nel periodo 2–8 dicembre 1975*, folder II, c.n.n.; cf. Positio III, *Summarium documentorum*, no. 87, p. 1340.

333. ArPost, *Documenti personali – documentazione clinica, Documentazione del ricovero del patriarca Luciani nei giorni 2–8 dicembre 1975 presso la divisione di Oculistica dell'Ospedale generale provinciale di Mestre*, folder II, c.n.n.

334. Positio II, *Testimonia extraprocessualia*, T. XVIII, p. 1179.

335. Ibid.

336. ArPost, *Documenti personali – documentazione clinica, Documentazione del ricovero del patriarca Luciani nei giorni 2–8 dicembre 1975 – Diario Clinico*, folder II, c.n.n.; Positio III, *Summarium documentorum*, no. 96, p. 1352.

337. Positio II, *Testimonia extraprocessualia*, T. XVIII, p. 1180.

338. Ibid. As reported in M. Roncalli, *Giovanni Paolo I*, p. 660,

the secretary, Fr. Diego Lorenzi, affirmed that he "suffered from hypertension" and that this state "worried him, as shown by his constant thoughts of death."

339. Cf. ArPost, *Documenti personali – documentazione clinica, Olografo del prof. Giovanni Rama, primario di Oculistica, con testimonianze personali del suo rapporto con il Servo di Dio*, folder II, c.n.n.; cf. Positio III, *Summarium documentorum*, no. 111, pp. 1379–1380.

340. Cf. Positio II, *Testimonia extraprocessualia*, T. XVIII, p. 1180.

341. From all the documentation, his niece Lina Petri arrived at the hypothesis that Professor Rama had reported to the patriarch regarding the risks of the circulatory disturbance affecting the ocular retina. In fact, on the following January 6, in answer to questions posed by his sister, Antonia, regarding his hospitalization and the therapy in progress, Luciani replied: "Dear Nina, the doctor told me that if this thing I had in my eye had ever reached my heart, I could have died. Moreover, to avoid possible relapses I am doing this cure. But do not worry because it will be resolved" (ibid.). His other niece, Pia Luciani, accepted this reconstruction as well: "Personally, I immediately thought of an embolism as the cause of death. There was, in fact, precedent. When he returned from Brazil, back in 1975, my uncle told me that there had been pressurization problems on the plane and a red dot appeared in his eye. Father Mario had him examined by the well-known ophthalmologist from Venice, Professor Rama, who told him that it was an embolus and that if it had lodged somewhere else, he would probably have died without even noticing. Even my cousin Lina, the daughter of my Aunt Antonia, who is a doctor, and was able to see our uncle while he was still in his room that same morning, told me that our uncle had a serene and relaxed face, and she too thought he had died of an embolism." (Positio II, *Depositiones testium*, T. XXVI, § 494, p. 435).

342. Positio II, *Testimonia extraprocessualia*, T. XVIII, p. 1177.

343. Positio II, *Depositiones testium*, T. LIV, § 987, p. 592.

344. ArPost, *Documenti personali – documentazione clinica, Appunti del dott. Antonio Da Ros, medico curante del Servo di Dio, relativi ai contatti con il Papa e alle visite occorse durante il pontificato*

[s.d.], folder II (Positio III, *Summarium documentorum*, no. 114, p. 1383).

345. Positio II, *Depositiones testium*, T. LIV, § 987. Sr. Margherita Marin's testimony confirms what the doctor said: "The first time, I think, was at the beginning, then I saw him come in mid-September, and the last time, I remember, was on September 23. Regarding his last visit, Sister Vincenza told us that the doctor determined that the Holy Father was well, very well, so much so, she said, that the doctor had also taken away his medication. However, I could not say which medication, or if he took away more than one; that was just the way she said it" (Positio II, *Testimonia extraprocessualia*, T. XV, no. 10, p. 1152). Therefore, there was no medical evidence regarding the concern for the pope's "ashen, nearly exhausted" appearance during the celebration of his installation at the Lateran, which some people had noticed, including Prime Minister Giulio Andreotti (G. Andreotti, *A ogni morte di Papa*, p. 161; other published testimonies are collected in M. Roncalli, *Giovanni Paolo I*, p. 639).

346. Positio II, *Depositiones testium*, T. XVII, § 350, p. 380.

347. Cf. Positio II, *Testimonia extraprocessualia*, T. XV, no. 21, p. 1115; T. XX, p. 1185.

348. Positio II, *Depositiones testium*, T. LIV, § 987, p. 592.

349. ArPost, *Documenti personali – documentazione clinica, Lettera del dott. Renato Buzzonetti, medico in seconda, al Sostituto della Segreteria di Stato mons. Giuseppe Caprio, per la trasmissione della documentazione relativa alla morte di Giovanni Paolo I e ai pregressi accordi intercorsi tra i medici curanti, in data 9 ottobre 1978*, folder II, c.n.n.; cf. Positio III, *Summarium documentorum*, no. 100, p. 1357.

350. Cf. ArPost, *Documenti personali – documentazione clinica, Relazione del dott. Buzzonetti indirizzata a mons. Giuseppe Caprio con data 9 ottobre 1978, in merito alla constatazione del decesso di Giovanni Paolo I la mattina del 29 settembre 1978, in data 9 ottobre 1978*, folder II; Positio III, *Summarium documentorum*, no. 101, p. 1359.

351. Positio II, *Testimonia extraprocessualia*, T. XX, p. 1188.

352. ArPost, *Documenti personali – documentazione clinica, Relazione del dott. Buzzonetti indirizzata a mons. Giuseppe Caprio con*

data 9 ottobre 1978, in merito alla constatazione del decesso di Gio-vanni Paolo I la mattina del 29 settembre 1978, in data 9 ottobre 1978, folder II; cf. Positio III, *Summarium documentorum*, no. 101, p. 1359; cf. Positio IV, *Biographia ex documentis*, cap. XII, *infra* Documents no. 4 at the end of the chapter.

353. Cf. Positio II, *Testimonia extraprocessualia*, T. XX, p. 1188.

354. Positio IV, *Biographia ex documentis*, p. 2989.

355. Positio II, *Testimonia extraprocessualia*, T. XX, p. 1188.

356. "It was also inappropriate because of the respect due to the person of the Holy Father and the religious and traditional venera-tion of the pope's mortal remains," Positio IV, *Biographia ex docu-mentis*, p. 2989.

357. Positio II, *Testimonia extraprocessualia*, T. XX, pp. 1180–1181.

358. Cf. ArPost, *Documenti personali – documentazione clinica, Relazione del dott. Buzzonetti indirizzata a mons. Giuseppe Caprio con data 9 ottobre 1978, in merito alla constatazione del decesso di Giovanni Paolo I la mattina del 29 settembre 1978, in data 9 ottobre 1978*, folder II; Positio III, *Summarium documentorum*, no. 101, p. 1358.

359. Positio II, *Testimonia extraprocessualia*, T. XVIII, p. 1187.

360. ArPost, *Documenti personali – documentazione clinica, Olo-grafi s.d. a. 1988 del prof. Giovanni Rama, primario di Oculistica, in merito all'episodio di trombosi retinica del 1975 e all'uso disonesto fat-to da David Yallop delle informazioni assunte*, folder II, c.n.n.; Positio III, *Summarium documentorum*, no. 110, p. 1137.

361. Positio II, *Testimonia extraprocessualia*, T. XX, p. 1187.

362. ArPost, *Documenti personali – documentazione clinica, Re-lazione in data 10 ottobre 1978 del prof. Mario Fontana, archiatra pontificio, sulla constatazione del decesso di papa Giovanni Paolo I*, folder II, c.n.n.; Positio III, *Summarium documentorum*, no. 105, pp. 1366–1367.

363. ArPost, *Documenti personali – documentazione clinica, Ap-punti senza data e senza firma inviati al dott. Buzzonetti dalla Segre-teria di Stato, ottobre 1978*, folder II, c.n.n.; Positio III, *Summarium documentorum*, no. 102, p. 1362.

364. ArPost, *Documenti personali – documentazione clinica, Relazione del dott. Buzzonetti sulla constatazione del decesso del Santo Padre Giovanni Paolo I del 10 ottobre 1978*, folder II, c.n.n.; cfr Positio III, *Summarium documentorum*, no. 104, pp. 1364–1365.

365. ArPost, *Documenti personali – documentazione clinica, Lettera del 11 ottobre 1978 del dott. Buzzonetti a mons. Caprio con cui trasmette le relazioni cliniche sua e del prof. Fontana in merito alla constatazione del decesso del Servo di Dio*, folder II, c.n.n.; Positio III, *Summarium documentorum*, no. 103, p. 1363.

366. ArPost, *Documenti personali – documentazione clinica, Richiesta del 12 gennaio 2013 da parte di mons. Marcello Bartolucci a mons. Giovanni Angelo Becciu per l'autorizzazione al dott. Buzzonetti a rendere disponibile documentazione riservata in suo possesso*, no. 2254–14/13. *Ivi, Assenso concesso in data 29 gennaio 2013 a firma di mons. Giovanni Angelo Becciu a mons. Marcello Bartolucci*, no. 47062.

367. Positio II, *Depositiones testium*, T. XXVI, § 494, p. 435.

368. Cf. ibid., T. XVII, § 350, p. 380.

369. ArPost, *Documenti personali – documentazione clinica, Lettera autografa del dott. Caprioglio, dopo sollecitazione della famiglia, in merito alla morte improvvisa del Servo di Dio*, folder II, c.n.n.; Positio III, *Summarium documentorum*, no. 116, p. 1385.

370. ArPost, *Documenti personali – documentazione clinica, Dichiarazione del 24 giugno 2010 a firma del dott. Luciano Caprioglio, primario della Divisione medica I Ospedale civile di Mestre, in merito alla morte del Servo di Dio*, folder II, c.n.n.; Positio III, *Summarium documentorum*, no. 115, p. 1384.

371. This famous book was the progenitor of the successful conspiracy literature. Published by David Yallop in 1984, entitled *In God's Name* (Bantam Books), and published the following year in Italy (*In nome di Dio. La morte di Papa Luciani*, Pironti), the book alleged that Luciani's death was the result of a plot by the Vatican Curia, which was in the hands of the Freemasons and hostile to the changes envisaged by the new pope. Next in this series was *The Company* by Robert Littell (Penguin Press, 2002), which imagined that the pope was killed by the KGB, who had been using the Vatican Bank and the

Banco Ambrosiano to pass an enormous quantity of dollars through Western accounts, with the objective of overwhelming the American currency. The latest novel on the matter was *The Last Pope* by Luis Miguel Rocha (G. P. Putnam's Sons, 2008). Fanciful conspiracy narratives still generate interest today, as proven in 2012 by the book *33 Days in the Vatican* (Segno) by Sergey Shkarovskij, from the Moscow State University of Management. The book endorsed the hypothesis that Luciani did not die a natural death. Various authors, less fortunate than Yallop, have tried to refute his hypothesis. The first, in order of publication, is Victor Willi who published *Im Namen des Teufels?* in 1987 (ed. Christiana Verlag). Lucio D'Orazi, a magistrate, tried the same with *In nome di Dio o del diavolo? La morte di papa Luciani* (Logos, 1988). The Vatican itself, aware of the damage being done to its image by Yallop's book, gave carte blanche to an English journalist, John Cornwell, to respond to Yallop's theses. In 1989, Cornwell's investigations resulted in the book, *A Thief in the Night* (Viking, 1989, Italian edition: *Un ladro nella note*), which, in terms of the type of book it was and its conclusion, proved to be as fictional as Yallop's book.

372. ArPost, *Documenti personali – documentazione clinica, Olografi s.d. a. 1988 del prof. Giovanni Rama, primario di Oculistica, in merito all'episodio di trombosi retinica del 1975 e all'uso disonesto fatto da David Yallop delle informazioni assunte*, folder II, c.n.n.; Positio III, *Summarium documentorum*, no. 110, p. 1377.

373. Positio II, *Testimonia extraprocessualia*, T. XX, pp. 1190–1191.

374. Ibid., In the written report released on February 28, 2013, the former Primary Pontifical Physician, Doctor Buzzonetti concluded as follows: "In hindsight, I believe that if — together with the official communication of the diagnosis of death — someone who had the authority to do so (family members or legal heirs) had released the doctors from professional secrecy (binding even after the death of the patient), authorizing them to report the convincing story of recurrent precordial pain, many posthumous interpretations would have vanished" (ibid., T. XX, p. 1188).

375. Ibid., T. XXI, no. 14, p. 1192/6.

376. *Depositio et tumulatio,* in *AAS,* 70 (1978) 12, p. 808. Cardinal Antonio Samorè presided over the rite.

377. Ibid. Cf. F. Ruozzi, *"Un papa più mostrato che dato?",* p. 551.

378. Positio II, *Testimonia extraprocessualia,* T. XXI, no. 15, p. 1192/6.

379. F. Ruozzi, *"Un papa più mostrato che dato?",* p. 551.

380. The television stations of thirty-one countries were present at the funeral, along with seventeen other radio networks; cf. G. CAPRILE, *L'inattesa scomparsa di Giovanni Paolo I,* in *La Civiltà Cattolica,* 3080 (1978) 9, pp. 162–163.

381. Ibid., p. 166.

382. Ibid.

383. Ibid., p. 165.

384. *Depositio et tumulatio,* in *AAS,* 70 (1978) 12, p. 809.

385. The Greek marble sarcophagus was made according to a design by Francesco Bacchini. The two reliefs with "praying angels" belonged to one of the facades of the renaissance tabernacle that held the Holy Lance, made in 1495 by Cardinal Lorenzo Cybo de Mari, on the orders of his late uncle, Innocent VIII, who had received the relic in Rome. The two sculptures, originally facing the Holy Lance, are attributed to the late school of Andrea Bregno (1418–1503). Cf. V. Lanzani, *Il sepolcro di Giovanni Paolo I,* in *Roma sacra. Guida alle chiese della Città eterna,* 26–27 (2003), p. 115.

386. Cf. *Depositio et tumulatio, AAS,* 70 (1978) 12, pp. 807–810.

387. J. Ratzinger, *Omelia del pontificale in suffragio di papa Giovanni Paolo I. Duomo di Monaco, 6 ottobre 1978,* in *Bollettino dell'arcidiocesi di Monaco e Frisinga,* 26 (1978), p. 3. Cf. Positio II, *Documenta testimonialia,* no. 2.1, p. 1213.

388. Positio II, *Testimonia extraprocessualia,* T. XXI, nos. 16–18, p. 1192/6.

389. Positio II, *Documenta testimonalia,* no. 2.1, p. 1213.

390. A. Luciani, *Omelia nella festa di san Rocco,* in *OpOm,* VIII, p. 194.

391. Positio II, *Documenta testimonalia,* no. 2.1, p. 1213.

392. A. Luciani, *Omelia per il 750° anniversario della morte di san Francesco,* in *OpOm,* VII, p. 464.